MW00882038

"Is God Really Like That?"
Is God Really Angry?

Bible Study Guides regarding God's character;
how He thinks and acts.

by

Paul G. Sweitzer

authorHOUSE™

1663 Liberty Drive, Suite 200
Bloomington, Indiana 47403
(800) 839-8640
www.AuthorHouse.com

© 2004 Paul G. Sweitzer
All Rights Reserved.

No part of this book may be reproduced, stored in a retrieval system, or transmitted by any means without the written permission of the author.

First published by AuthorHouse 11/09/04

ISBN: 1-4184-2152-9 (sc)

Printed in the United States of America
Bloomington, Indiana

This book is printed on acid-free paper.

<u>Dedication</u>

Dedicated to God,
in the name of Jesus regarding His reputation.

Table of Contents

x

Suggestions for Bible Students

The following 30 Bible Study Outlines contain many thought provoking ideas that are easy to understand. However, these 30 Outlines should be studied in the order given – without skipping ahead.

Why? Because some topics can be understood only with proper background support. It is something like studying algebra. An algebra teacher would not ask his or her students to begin with the last chapter of the text book! By comparing Holy Scripture, the Bible explains itself. Your Bible will become its own encyclopedia or dictionary.

In other words, you will cheat yourself and lose out on extremely important truths unless you study these Outlines in the proper sequence. You will avoid coming to any wrong conclusions based upon a wrong premise not coming from Holy Scripture.

IMPORTANT POINT:

Certain Old Testament ideas cannot be properly understood without comparing them with what Jesus did and said in the New Testament. The reason for this will become crystal clear as you continue your Bible research.

When you complete these Outlines, in order, you will then <u>know</u> <u>much</u> <u>more</u> <u>than</u> <u>most</u> <u>preachers</u> about how God thinks and acts. Then you can teach your children and grandchildren about a God of love whom they will never need to fear.

"Is God Really Like That?"

Bible Study Guides on the Subject of God
By Paul G. Sweitzer, BA, MA

All honest Christians, including preachers and priests, change their minds from time to time as they continue to study Holy Scripture.

Why? Because the revelation of Bible truth is progressive. Jesus told His disciples:

John 16:12,13

"I have yet many things to say to you, but you cannot bear them now. When the Spirit of truth comes, he will guide you into all truth."

People from different denominations [including preachers] teach direct opposites regarding some Bible doctrines, yet all study from the same Bible!

Most people who are raised Baptist remain Baptists all of their lives. Most who are raised Pentecostal remain Pentecostals all of their lives. Most Methodists remain Methodists, etc. Yet all say they are following the Bible. What does this tell us? It tells us that we might not understand everything there is to know on every subject.

Buried deeply within our subconscious minds are ideas we have been taught since we were 3 years old; therefore, everyone feels a little uncomfortable when introduced to new ideas. Some are afraid they will be deceived into believing doctrines of devils! The fact is that God will reveal new truth to everyone who studies prayerfully with an open mind.

Why would I have someone else tell me what God is like when I can read it for myself in my own Bible? A couple hundred years ago people had to depend upon their parents and preachers to tell them what the Bible taught. Now, ALL can read the Bible for themselves.

God really does answer the prayers of ordinary people – people who are caught up in the "rat race" of trying to make a living. Getting to know what God is really like will be of great help as you continue the "rat race."

The outlines that follow are truly Bible outlines. People who have studied the Bible all their lives are very pleased with what they have gained from this study.

Is God Really Like That?
Outline No. 1

One day while making a pastoral visit in Baytown, Texas, during a severe thunderstorm I observed three young children playing in a bedroom adjacent to the living room where their mother and I were talking. As the storm grew worse it produced thunder and lightning. To my surprise, in response to the thunder, the three children hid under a bed! When I questioned their mother as to why, she informed me that she was "teaching them to fear God, just as the Bible says." These three children could never learn to genuinely love God with such misguided training.

To "fear" God is to respect Him, yet some places in your Bible seem to portray God as vengeful, harsh, cruel, exacting, and/or dictatorial. Because of this, today's generation has a tendency to reject the idea that Bible writers were inspired by a "God of love" [1 John 4:8,16]. For example, one of the Old Testament laws given to Israel was the "eye for an eye" law:

Exodus 21:23-25

If any harm follows, then you shall give life for life, eye for eye, tooth for tooth, hand for hand, foot for foot, burn for burn…

Leviticus 24:19,20

Anyone who maims another shall suffer the same injury in return: fracture for fracture, eye for eye, tooth for tooth…

Yet in the New Testament Jesus said:

Matthew 5:38, 43-45, 48

"You have heard that it was said, 'An eye for an eye and a tooth for a tooth.' **But I say** to you, Do not resist one who is evil. But if any one strikes you on the right cheek, turn to him the other also… "You have heard that it was said**, 'You shall love your neighbor and hate your enemy.' **But I say to you, Love your enemies** and pray for those who persecute you, so **that you may be children of your Father in heaven;** for he makes his sun rise on the evil and on the good, and sends rain on the righteous and on the unrighteous. **Be perfect, as your heavenly Father is perfect."**

Note, in Matthew 5:43-48, how diplomatic Jesus was when He referred to this Old Testament "eye for an eye" get even law: "You have heard that it was said… but I SAY to you, "Love your enemies." WHY? "So that you may be children of your Father in heaven." When Jesus said, "But I SAY," He was claiming to have greater authority than the source of this particular Old Testament "eye for an eye" law!

These words of Jesus in Matthew 5:38-48 [Above] show that all of the O.T. laws did not originate with God. Who was the true lawgiver? Who was it that led Israel through the desert?

James 4:12

There is one lawgiver and judge who is able to save and destroy.

1 Corinthians 10:1-4

I do not want you to be unaware, brothers and sisters, that our ancestors were all under the cloud, and all passed through the sea, and all were baptized into Moses in the cloud and in the sea, and all ate the same spiritual food, and all drank the same spiritual drink.. For they drank from the spiritual rock that followed them, and the rock was Christ.

Exodus 3:14

God said to Moses, "I AM WHO I AM." He said further, "Thus you shall say to the Israelites, "I AM has sent me to you."

John 8:57-59

Then the Jews said to him, "You are not yet fifty years old, and have you seen Abraham?" Jesus said to them, "Very truly I tell you, before Abraham was, I am." So they picked up stones to throw at him, but Jesus hid himself and went out of the temple.

The Jews knew that Jesus was claiming to be the great God of the Old Testament who guided the nation of ancient Israel through the desert after they escaped from Pharaoh; therefore, they tried to stone Him for blasphemy!

The true Lord God of the Old Testament thought exactly like **Jesus** of the New Testament. God's attitude is always the same. **Always!**

Malachi 3:6

"For I the Lord do not change."

Hebrews 13:8

"Jesus Christ is the same yesterday and today and for ever."

James 1:17

"…every perfect gift is from above, coming down from the Father of lights with whom there is no variation or shadow due to change."

Revelation 22:13,16

"I am the Alpha and the Omega, the first and the last, the beginning and the end… It is I, Jesus, who sent my angel to you with this testimony for the churches. I am the root and descendant of David, the bright morning star."

Hebrews 1:1,2

"In many and various ways God spoke of old to our fathers by the prophets; but **in these last days he has spoken to us by a Son,** whom he appointed the heir of all things, through whom also he created the world.

Jesus came and lived as a human being in this world in order to demonstrate what God is really like. Jesus, in **John 8:44**, accused the devil of being a **murderer** and a **liar** from "the beginning." **Satan [with the help of the clergy] has succeeded in giving God a bad name.** By carefully and prayerfully studying your Bible with an open mind, you can learn what God is <u>really</u> like – you will learn that **God is not the terrible Being Satan has made Him out to be.**

The reason for our study of God is to learn how He <u>really</u> thinks and acts. The forces of evil have succeeded in giving God a bad name. When an **earthquake** hits, the newspapers and many religious leaders say, "God did it." If earthquakes <u>do</u> come from God as punishment, **how is it that a third grader can tell you what causes an earthquake?!**

> <u>FACT</u>: **Everything written in the Old Testament should be compared with what Jesus did and said in the New Testament.**

The above **"FACT"** is a **RULE** that will be applied to any idea presented in these outlines. When we apply this rule to the Old Testament **"eye for an eye"** law, we understand that Jesus did <u>not</u> regard this philosophy as coming from the true God of the O.T. **Bible proof** of the **source** of this counterfeit "eye for an eye" law will be given to you before you complete these outlines.

As we progress in our study, certain ideas will be declared **"facts."** You may, at first, disagree with some of the **so-called "facts."** And **with some you may never agree;** however, **a study with no new thoughts is a waste of time.**

THE <u>AUTHORITY</u> FOR THE IDEAS PRESENTED IN THESE OUTLINES:

<u>No. 1</u> --Holy Scripture
<u>No. 2</u> –Logic & common sense

For example, how can God really be **"love"** as the apostle John claimed [1 John 4:8,16], and still be the **vengeful "get even" God** most people, including Christians, make Him out to be?

> **FACT: God never changes.**

God, who knows everything [omniscient] and is all powerful [omnipotent], did not have to learn by trial and error the best ways to deal with sinners:

<u>Malachi 3:6</u>
"For I the Lord do not change."

We cannot overemphasize the fact that God <u>never</u> changes! He is not moody! He does not get angry in the same way people do.

<u>Mature</u> Christians choose to think, speak, and act like their example, Jesus. In Romans chapter 12 the apostle Paul reflects the thinking of Jesus:

Romans 12:20,21

If your enemies are hungry, feed them; if they are thirsty, give them something to drink; for by doing this you will heap burning coals on their heads. Do not be overcome by evil, but overcome evil with good.

Old Testament theology: **"Our God is one."** They believed everything, either good or bad, came directly from the <u>one</u> God. Does God actually **cause** punishment [earthquakes, hurricanes, sickness, etc.], or does He merely **allow** them to take place? The answer will become crystal clear as we continue to carefully examine what your <u>Bible</u> says about God.

Each generation learns more about God and how He works by:
    [a] studying more for themselves.
    [b] by comparing Scripture.
    [c] by comparing Bible propecy with the <u>fulfillment</u> of Bible prophecy.

Is it possible that I, as an individual, could be prejudiced in my thinking about God? Is it possible that I believe what I believe because of preconceived ideas taught to me before I began to think and study for myself? **How could such a thing be possible** – after all, I was taught by good, honest conscientious parents, and by educated religious leaders who would never teach anything but the Truth of the Bible!

Stop and honestly consider the **reality** of our present religious world. **There are honest, genuine Christians in <u>every</u> denomination.** They pray before they study their Bibles, asking God for guidance from His promised Spirit. How, then, could I possibly <u>not</u> know <u>everything</u> there is to know about God that is important?

The fact is that **most people remain in the denomination in which they were raised.** Most people who were raised in the Baptist church stay Baptists; most Roman Catholics stay Roman Catholics; most Mormons remain Mormons; Methodists remain Methodists; most Seventh-day Adventists stay Seventh-day Adventists; and most Lutherans remain Lutherans! Therefore, it becomes obvious that **most people believe [at least in part] what they believe because of earlier influences.**

Even religious leaders **within their own denomination** disagree on many issues!

It only makes sense to study with an open mind, asking God to guide you into a more progressive Truth, <u>as an individual</u>, especially concerning God and how He thinks and acts.

Your Bible says that in the last days, before Jesus returns, people will learn more and more about the real Truth:

Daniel 12:4 Amplified Bible

But you, O Daniel, shut up the words and seal the book until the time of the end. [Then] many shall run to and fro *and* search anxiously [through the Book], and knowledge [of God's purposes as revealed by his prophets] shall be increased *and* become great.

Before Jesus returned to heaven notice what He told His disciples:

John 16:12,13

"I have yet many things to say to you, but you cannot bear them now. When the Spirit of truth comes, he will guide you into all the truth."

Some ideas once considered **"undeniable facts"** are now being questioned. Today's generation does not accept **"facts"** just because father, mother, teachers, and/or preachers are convinced they are true. Adults, as a whole, are more tolerant of different views of various religious organizations.

Sometimes it is considered "politically incorrect" to speak against the beliefs of another religion – like the fact that the Koran teaches that Moslems should kill others around them that refuse to accept their religious beliefs. Most Moslems, of course, do not attempt to kill people of other religions, even though such a philosophy is taught in their "Bible." That is why there are so many "suicide bombers" in the Arab countries.

In the past Satan has, and still does, imitate the true Lord. Satan is very good at pretending to be God:

2 Cor 11:13,14

For such men are false apostles, deceitful workers, disguising themselves as apostles of Christ. And no wonder, for **even Satan disguises himself as an angel of light.**

According to Jesus Himself, even **religious leaders** sometimes teach **tradition** rather than teaching God's truth or His commands:

Mark 7:9

And he said to them, "You have a fine way of rejecting the commandments of God, in order to keep your tradition."

Because God seems to be portrayed, in some places in the Bible, as harsh and cruel, and because of what seems to be Bible contradictions, today's younger generation has a tendency to reject the idea that the Bible writers were inspired by a **"God of love"** [1 John 4:8,16].

Unless we understand how Bible writers wrote, it appears that the Bible contradicts itself. For example, compare **Ezekiel 20:25,26** with **Jeremiah 32:35:**

Ezekiel 20:25,26

Moreover **I gave them** statutes that were not good and ordinances by which they could not have life; and **I defiled them** through their very gifts in **making them**

offer by fire all their first-born, that I might horrify them; I did it that they might know that I am the LORD.

Jeremiah 32:35

They [Israel & Judah] built the high places of **Baal** in the valley of the son of Hinnom, to **offer up their sons and daughters to Molech,** though **I did not command them,** nor did it enter into my mind, that they should do this **abomination,** to cause Judah to sin.

In the preceding Bible texts **Ezekiel and Jeremiah contradict each other!** Ezekiel claimed that God made them offer their babies as human sacrifices. Jeremiah wrote just the opposite! Jeremiah said that God did not command them to offer their children as human sacrifices, and that it never even entered His mind that they should do such an "abomination."

The preceding contradiction comes as a shock to some individuals who have always believed that every word in the Bible came directly from God without any human thought.

What really happened was that Bible writers expressed, in their own words and way of thinking, the ideas that were impressed upon their minds by God's Spirit. Each Bible writer had to rely upon his own education and background; otherwise, everything written in the Bible would have

consisted of the same grammar and vocabulary. We can tell by the style and vocabulary that the writer of the book of Hebrews had much more formal education than the apostle John. This, of course, does not mean that the writer of Hebrews understood God better than the apostle John. It only means that different writers expressed themselves in different ways, according to their individual backgrounds. Even Bible records of the Ten Commandments are a little different in Exodus 20 and Deuteronomy 5.

There is no contradiction when we understand how Bible writers wrote.

FACT: Bible writers wrote as if God actually DID things which He merely ALLOWED.

For example: Most children have learned in S.S. class that **King Saul** committed suicide. But how did **King Saul die** according to the following Bible text?

1 Chronicles 10:13,14

So Saul died for his unfaithfulness; he was unfaithful to the Lord in that he did not keep the command of the Lord; more-over, he had consulted a medium, seeking guidance, and did not seek guidance from the Lord. Therefore **the Lord put him to death** and turned the kingdom over to David son of Jesse.

The above Bible verse states clearly that **"the Lord put him to death."** Is that how it <u>really</u> happened? Did the Lord <u>really</u> kill King Saul? To find the answer we must **compare Scripture:**

1 Chronicles 10:4,5

Then Saul said to his armor-bearer, "Draw your sword, and thrust me through with it, so that these uncircumcised may not come and make sport of me." But his armor-bearer was unwilling, for he was terrified. So **<u>Saul took his own sword and fell on it</u>.** When his armor-bearer saw that Saul was dead, he also fell on his sword and died.

Do the preceding Bible texts contradict themselves? They do **not** IF and ONLY IF you accept the fact that Bible writers wrote as if God actually did things which He merely allowed.

ANOTHER EXAMPLE:

1 Kings 16:1-3

The word of the Lord came to Jehu... **"I will consume Baasha and his house..."**

This preceding Bible verse quotes the Lord as saying, **"I will consume Baasha."** Now compare the following Bible verses to determine exactly **<u>how</u>** God did it:

1 Kings 16:8-12

"...Elah... began to reign over Israel... But his servant <u>Zimri</u>, commander of half his chariots, conspired against him. When he was... drinking himself drunk... **Zimri** came in and... **killed him...** Thus <u>Zimri</u> <u>destroyed</u> all the house of <u>Baasha, according to the word of the Lord, which he spoke against Baasha by the prophet Jehu.</u>

<u>No. 1</u> – **The Lord told Jehu, "I will consume Baasha."**
[1 Kings 16:1-3]

<u>No. 2</u> – **"<u>Zimri</u> destroyed all of the house of Baasha."**
[1 Kings 16:8-12]

<u>No. 3</u> – **When "Zimri destroyed," it fulfilled the Lord's saying, "I will consume Baasha."**
[1 Kings 16:12]

Bible writers plainly quote God as saying, "I kill... I make people rich. I make people poor... I punish..." **But knowing <u>how</u> God kills or punishes is the <u>key</u>** to understanding His loving nature. Unless we always remember the fact that Bible writers wrote as if God actually <u>did</u> things which He merely <u>allowed</u>, God will always appear to be two-faced. **God is not two-faced!** He never was and

He never will be! God is the same "yesterday, today, and forever" [James 1:17; Mal. 3:6; Heb. 13:8].

God is not two-faced!

FACT: God "punishes" and "kills" by **ALLOWING** evil men to do their evil, and by **ALLOWING** nature out of control to destroy.

You, as a Bible student, can figure out for yourself how God "kills" by concentrating on what your Bible really says when it describes how God "kills." **Apply logic** to the following Bible texts:

Psalm 5:10 [KJV]

Destroy thou them, O God: let them fall by their own counsels:

Exodus 22:24

…my wrath will burn, and I will kill you with the sword.

Here we have **"Bible proof"** that God kills! It plainly says, "I will kill you." Then it says **how** God will kill. He will kill, according to this Bible verse, with a **"sword."** The book of Revelation speaks about a symbolic **"sword"** that God carries **in His mouth!** [See Rev 1:16; 2:12,16; Eph 6:17; Heb 4:12; Matt 26:51,52]

Jeremiah 11:22

…says the Lord of hosts: **I am going to punish them**; the young men shall die by the **sword**; their sons and daughters shall die by **famine.**

Ezekiel 30:22-26

…says the Lord God: I am against Pharaoh king of Egypt, and **will break his arms…** I will make the sword fall from his hand… I will strengthen the arms of the king of Babylon, and put **my sword in his hand;** but I will break the arms of Pharaoh… And they shall know that I am the Lord, **when I put my sword into the hand of the king of Babylon… and I will scatter the Egyptians** among the nations… Then they shall know that I am the Lord.

Even if Ezekiel had not explained exactly what God would do, **common sense** would tell us that God would not literally break Pharaoh's arms! God only "broke Pharaoh's arms" by **allowing** the king of Babylon to conquer Egypt.

FACT: The "sword" of God is, in reality, the sword (or weapons) of men.

REVIEW

[1] When we compare Scripture, the Bible will explain itself.

[2] Even though Bible <u>scholars</u> do not agree as to how God thinks and acts [even within the same denomination] God has promised to guide <u>our</u> minds as we study <u>personally</u>, for ourselves.

[3] It is impossible to genuinely love God if we fear that He will torment us in "hell" if we fail to follow all of His rules, in the same way we could not genuinely love an <u>earthly</u> father who tortured us every time we broke one of his rules!

[4] Holy Scripture will appear to contradict itself unless we understand that Bible writers wrote as if God actually <u>did</u> things which He merely <u>allowed</u> to happen.

[5] Even though the Bible says that God killed king Saul, we know by comparing Scripture, that Saul actually committed suicide.

[6] God "kills" and "punishes" by <u>allowing</u> evil men to do evil, and by <u>allowing</u> nature out of control to destroy. God can, at any time, <u>prevent</u> nature out of control from destroying, as He did when the storm arose while He and His disciples were in a boat on the Sea of Galilee [Mark 4:39].

[7] When the Bible quotes God as saying, "I will kill you with the sword," it does <u>not</u> mean that God carries a <u>literal</u> sword to kill His enemies. "God's sword" was put into the hand of the king of Babylon! [See Ezekiel 30:22-26] The "sword" of God by which He kills His enemies is, in reality, the swords or weapons of men.

PREVIEW

As we continue to study from Holy Scripture, we will come to know for sure that "God is love," and that He <u>always</u> acts that way. <u>Always</u>!

We will learn from Scripture <u>when</u> God uses force, and for <u>what reasons.</u>

Is God Really Like That?
Outline No. 2

DOES GOD EVER USE FORCE?

Of course He does! If God and/or His holy angels did not use force, how would we be protected from evil angels and evil men?

1 Peter 5:8
Like a roaring lion your adversary the devil prowls around, looking for someone to devour.

The question is not whether or not God uses force, but **how, when**, and **why** He uses force. **God uses force only:**

[1] - To protect people from evil angels.
[2] - To protect people from evil men.
[3] - To get people's attention.

There is a big difference in using force to protect, and in using force to kill or to seek revenge!

AN EXAMPLE **of how and why God uses force is when holy angels caused evil men to become blind when they were attempting to force their way into Lot's home in Sodom:**

Genesis 19:1-11
Now the **two angels** came to **Sodom** in the evening as **Lot** was sit-ting in the gate... they... entered his house, and he prepared a feast for them… Before they lay down, the men of the city, the **men of Sodom,** surrounded the house... and they **called to Lot** and said to him,

"Where are the men who came to you tonight? Bring them out to us that we may have relations with them." But **Lot** went out to them at the doorway, and shut the door behind him, and **said, "Please, my brothers, do not act wickedly...** But they said, "Stand aside."... So they pressed hard against Lot and came near to break the door. But the men [angels] reached out their hands and brought Lot into the house with them, and shut the door. And **they struck the men who were at the doorway of the house with blindness,** both small and great, so that they wearied themselves trying to find the doorway.

In a future chapter you will consider how Sodom and Gomorrah were destroyed. Remember that Bible writers wrote as if God directly did things that He had merely allowed.

1 Kings 13:1-6 [below] tells the story of **Jeroboam,** the first king of the ten tribes of Israel, whose **arm was made paralyzed temporarily** in order for God to get His point across. **Jeroboam was not hurt** -- except for his pride!

1 Kings 13:1-6
And behold, a man of God came out of Judah by the word of the LORD to Bethel. Jeroboam was

standing by the altar to burn incense... [3] And he gave a sign the same day, saying, "This is the sign that the LORD has spoken: 'Behold, the altar shall be torn down, and the ashes that are upon it shall be poured out.'"

[4] And when the king heard the saying of the man of God... Jeroboam stretched out his hand from the altar, saying, "Lay hold of him." And his hand, which he stretched out against him, dried up, so that he could not draw it back to himself. [5] The altar also was torn down, and the ashes poured out from the altar, according to the sign which the man of God had given by the word of the LORD. [6] And the king said to the man of God, "Entreat now the favor of the LORD your God, and pray for me, that my hand may be restored to me." And the man of God entreated the LORD; and the king's hand was restored to him, and became as it was before.

To get Saul's attention, before he was renamed Paul, he was struck down with blindness:

Acts 9:3-9

As he journeyed he came near Damascus, and suddenly a light shone around him from heaven. Then he fell to the ground, and heard a voice saying to him, "Saul, Saul, why are you persecuting Me?" And he said, "Who are You, Lord?" Then the Lord said, "I am Jesus, whom you are persecuting... For three days he was without sight..."

God sent **Jonah** to preach to the people of **Nineveh**, to warn them to repent in order to avoid destruction. **Jonah was afraid to go to Nineveh,** so he tried to run away by boarding a ship to Tarshish [Jonah 1]. It was then that **God used the force of the wind to get Jonah's attention.** As soon as Jonah was thrown overboard the wind ceased, just as it had done when Jesus rescued His disciples from the Sea of Galilee [Matt. 8:23-27].

Nevertheless, **no life was lost. No one was hurt. One of the Assyrian gods was a fish god.** Possibly Jonah was seen coming out of the mouth of the big fish which certainly would have gotten the Ninevites' attention! As a result the city "repented" when they heard Jonah's warning. **And what is God's attitude toward the heathen?**

Jonah 4:10,11

And the LORD said,... "Should not I pity Nineveh, that great city, in which there are more than 120,000 persons who do not know their right hand from their left."

Few people in the history of the world were more cruel than the Assyrians, yet God had regard for them also. Their "repentance" lasted only a short time. How the Assyrians were destroyed will be covered in detail in a later outline.
Another example of how and why God uses force is when Elisha and Israel were threatened by the Syrian army:

2 Kings 6:18-23

And when the Syrians came down against him, Elisha prayed to the LORD, and said, "Strike this people, I pray thee, with blindness." So he struck them with blindness in accordance with the prayer of Elisha... As soon as they entered Samaria, Elisha said, "O LORD, open the eyes of these men, that they may see." So the LORD opened their eyes, and they saw; and lo, they were in the midst of Samaria... And the Syrians came no more on raids into the land of Israel.

Revelation 7:1-3 [below] describes, in symbols, how God used force to prevent the forces of evil from hurting people. [Wind = destruction. Trees = people]

Revelation 7:1-3

After this I saw four angels standing at the four corners of the earth, holding back the four winds of the earth, that no wind might blow on earth or sea or against any tree... "Do not harm the earth or the sea or the trees, till we have sealed the servants of our God upon their foreheads."

When **Jesus** lived here on earth the people were taught that if something bad happened to anyone, it was because God was getting back at him for doing some evil thing. **Jesus** made it clear that God did not act this way toward sinners. **God treats everyone alike:**

Matthew 5:43-45

"You have heard that it was said, 'You shall love your neighbor and hate your enemy.' But I say to you, Love your enemies and pray for those who persecute you, so that you may be sons of your Father who is in heaven; for he makes his sun rise on the evil and on the good, and sends rain on the just and on the unjust."

God hates sin, but He loves the sinner!

God loves everyone, good or bad; however, each individual must choose for himself whether or not he is on God's side. **Notice the attitude of God** [in the form of a warrior] **when He talked to Joshua:**

Joshua 5:13-15

When Joshua was by Jericho, he lifted up his eyes and looked, and behold, a man stood before him with his drawn sword in his hand; and Joshua went to him and said to him, "Are you for us, or for our adversaries?" And he said, "No; but as commander of the army of the LORD I have now come." And Joshua fell on his face to the earth, and worshiped, and said to him, "What does my lord bid his servant?" And the commander of the Lord's army said to Joshua, "Put off your shoes from your feet; for the place where you stand is holy."

The "commander of the Lord's army" was not for either side! The fact that this "man" allowed Joshua to worship him indicates that **it was God Himself, in the form of a man,** who appeared to Joshua. In Rev 22:8,9 the apostle John was forbidden to worship at the foot of even an angel!

Revelation 22:8,9

I John am he who heard and saw these things. And when I heard and saw them, **I fell down to worship at the feet of the angel** who showed them to me; but he said to me, **"You must not do that!** I am a fellow servant with you and your brethren the prophets, and with those who keep the words of this book. Worship God."

Do people who have Jesus as their example have a right to get even with those who hurt them? **Yes!** But exactly **HOW** MAY WE GET EVEN, according to the apostle Paul?

Romans 12:14-21

Bless those who persecute you; bless and do not curse them... Repay no one evil for evil... No, "if your enemy is hungry, feed him; if he is thirsty, give him drink; for by so doing you will heap burning coals upon his head." Do not be overcome by evil, but overcome evil with good.

Daniel 10:13 [below] **gives an example of how God uses force when He finds it necessary to further His plans:**

Daniel 10:13

The prince of the kingdom of Persia withstood me twenty-one days; but **Michael,** one of the chief princes, came to help me, so I left him there with the prince of the kingdom of Persia.

This **"prince"** of Persia was **either Cyrus,** king of Persia, **or Satan,** the "prince of the power of the air" [Eph. 2:2] who was influencing the Persian king. An angel was sent with a message to Daniel -- possibly Gabriel. **Michael was Jesus.**

The problem: Prophecy regarding the nation of Israel needed to be fulfilled. **Can you imagine either God or holy angels taking 21 days to persuade Cyrus to act according to prophecy?! If physical force was heaven's method, only 21 seconds would have been needed!** Yet "21 days" was not enough! Therefore, Michael Himself was called. **Even Satan yields in the presence of Jesus.**

"Michael" = Jesus

The Hebrew meaning of "Michael" is "who like God" or "who is like God." "Michael" is referred to as the "archangel" – the angel of highest rank:

1 Thessalonians 4:16

For the **Lord himself** will descend from heaven with a cry of command, **with the archangel's call...**

Jude 1:9

But when the **archangel Michael,** contending with the devil, **disputed about the body of Moses...**

Revelation 12:7-9

Now **war** arose in heaven, **Michael and his angels** fighting against the **dragon; and the dragon and**

his angels fought, but they were defeated and there was no longer any place for them in heaven. And the great **dragon** was thrown down, that ancient **serpent,** who is called the **Devil** and **Satan,** the deceiver of the whole world – he was thrown down to the earth, and his angels were thrown down with him.

The great controversy is between Jesus and Satan. Note, above, that both Michael and Lucifer [Satan] have their angel followers. And who is it that is coming from heaven to raise the dead? **None other than** Michael:

Daniel 12:1,2

At that time shall arise **Michael, the great prince who has charge of your people.** And there shall be a time of trouble, such as never has been… but at that time **your people** will be delivered, everyone whose name shall be found written in the book. And many of **those who sleep** in the dust of the earth **shall awake,** some to everlasting life, and some to shame and everlasting contempt.

Some believe that **Jesus,** before man was created, took the form of an angel in order to identify with the angels, in the same way Jesus took the form of a man in order to identify with man. There is <u>no Scripture</u> that says this; nevertheless, this may or may not explain why Jesus is referred to as the "archangel." Even though Jesus **may** have assumed the form of an angel,

it does not change the fact that Jesus was still God – in the same way that **Jesus was still God even though He took the form of a man when He came to redeem man.**

You and I make many choices every day. Our choices and our attitudes make a difference in our personal success or failure.

<u>**Willful**</u> **and** <u>**continued**</u> **rebellion** against God or His law will result in the <u>**lowering of the "hedge" of holy angels**</u> [See Job 1 & 2]. This does <u>**not**</u> mean <u>**all**</u> protection is removed permanently. God is always ready and willing to help whenever people either ask for help or discontinue their willful rebellion. **Trials** and hardships brought about as **a** <u>**natural result**</u> of our breaking the rules should cause us to reform!

> **FACT: If force had been the method used to overcome evil, it would have been accomplished long ago.**

Most of our problems we have brought upon ourselves because of wrong choices concerning marriage, education, eating, drinking, etc. Your Bible speaks of **"the sins of the fathers… unto the third and fourth**

generations." These negative effects are the **natural** **results** of generation after generation making the same poor choices.

Example:

800 cats were divided into **two groups**. **400** cats were fed only **raw foods**. All **400** remained healthy over their normal life spans for the next three generations. The second study group ate only **cooked foods** [all enzymes are destroyed when food is heated over 120 degrees]. The **first generation** of this **second group,** that ate only cooked foods, developed diseases near the **end** of their life spans – like cancer. The **second generation** on cooked foods developed disease during the **middle** of their life spans. The **third** generation developed disease **early**. **Some were born with disease. Some were born deformed**.

Example:

A father advised his son to stay out of fights. One day his father, from afar, saw his son getting "beat up" in a fight! Instead of saying to himself, "I told him not to fight; it serves him right; I'll see him in the hospital," he went over and stopped the fight. His son was inclined to learn his lesson the hard way. This is how God works with people. **Most people choose to learn the hard way;** however, **God would much prefer that we learn the easy way.**

> **FACT: God always gives us liberty to do what we knowingly choose to do.**

The study of God should be taken seriously. Unless we know what God is really like – how He thinks and how He acts – it would be impossible to judge Him rightly.

The younger generation wants nothing to do with a God who would do, and command to be done, the terrible things attributed to Him in the Old Testament! Many have put their frustration in words: "Who wants to have anything to do with a God like that?"

But doesn't the Bible say that <u>ALL SCRIPTURE</u> is inspired by God?

It depends on <u>which</u> <u>translation</u> you read. In most translations it reads as follows:

2 Timothy 3:16 [RSV]

"All scripture *is* inspired by God and is profitable..." [Margin: "Or, every scripture inspired by God is..."]

In the original Greek, **"is"** is <u>not</u> included. The **"is"** was **added** by the Bible translators. In other words, Bible translators <u>thought</u> the word should be added to make the text say what <u>they</u> thought it should say!

Some translations have it as it was In the original Greek:

2 Tim. 3:16

Revised Version
"Every scripture inspired of God is profitable for teaching, for reproof..."

American Standard
"Every scripture inspired of God is also profitable..."

New English Bible
"Every inspired scripture has its use for teaching the truth and refuting error..."

REVIEW

[1] **God does use force to protect people from evil angels and evil men, and to get people's attention.**

[2] **There is a big difference in using force to protect, compared to using force to kill or to seek revenge.**

[3] **Examples of how God used force:**
[a] To protect Lot from the evil men of Sodom.
[b] Making king Jeroboam's arm dry up temporarily.
[c] Using wind and a large fish to get Jonah's attention.
[d] Saul [Paul] was made temporarily blind before his conversion.

[e] Syrian army made blind for a short time to protect Israel.

[4] God expects us to treat others well even if they do not treat us well. We are to return good for evil.

[5] God never forces us to do anything!

Is God Really Like That?
Outline No. 3

"WRATH OF GOD"

Many times we jump to the conclusion that a word in the Bible means the same as it does in our own society. When we do not **allow the Bible to serve as its own encyclopedia or dictionary,** by comparing Scripture, we often come to wrong conclusions.

For example, do you really believe that our "God of love" Creator actually loses control of His emotions, and becomes violently angry? Does God stoop to man's level?! What is your Bible talking about when it refers to **"God's wrath"?**

To the apostle Paul, the "wrath of God" was when "God gave them up." Paul used this exact expression three times in

Romans 1:18-32

For **the wrath of God** is revealed from heaven against all ungodliness and wickedness of those who by their wickedness suppress the truth. For what can be known about God is plain to them, because God has shown it to them. Ever since the creation of the world his eternal power and divine nature, invisible though they are, have been understood and seen through the things he has made. So **they are without excuse...** Therefore **GOD GAVE THEM UP** in the lusts of their hearts to impurity, to the degrading of their bodies among themselves, because they exchanged the truth about God for a lie and worshiped and served the creature rather than the Creator, who is blessed forever! Amen. For this reason **GOD GAVE THEM UP** to degrading passions. Their women exchanged natural intercourse for unnatural, and in the same way also the men, giving up natural intercourse with women, were consumed with passion for one another. Men committed shameless acts with men and received in their own persons the due penalty for their error. And since they did not see fit to acknowledge God, **GOD GAVE THEM UP** to a debased mind and to things that should not be done...

Psalm 78:48,49

He gave over their cattle to the **hail,** and their flocks to **thunderbolts.** He let loose on them his fierce anger, **wrath,** indignation, and **distress**, a company of **destroying angels.**

God's wrath was when **"He gave over"** their cattle to the **hail. "He let loose on them... destroying angels.** God did this by giving evil angels **permission** to do harm. In the following text [Mark 5:1-13] the evil spirits had to get **permission** from Jesus: **"Send us to the swine, let us enter them." "So He gave them leave..."**

Mark 5:1-13

...Jesus asked him, "What is your name?" He replied' "My name is Legion; for we are many." And he **begged him** eagerly **not to send them** out of the country. [11] Now a great herd of swine was feeding there on the hillside; and **they begged him, "Send us to the swine, let us enter them."** And the **unclean spirits** came out, and entered the swine; and the herd, numbering about **two thousand...** drowned in the sea.

Jesus Himself experienced God's "wrath."
Isaiah prophesied that Jesus would be killed by God!

Isaiah 53:4-10

Surely he has borne our infirmities and carried our diseases; yet we accounted him stricken, **smitten by God**, and afflicted... **Yet it was the will of the LORD to crush him with pain. When you make his life an offering for sin...**

FACT: The "wrath of God" is what people experience when God withdraws His supernatural protection.

But **how** did God **"bruise"** Jesus? **How** was Jesus **"struck down by God"?** Jesus, using the words of King David, gives us a clue:

Psalm 22:1

My God, my God, why have you forsaken me? Why are you so far from helping me, from the words of my groaning?

Matthew 27:46 & Mark 15:34

And about three o'clock Jesus cried with a loud voice, "Eli, Eli, lema sabachthani?" that is, **"My God, my God, why have you forsaken me?"**

Notice that **Jesus did not ask God, "Why are You killing Me?"** or "Why are You tormenting Me?" On the cross Jesus experienced what all sinners will experience when they die the eternal death [second death] -- the experience of the dying when they feel there is no more hope. Jesus died on the cross without conscious communication with God, angels, or anyone!

The **"wrath of God"** is what people experience when **God withdraws** His presence and supernatural protection. **The withdrawing** of God's protection is a matter of **cause and effect;** when people knowingly and willingly choose to go against God and/or His laws. This is **not the same** as when a **parent** does not allow a disobedient child to unnecessarily harm himself. God withdraws His protection only when His adult children choose to rebel against Him.

Isaiah 34:2

For the **LORD is enraged** against all the nations, and **furious** against all their hoards; he has doomed them, has **given them over for slaughter.**

The preceding Bible text speaks about an **"enraged"** or **angry** Lord who is **"furious."** And how does the Lord act when He is "enraged" and "furious"? **He merely refuses to work miracles to save people from their enemies!**

Jeremiah 18:17

Like the wind from the east, I will scatter them before the enemy. I will show them my back, not my face, in the day of their calamity.

Ezra 5:12

But because our ancestors had angered the God of heaven, he gave them into the hand of King Nebuchadnezzar of Babylon.

2 Chronicles 24:20

Because you have forsaken the Lord, he has also forsaken you."

Please notice in the following Bible text exactly what happens when God says, "I am bringing punishment."

Jeremiah 46:25,26

The LORD of hosts, the God of Israel, said: See, I am bringing punishment... **I will hand them over** to those who seek their life, to King Nebuchadnezzar of Babylon and his officers.

Isaiah 10:5,6,7

Ah, **Assyria,** the rod of my anger-- the club in their hands is my fury! Against a godless nation I send

him, and **against the people of my wrath** I command him, to take spoil and seize plunder... **but it is in his heart to destroy...**

Always keep in mind that Bible writers wrote as if God actually did things which He merely allowed. Old Testament writers **believed in only one God** -- a God that brought both good and evil.

Isaiah 37:7

...king of Assyria... I myself will put a spirit in him, so that he shall hear a rumor, and return to his own land; I will cause him to fall by the sword in his own land.'"

God, according to Isaiah, **said that He would** cause the king of Assyria to **"fall by the sword."** What happened, according to history? **His sons killed him!** Why he returned home is very interesting, and will be studied in detail in another outline.

FACT: GOD'S "PUNISHMENT" IS GOD ALLOWING ENEMIES TO DO WHAT COMES NATURALLY.

Does God break His own law?

Most Christians teach that the **Ten Commandment law** ["Moral Law"] is **a reflection of God's character.** One of the **Ten Commandments** says that it is **wrong to kill. God does not break His own law?.**

More Bible proof will be given as we continue our studies.

IMPORTANT NOTE:

When faced with a serious hardship we are inclined to think, "What have I done to deserve this?" We have been taught that God is out to get us; that we must "reap what we sow." Most of the time **we do have to pay the natural results** of foolish actions.

For example, a Christian who marries a non-Christian can expect **marriage problems**, not because God is punishing him or her, but because of the natural result of trying to mix water with oil.

The further away we get from **God's original diet** as recorded in Genesis chapter one, the more sickness we will experience. **God is never responsible for getting us sick!** We live in a world in which people bring disease upon themselves. **We cannot rightfully blame God when we break health laws.** Modern research has proven to us scientifically that God's health rules found in the Bible are inspired. People are brainwashed with thousands of **commercials** which tell them that devitalized and high fat foods are "good for you." And **whose fault is it** when we allow others to sell us things which hurt us and our families?

God never zaps anyone with **lung cancer** because He catches him **smoking!** On the other hand, He does not prevent it! Every person, young or old, chooses for himself whether or not to treat the body as a "temple" of God [1 Corinthians 6:19].

All people, Christians and non-Christians alike, live in an imperfect world. God never promised us a life without heartaches. What He has promised us is **supernatural help** so that no trial or temptation will be too much for us to handle:

1 Corinthians 10:13

> No temptation has overtaken you that is not common to man. God is faithful, and he will not let you be tempted beyond your strength, but with the temptation will provide the way of escape, that you may be able to endure.

God "punishes" people who underlineddeliberately and continually rebel against Him or His laws, **by removing some or all of His supernatural protection.** Without divine protection and guidance, man will self-destruct, as a natural consequence.

However, **only God can judge** a person's heart and know for sure whether or not a person is doing what he is doing because of human weakness, or because of willful rebellion. And no one should get the idea that those hurt in hurricanes, tornadoes, floods, wars, or crime are terrible sinners. **God has more than one reason for allowing bad things to happen to good people.**

FACT: GOD ALWAYS GIVES US LIBERTY TO DO WHAT WE INSIST UPON DOING.

The "wrath of God" is God withdrawing His presence from individuals, groups, or countries when they knowingly rebel against Him or His laws. However, God only allows evil men and evil angels to have **partial control** of individuals. groups, or countries – only **partial control** of the forces of nature. God's **"strange act"** is <u>not</u> killing people, but leaving people to themselves when they cry for help. This only happens when people knowingly and willfully separate themselves from God or His laws.

No one has committed the **"unpardonable sin"** who has **any** desire for God's love or forgiveness.

Perhaps a good example of how God treats His children is when an earthly parent uses what is called, **"tough love."** At times parents, even though it bothers them, refuse to post bail for a son or daughter who has been in trouble with the law one or more times.

Even though some people, young or old, never seem to learn that breaking the laws of the land and the laws of God works against them, there are <u>some</u> who <u>do</u> learn the hard way! Some alcoholics <u>do</u> stop drinking. Some married individuals <u>do</u> learn, the hard way, that being unfaithful to a spouse, in the end, brings heartache; in addition to more financial difficulties!

In the very same way people experience the **"wrath of God."** They experience what it is like for God to allow them to do it <u>their</u> way rather than His way. **God merely withdraws a portion of His supernatural protection = Job's "hedge"** until they wake up to the fact that God's ways are for their benefit. God <u>never</u> gives us a law that is not for our own good.

Another way of putting it: People who <u>deliberately</u> choose to follow God's **permissive will** rather than His **perfect will,** experience more trouble in this life than they would if they followed God's **perfect will.** God and His holy angels are delighted when individuals choose His **perfect will. The difference in God's perfect will and His permissive will is covered in detail in chapter 4.**

REVIEW

[1] The apostle Paul wrote that the "wrath of God" was shown when "God gave them up."

[2] God does not make anyone sick. He does not zap people with lung cancer because He catches them smoking.

[3] Sickness comes as a result of:
a) Wrong eating and drinking
b) Negative thinking
c) Not being willing to forgive self
d) Not being willing to forgive others
e) Living in an imperfect world

[4] God always gives us liberty to do what we <u>insist</u> upon doing.

[5] Jesus was, according to Isaiah, "struck down by God" and "crushed" by God, who made Him "an offering for sin." This was accomplished only by with-drawing His presence so that Jesus felt no conscious communication with God.

[6] When Jesus died on the cross without any conscious hope, He experienced what all the unsaved will experience as they die knowing they have not accepted the free gift of eternal life.

[7] God is love, and He always acts that way. Always!

PREVIEW

[1] The destruction at the time of Noah's flood, and the destruction of Sodom and Gomorrah will be studied in detail in later outlines.

[2]

1 Corinthians 2:9-12

"Eye has not seen, nor ear heard, nor have entered into the heart of man the things which God has prepared for those who love Him." But God has revealed them to us through His Spirit. For the Spirit searches all things, yes, the deep things of God... Now <u>we</u> have received, not the spirit of the world, but the Spirit who is from God, that we might know the things that have been freely given to us by God.

Most of the time the above Bible text is applied incorrectly. It <u>is</u> true that we do not know what awaits us in heaven; however, <u>this</u> Bible text tells us that we, as Bible students, have the opportunity to know more than those who do not allow God to guide them. In other words, Christians who study with an open mind have the ability to understand spiritual things not understood by those who do not allow God to teach them. When you complete these studies, you will know much more than the average Christian about how God thinks and acts.

Is God Really Like That?
Outline No. 4

Perfect Will vs. Permissive Will

God's permissive will is what God **allows** but **does not like** nor **sanction**.

Several practices were **allowed** by God of which **He did not approve;** especially in Old Testament times.

A GOOD EXAMPLE of His **PERMISSIVE WILL** is when ancient **Israel** was **allowed to have a king.** They were fully aware that being ruled by a king was not God's desire; yet **they insisted.** As a result, Israel suffered the **natural consequences** of their rebellion.

It is extremely important to keep in mind that God never forces individuals to do His perfect will.

1 Samuel 8:4-22

Then **all the elders of Israel...** said... **appoint for us,** then, **a king** to govern us, like other nations."... Samuel prayed to the LORD, and the LORD said to Samuel, "Listen to the voice of the people in all that they say to you; for they have not rejected you, but **they have rejected me** from being king over them.... you shall solemnly

warn them, and show them the ways of the king who shall reign over them."... But **the people refused to listen** to the voice of Samuel; they said, "No! but **we are determined to have a king over us, so that we also may be like other nations,** and that our king may govern us and go out before us and fight our battles."

The same lord who told Samuel to anoint Saul as king, also told Saul to slaughter the Amalekites, not for what they had done, but **for what their ancestors** had done! What did **King Saul** do? He killed every man, woman, and even every **infant!**

1 Samuel 15:1-3

And Samuel said to Saul, "The Lord sent me to anoint you king over his people Israel; now therefore hearken to the words of the Lord. Thus says the Lord of hosts, **'I will punish** what Amalek did to Israel in opposing them on the way, **when they came up out of Egypt.** Now go and smite Amalek, and utterly destroy all that they have; do not spare them, but **kill** both **man** and **woman, infant** and **suckling**, ox and sheep, camel and ass.'"

One lady told me that, because of the above story, [about the "Lord" commanding that little children should be killed] she hated God. Now that she knows the Truth of what really happened, she "no longer hates God."

FACT: GOD DOES NOT FORCE US TO CHOOSE HIS WAY.

As far as our personal lives are concerned, God makes His perfect will known to us through Holy Scripture. Those who knowingly disregard God's perfect will should not expect divine miracles! Such people must continue to wrestle with natural consequences. Most of our trials could have been prevented with emotional control or tongue control.

God is not the problem!

A few Christians claim that, in the case of incest, "God creates the baby." No, He does not. Neither does God create babies with no arms, legs, brains, etc. who are born because, among other things, expectant mothers use legal and illegal drugs. What God <u>does</u> do is to give people the ability to reproduce -- along with the laws as to how and when this should be done. A baby born with a low IQ because the mother smoked cigarettes is not God's doings -- except that He <u>allows</u> the mother to treat her body in such a way as to reproduce a less than perfect baby. Neither is a retarded baby born of a mother who is a slave to cocaine a creation of a God of love! One way that "God creates evil" is by allowing people to choose for themselves.

"You can't cram your religion down my throat!"

This would be the cry of millions of people **IF** God tried to **FORCE** them to do things His way. Yet millions are frustrated with God because He does not exercise enough control over **OTHER** people!! Many are angry with a God who appears to shirk His responsibility. It seems that either:

[a] A fictitious "God of love" has purposefully deceived us,
or
[b] Theologians have sold us a counterfeit bill of goods.

If our "God of love" is all powerful, and if He is in control, **why does He tolerate the misery** inflicted by individuals and nations?

It <u>seems</u> that if God had any sense at all, He would eliminate the <u>cause</u> of evil. The evidence <u>seems</u> to indicate that God is doing an irresponsible job of keeping law and order.

FACT: GOD HAS CHOSEN <u>NOT</u> TO BE IN COMPLETE CONTROL.

God has, by design, put people in control. People choose. Each individual chooses, as does each city, state, and country. Every choice helps to determine success or failure, poverty or wealth, life or death.

But is not God responsible if I make unwise choices because I was raised in an insecure environment? Ask the same question a different way. **Is it God who is responsible or am I** responsible if I raise **my** children in an insecure home environment resulting in my children making unwise choices?

FACT: FREEDOM OF CHOICE IS SOMETHING GOD INSISTS UPON.

God is not interested in followers who have no choice but to do as He says. That would be like manufacturing a **mechanical dog** that wags his tail automatically whenever a door opens!

Slavery
WAS NEVER PART of GOD'S PERFECT WILL.

It was never God's intention that one person be a slave to another. Anyone who would argue this point has not the slightest idea of what God is really like. God does not value one race above another.

Romans 10:12

For there is no distinction between Jew and Greek; the same Lord is Lord of all and is generous to all who call on him.

Acts 10:34,35

Then Peter began to speak to them: "I truly understand that God shows no partiality, but in every nation anyone who fears him and does what is right is acceptable to him.

Polgamy
WAS NEVER PART of GOD'S PERFECT WILL.

At **Creation** God gave Adam **one wife,** not two or more. The first person mentioned in the Bible to have two wives was Lamech, the great, great grandson of Cain [Adah and Zillah Genesis 4:17-19].

1 Timothy 3:2,12

Now a bishop must be above reproach, the husband of one wife... Let deacons be the husband of one wife...

King David and **King Solomon** had many wives; however, this was **not God's perfect will.** It was not until New Testament times that God's perfect will was vigorously promoted.

It is almost impossible for a husband to devote himself equally to two wives.

We see the sad plight of women in the Moslem countries where each man can legally have up to four wives. The only exception is the country of **Turkey** where only one wife is legal.

Divorce
WAS ALLOWED,
BUT WAS NEVER PART
OF GOD'S PERFECT WILL.

Jesus Himself spoke of the divorce situation. Jesus stated that the only reason **Moses** allowed divorce was because of their **"hardness of heart."** Jesus made it clear that divorce was never part of God's perfect will:

Matthew 19:7,8

They said to him, "Why then did Moses command us to give a certificate of dismissal and to divorce her?" He said to them, "It was because you were so hard-hearted that Moses allowed you to divorce your wives, but from the beginning it was not so.

Matthew 19:4-6

He answered, "Have you not read that the one who made them at the beginning 'made them male and female,' and said, 'For this reason a man shall leave his father and mother and be joined to his wife, and the two shall become one flesh'? So they are no longer two, but one flesh. Therefore what God has joined together, let no one separate."

Sometimes divorce is necessary, and becomes the lesser of two evils.

"EYE FOR AN EYE"
WAS NEVER PART OF
GOD'S PERFECT WILL

Jesus made it **crystal clear** that the **"eye for an eye"** laws were **not from God!** This is an extremely important fact. The words of **Jesus in the New Testament** teach a **direct opposite** of the counterfeit Old Testament laws [See Matt 5 below] Remember that **Jesus is "the same yesterday, today, and forever."**

JESUS SAID:

Matthew 5:38,39; 43-45

"You have heard that it was said, 'An eye for an eye and a tooth for a tooth.' But I say to you, Do not resist an evildoer. But if anyone strikes you on the right cheek, turn the other also; "You have heard that it was said, 'You shall love your neighbor and hate your enemy.' But I say to you, Love your enemies and pray for those who persecute you, so that you may be children of your Father in heaven; for he makes his sun rise on the evil and on the good, and sends rain on the righteous and on the unrighteous.

Stoning People to Death
NOT PART OF GOD'S
PERFECT WILL

Stoning people to death for **adultery [Deut 22:13-21]** or for **not keeping the Sabbath as a holy day [Numbers 15:32-36]** was never a part of God's perfect will.

Today some Christians sanction the **death penalty;** others do not. However, no Christian who reflects the thinking of Jesus would sanction the death penalty for adultery or for not keeping the Sabbath as a holy day!

The **origin** of these old **counterfeit laws,** which contradict God's true character of love, are studied in detail in a later chapter. **Jesus** Himself taught against these laws even <u>before</u> He was nailed to the cross:

John 8:3-11

The scribes and the Pharisees brought a woman who had been caught in adultery; ...they said to him, "Teacher, this woman was caught in the very act of committing adultery. Now in the law Moses commanded us to stone such women. Now what do you say?" ...Jesus bent down and wrote with his finger on the ground... said to them, "Let anyone among you who is without sin be the first to throw a stone at her." ...they went away, one by one... Jesus... said to her, "Woman, where are they? Has no one condemned you?" She said, "No one, sir."　　　And Jesus said, "Neither do I condemn you. Go your way, and from now on do not sin again."

Circumcision
<u>NEVER</u> PART OF GOD'S PERFECT WILL – IT DID NOT ORIGINATE WITH MOSES

John 7:22

[Jesus speaking]
Moses gave you circumcision (it is, of course, not from Moses, but from the patriarchs)...

According to the apostle **Paul,** circumcision has nothing whatsoever to do with the spiritual life:

1 Corinthians 7:19

Circumcision is nothing, and un-circumcision is nothing; but obeying the commandments of God is everything.

Galatians 6:15

For neither circumcision nor uncircumcision is anything; but a new creation is everything!

The idea of cutting the "flesh" for religious reasons originated with **heathen** religions:

Leviticus 19:28

You shall not make any gashes in your flesh for the dead or tattoo any marks upon you: I am the LORD.

Vegetarian Diet
WAS GOD'S PERFECT DIET AT CREATION

Genesis 1:29-30

God said, "See, I have given you every plant yielding seed that is upon the face of the earth, and every tree with seed in its fruit; you shall have them for food. And to every beast of the earth… I have given every green plant for food."

God's Permissive Will took over after Noah's Flood, when He allowed people to eat flesh:

Genesis 9:3,4

Every moving thing that lives shall be food for you; and just as I gave you the green plants, I give you everything. Only you shall not eat flesh with its life, that is, its blood.

The eating of flesh foods was one of the reasons why man's life span was reduced from 900+ years before Noah's flood to 600 to 200 years within six generations after Noah's flood.

Because God refused to force people to obey all of His laws, and because God insisted that you and I, as well as the people who lived in Old Testament times, have freedom of choice, **today** we have slavery, bigamy, divorce, etc.

REVIEW

[1] During Old Testament times God did not **force** people to follow His perfect will.

[2] Neither does God force people **today** to follow His perfect will, even though people would experience much less heartache if they would do so.

[3] **A good example** of how God lets people know His **perfect** will but allows people to choose His **permissive** will, is when ancient **Israel demanded a king.**

[4] Ancient **Israel suffered** greatly because they insisted upon doing things their own way.

[5] Because God does not force us to do things His way, **most of us have to learn the hard way – if we ever learn at all!** Life is much more pleasant when we learn the easy way, by following God's **perfect** will.

[6] By allowing people to learn by **trial and error,** God is developing the type of people that He can trust to take to heaven – people who will love and obey Him, not because they have to, but because they want to do so.

[7] **Slavery** was never God's perfect will.

[8] **Polygamy** was never God'sperfect will.

[9] Divorce was never God's perfect will.

[10] The **"eye for an eye"** philosophy was one of several counterfeit laws. **Jesus** made it clear that He was <u>not</u> the one who gave the "eye for an eye" law.

[11] Stoning people to death for **adultery** was never part of God's perfect will.

[12] Stoning people to death for not keeping the **Sabbath** as a holy day, was never part of God's perfect will.

[13] Circumcision was not part of God's perfect will.

[14] Vegetarianism was God's perfect plan at Creation.

The whole purpose of these Bible study outlines is to prove, from the Bible, that **God is certainly <u>not</u> the vengeful, get even, two-faced God** that most people, including Christians, have made Him out to be.

Today, **our children and youth have been taught to think for themselves,** and many of them have decided that they want no part of a God who thinks and acts like He is presented in the Old Testament. They no longer accept ideas as fact just because Dad, Mother, preacher, or priest say they

are facts. **They want and deserve Bible proof that God really is love as the apostle John claims he is [1 John 4:8,16].**

PREVIEW

At the **dedication of Solomon's Temple,** Solomon sacrificed 120,000 sheep and **22,000 oxen,** as **"peace offerings"** [1 Kings 8:63]. In **Outline No. 5** you will learn what the Old Testament prophets wrote about animal sacrifices. **To most of you it will be a surprise!**

Is God Really Like That?
Outline No. 5

Perfect Will vs. Permissive Will

Part II

Remember that **God's permissive will** is what **God allows but does not sanction.**

It is extremely important to keep in mind that God never forces individuals to do His perfect will.

In our last outline we studied several things that God permitted, in OT times, that were not part of His perfect will:

a) A king for Israel
b) Slavery
c) Bigamy
d) Divorce
e) Circumcision
f) "Eye for an eye" policy
g) Stoning people to death

Animal Sacrifices
WERE PART OF GOD'S PERMISSIVE WILL ONLY

The idea that animal sacrifices were part of God's permissive will, rather than part of His perfect will, comes as a **big surprise** to many Christians who understand why **Jesus** is called **"the Lamb of God."** Conclusions as to the significance of killing lambs in Genesis, and the Passover lambs in Exodus, will come in a later outline. For now, consider the fact that **God did not regulate the killing of animals until AFTER Israel insisted upon doing it the heathen way!**

The prophet **Jeremiah wrote plainly** about what God did **NOT** command when He brought Israel out of Egypt:

Jeremiah 7:21-24

Thus says the LORD of hosts, the God of Israel: Add **your** burnt offerings to your sacrifices, and eat the flesh. For in the day that I brought your ancestors out of the land of Egypt, **I did not speak to them or command them concerning burnt offerings and sacrifices.** But this command I gave them, "Obey my voice, and I will be your God, and you shall be my people; and walk only in the way that I command you, so that it may be well with you. "Yet they did not obey or incline their ear, but, in the **stubbornness of their evil will, they walked in their own counsels,** and looked backward rather than forward.

In verse 21 [above] Jeremiah portrays God as being sarcastic. Jeremiah quotes God as saying, in effect, "If you insist on doing it your way, then go right ahead and do it your way." = God's permissive will only.

> **Fact:** The idea of sacrificing animals came, not from God, but from Egypt and paganism.

Hosea 6:4-7

What shall I do with you, O Ephraim?... O Judah? Your love is like a morning cloud, like the dew that goes away early... For I desire steadfast love **and not sacrifice,** the knowledge of God **rather than burnt offerings.** But at Adam [Hebrew = like Adam] they transgressed the covenant; there they dealt faithlessly with me.

Stephen explained to the Jewish leaders of his day **how and why animal sacrifices began at Sinai,** and **they murdered him!** Stephen's explanation was that **Israel,** in their hearts, had **"turned back to Egypt"** and **worshiped Rephan and Moloch.** Stephen also told them **that God "gave them over to worship the host of heaven"** [like Baal worship]:

Acts 7:39-43

Our ancestors were unwilling to obey him; instead, they pushed him aside, and in their hearts they turned back to Egypt, saying to Aaron, 'Make gods for us... At that time they made a calf, offered a sacrifice to the idol... But **God turned away from them and handed them over to worship the host of heaven,** as it is written in the book of the prophets: 'Did you offer to me slain victims and sacrifices forty years in the wilderness, O house of Israel? No; you took along the **tent of Moloch,** and the star of **your god Rephan,** the images that you made to worship; so I will remove you beyond Babylon.'

Today, when newsmen report that certain cults are **sacrificing animals** during their religious services, we assume that they are speaking of **devil worship.** Even though the people of Israel directed their burnt offerings to God, their rituals were carried over from heathen practices of Egypt.

Ezekiel 20:24-26

...because they... had rejected my statutes... I gave them statutes that were not good and ordinances by which they could not live. I defiled them through their very gifts, in their offering up all their firstborn, in order that I might horrify them, so that they might know that I am the LORD.

You and I know that God never really forced or commanded Israel to offer their firstborn as human sacrifices, yet Bible writers wrote as if He had! [See Jeremiah 32:35].

The killing of millions of animals did not serve to make the people of Israel more loving and kind! It did not cause them to love God more. Evidently they missed the fact that **the blood of animals did not take away sin. Only the blood of Jesus took care of all sins** of the "saved" from Adam to the second coming.

Hebrews 10:4-6

For it is **impossible** for the blood of bulls and goats to take away sins. Consequently, when Christ came into the world, he said, "Sacrifices and offerings you [God] have not desired, but a body you have prepared for me; **in burnt offerings and sin offerings you [God] have taken no pleasure.**

Matthew 9:13

"Go and learn what this means, '**I desire mercy, not sacrifice.**' For I have come to call not the righteous but sinners."

> ## FACT: The blood of animals never took away ANY sin.
> ## The blood of Jesus took away ALL sin of the saved.

We have no record of Jesus telling anyone, **"go and kill a lamb,"** when He was living here on earth. He merely said, **"Your sins are forgiven." Jesus spoke these words of forgiveness long before He was nailed to the cross!** Following are examples of Jesus' attitude of forgiveness <u>before</u> He died on the cross:

Matthew 9:2-6

And just then some people were carrying a paralyzed man lying on a bed. When Jesus saw their faith, he said to the paralytic, "Take heart, son; your sins are forgiven." Then some of the scribes said to themselves, "This man is blaspheming...."

Mark 2:5-12

When Jesus saw their faith, he said to the paralytic, **"Son, your sins are forgiven...**

Luke 5:20-26

When he saw their faith, he said, "Friend, **your sins are forgiven you...**"

John 8:11

[To woman caught in adultery] ...Jesus said, **"Neither do I condemn you.** Go your way, and from now on do not sin again."

Jesus challenged the Pharisees to reconsider their attitudes toward sacrifices and the forgiveness of sins:

Matthew 9:13

[Jesus speaking]
"...Go and learn what this means, 'I desire mercy, not sacrifice'..."

The prophet **Isaiah understood** that **God was not pleased with animal sacrifices** -- that He merely wanted a common sense understanding between Himself and His people, just as He does today:

Isaiah 66:3,4

"He who slaughters an ox is like him who kills a man; he who sacrifices a lamb, like him who breaks a dog's neck; he who presents a cereal offering, like him who offers swine's blood; he who makes a memorial offering of frankincense, like him who blesses an idol. These have chosen their own ways, and their soul delights in their **abomination… they did what was evil in my eyes, and chose that in which I did not delight.**"

Isaiah 1:11-20

"What to me is the multitude of your sacrifices? says the LORD; **I have had enough of burnt offerings** of rams and the fat of fed beasts; **I do not delight in the blood of bulls, or of lambs,** or of goats… "Come now, let us reason together, says the LORD: though your sins are like scarlet, they shall be as white as snow; though they are red like crimson, they shall become like wool. If you are willing and obedient, you shall eat the good of the land; but if you refuse and rebel, you shall be devoured by the sword; for the mouth of the LORD has spoken."

The story of **Abraham** thinking that God wanted him to sacrifice **Isaac,** will be covered in detail in a future outline.

FACT: GOD NEVER <u>REQUIRED</u> ANIMAL SACRIFICES, YET HE <u>ALLOWED</u> THE STUBBORN PEOPLE TO DO IT THE HEATHEN WAY!

David understood this when he wrote:

Psalm 40:6

Sacrifice and offering **you do not desire,** but you have given me an open ear. **Burnt offering** and sin offering you have not required.

Psalm 50:13-15

Do I eat the flesh of bulls, or drink the blood of goats? Offer to God a sacrifice of thanksgiving, and pay your vows to the Most High. Call on me in the day of trouble: I will deliver you, and you shall glorify me."

Regardless of the fact that the writer of the book of Hebrews plainly states that it was **"impossible"** for the **"blood of bulls and goats"** to take away sin, some quote <u>Hebrews 9:22</u> [below] as "proof" that animal sacrifices were necessary during **O.T.** times:

Hebrews 9:22

Indeed, under the law almost everything is purified with blood, and without the shedding of blood there is no forgiveness of sins.

However, the verses **following** Hebrews 9:22 clearly show that the **only** blood that took away sin was the **blood of Jesus** when He died on the cross:

Hebrews 9:24-28

For Christ did not enter a sanctuary made by human hands, a mere copy of the true one, but he entered into heaven itself... But as it is, **he has appeared once for all** at the end of the age **to remove sin by the sacrifice of himself.**

Therefore, it **IS** true that no forgiveness of sin is possible **"without the shedding of blood."** But the **ONLY blood** that took away sin is the blood of Jesus. People were saved in Old Testament times in the very same way people are saved in our times – by the blood of Jesus. **People today look back to the cross. People in O.T. times looked forward to the coming of a Messiah. FOR EXAMPLE: Abraham,** according to the apostle Paul, was **saved by grace** through faith, the same as people are today:

Romans 4:2,3,9

For if **Abraham** was justified by works, he has something to boast about, but not before God. [3]For what does the scripture say? **"Abraham believed God, and it was reckoned to him as righteousness"...** **"Faith was reckoned to Abraham as righteousness."**

Today we have an advantage that people did not have a few years ago. Two hundred years ago people were forced to depend upon the clergy to tell them what was Truth and what was not Truth. Before the invention of the printing press people had no opportunity to study the Bible for themselves in their own homes. Now you can compare Scripture, check the context of the quoted verses, and determine for yourself whether or not the preacher is teaching according to the whole Bible.

A pastor's young daughter watched her father preparing a sermon. "Daddy," she asked, "Does God tell you what to say?" He responded, "Of course, honey. Why do you ask?" Her reply: "I was wondering why you scratch so much out."

> **FACT:** The revelation of truth is progressive to each of us as individuals, whether or not we are preachers.

Each new generation of genuine, mature, open-minded Christians has a better understanding of the Bible and its Author. According to the apostle Paul, **New Testament writers knew more than Old Testament writers:**

Ephesians 3:4-9

...which will enable you to perceive my understanding of the mystery of Christ. In former generations this mystery was not made known to humankind, as it has now been revealed to his holy apostles and prophets by the Spirit... and to make everyone see what is the plan of the mystery hidden for ages in God who created all things;

> ## FACT: God will keep His promise to lead you into all truth in His own way and His own time.

Perhaps God knows the time is right for **YOU,** by leading you to this Bible study of His true character. God <u>wants</u> you to know how He <u>really</u> thinks and how He <u>really</u> acts.

"<u>Lamb</u>" = <u>Jesus</u>

It was not until New Testament times that Jesus was referred to as the "Lamb." During Old Testament times the people of Israel, against the true Lord God's wishes, sacrificed as burnt offerings not only lambs, but sheep, kids, goats, rams, cows, bulls, calves, oxen, and doves! At the dedication of Solomon's temple:

1 Kings 8:63
Solomon offered as peace offerings to the Lord **22,000 oxen** and **120,000 sheep.**

> ## John the Baptist was the first person to refer to Jesus as a Lamb:

John 1:29
"Behold, the Lamb of God, who takes away the sin of the world!"

Because **John the Baptist** had been taught wrongly by the Jewish leaders from a child, he was deceived into thinking that **Jesus** would lead the army of Israel against their enemies; that He would set up His earthly kingdom! When **Jesus** did not have John the Baptist freed from prison, he was bitterly disappointed. John, from prison, sent two of his disciples to ask Jesus: **"Are you he who is to come, or shall we look for another?"** [Luke 7:19].

Two of God's greatest prophets, **John the Baptist** and **Elijah** did not understand how God thinks and acts! **Peter and John** wanted to call fire down from heaven **"like Elijah,"** to destroy some Samaritans who did not welcome **Jesus** into their village [Luke 9:52-55; 2 Kings 1:9-12].

John the Baptist, Peter, John, and Elijah were **sure** they knew how God operates! But they did not – just like most Christians today **think** they know that God torments, kills, and will "burn them in fire" for eternity if they do not obey Him! Church people back then, thought they knew what the coming **Messiah** would be like, just like most people today **"know"** what will happen when Jesus returns the second time**!**

Because Israel insisted upon offering animal sacrifices like the heathen**,** the true Lord allowed Satan to point the leaders of Israel in the wrong direction where they set up counterfeit rules. Even though the people of Israel sacrificed goats, sheep, **bulls,** doves, and lambs to "atone for sin**,"** God's permissive will allowed Israel to avoid total loss. God stepped in and declared that only the **lamb** represented **Jesus.**

Jesus, as the Lamb, is referred to in Acts 8:32, 1 Peter 1:19, and several times in the book of Revelation.

Remember that only **the blood of Jesus took away sin.** The sacrificing of animals in the Old Testament was the result of Israel being influenced by the pagans. **The many laws regarding the sacrificing of animals were given** after **Israel insisted on doing it the heathen way.** The Lamb representing Jesus was a **secondary plan** – not an original perfect plan.

The fact that Noah, Abraham, and possibly Abel offered animal sacrifices, does not prove that animal sacrifices were commanded by the true **Lord God. Jeremiah, Hosea, Stephen, Ezekiel, Isaiah, and David all wrote that animal sacrifices were** not **originally God's idea!**

Who Was/Is Jesus?

Jesus is the "first" and the "last":

Revelation 22:12,13

"Behold, **I am coming soon…** to repay every one for what he has done. I am the **Alpha** and the **Omega,** the **first** and the **last,** the **beginning** and the **end.**

Jesus was our Creator:

John 1:1-4,10,14

In the beginning was the **Word,** and the **Word** was with God [Yahweh]**,** and the **Word was God** [Elohim]**;** He was in the beginning with God [Yahweh]**;** **all things were made through him** [KJV: "by him"]**,** and without him was not anything made that was made. **In him was life,** and the life was the light of men**… He was in the world,** and the world was made through him [KJV: "by him"]**,** yet the world knew him not**…** And **the Word became flesh** and dwelt among us**…**

Colossians 1:14-16 KJV

In whom we have redemption through his blood, even the forgiveness of sins: [15] Who is **the image of the invisible God**, the firstborn [greatest] of every creature: [16] **For by him were** all things created, that are **in heaven,** and that are in the **earth, visible** and **invisible,** whether they be thrones, or dominions, or principalities, or powers**; all things were created by him and for him:**

Jesus was the God of the O.T.

1 Corinthians 10:1-4

...our fathers were all under the cloud, and all passed through the sea, and all were baptized into **Moses** in the **cloud** and in the **sea,** and all ate the same supernatural food and all drank the same supernatural drink. For they drank from the supernatural **Rock which followed them,** and **the Rock was Christ.**

John 8:57-59

The Jews then said to him. You are not yet fifty years old, and **have you seen Abraham?"** Jesus said to them, "Truly, truly, I say to you, **before Abraham was, I am."** So they took up stones to throw at him; but Jesus hid himself, and went out of the temple.

Exodus 3:14,15

God [Elohim] said to Moses, **"I AM WHO I AM."** And he said, "Say to the people of Israel, **'I AM** has sent me to you.'" God [Elohim] said to Moses, "Say to the people of Israel, 'The Lord **[Yahweh],** the God [Elohim] of your fathers, the God [Elohim] of Abraham, the God [Elohim] of Isaac, and the God [Elohim] of Jacob, has sent me to you': this is my name for ever, and thus I am to be remembered throughout all generations.

By comparing John 8:57-59 with Ex 3:14,15 we understand that Jesus Himself claimed to be the great **"I AM"** of the Old Testament.

Why was it only indirectly that Jesus referred to Himself as God? Stop and think. If someone who looked like an ordinary man met you on the street and claimed that he was "God," what would be y<u>our</u> reaction?! It was difficult enough for people to accept Jesus as the "Son" of God. Following are interesting texts which may shed some light on the subject:

Isaiah 9:6

"For to us a child is born, to us a son is given; and the government will be upon his shoulder, and his name will be called 'Wonderful Counselor, **Mighty God, Everlasting Father, Prince of Peace."**

Matthew 1:23

"Behold, a virgin shall conceive and bear a son, and his name shall be called **Emmanuel** (which means, **God with us.**)"

When did Jesus become the "Son of God"?

Adam, is called a **"son of God"** in Luke's chronology:

Luke 3:38

...the son of Enos, the son of Seth, the son of **Adam, the son of God."**

Adam was to be the representative of this world in meetings of the "sons of God" in heaven:

Job 1:6,7

Now there was a day when the **sons of God** came to present themselves before the Lord, and **Satan** also **came among them.** The Lord said to Satan, "Whence have you come?" Satan answered the Lord, "From going to and fro on the earth, and from walking up and down on it."

Jesus, the **"second Adam"** [1 Cor 15:45-49], paid the penalty for Adam's sin, thus He redeemed mankind, and **became the rightful and legal representative of this world. Jesus took Adam's place as the representative of this world – one of the "Sons of God" – when He raised Himself from the grave:**

John 10:17,18

"... I lay down my life, that I may take it again. No one takes it from me, but I lay it down of my own accord. I have power to lay it down, and I have power to take it again..."

God Himself, the invisible Spirit, came into Mary's womb to produce the body He called, "The Son of God." **Jesus is the <u>visible</u> "image of the <u>invisible</u> God"** [Col 1:15].

Mary became pregnant via **God's Holy Spirit** [Luke 1:35]. **Jesus** was the **"first-born of the dead"** [Rev 1:5] and the **"first-born of all creation"** [Colossians 1:15,16,18] in the same sense that **King David** was called the **"first-born"** when, in fact, he was the youngest of four sons [1 Samuel 17:13,14]. In other words, **Jesus and David were the greatest,** even though they were not the <u>literal</u> "first-born."

> # FACT: Our Creator Himself came to redeem us!

Is God Really Like That?
Outline No. 6

"Fire" in the Bible

Whenever people speak of fire in connection with the Bible, or in connection with God, a picture of "hell fire" comes into mind.

The idea that a "God of love" <u>could</u> do what most Christians say He does – torment in fire anyone who does not follow all of His rules – not just for 1,000 years, but "forever," is Satanic doctrine!

Would <u>YOU</u> be as cruel to one of <u>YOUR</u> children if he or she disobeyed you?! Your answer, we hope, is "No." Does that mean you think you are more loving and fair than God?

1 John 4:8,16
God is love… God is love.

Either God <u>is</u> love, or He isn't love. We cannot have it both ways. Yes, He is God, and God can do anything He wants – because He is God; however, **it is absolutely impossible for Him to be cruel and still be able to classify Himself as "love."**

In Outlines 12 thru 17 we will study, **from the Bible**, what will happen to both good people and bad people when they die.

In the next four outlines we will study about **eighteen different types** of "fire" mentioned in your Bible. Our study will demonstrate how God continues to be our "**God of love**" while allowing us to experience different types of **"fire."**

[1] Fire of the <u>TONGUE</u>

Children will sometimes tauntingly repeat, "Liar, liar, your **tongue** is on fire!"

James 3:5,6
So also the **tongue** is a small member, yet it boasts of great exploits. How great a forest is set **ablaze** by a small fire! And **the tongue is a fire.**

Proverbs 16:27
Scoundrels concoct evil, and their **speech** is like a **scorching fire.**

Proverbs 29:8
Scoffers set a city **aflame,** but the wise turn away wrath.

[2] Fire of
RETURNING
GOOD FOR EVIL

Romans 12:20,21
No, "if your enemies are hungry, feed them; if they are thirsty, give them something to drink; for by doing this you will **heap burning coals on their heads.**" [21]Do not be

overcome by evil, but overcome evil with good.

Proverbs 25:21,22

If your enemies are hungry, give them bread to eat; and if they are thirsty, give them water to drink; for you will **heap coals of fire on their heads,** and the LORD will reward you.

[3] Fire of
PASSION

1 Corinthians 7:9

But if they are not practicing self-control, they should marry. For it is better to marry than to be **aflame** with **passion.**

[4] Fire of
JEALOUSY

Song of Solomon 8:6 KJV

Jealousy is cruel as the grave: the coals thereof ar*e* coals of **fire,** which hath a most vehement **flame.**

Psalm 79:5

Will thy **jealous** wrath **burn like fire...?**

Deuteronomy 4:24 KJV

For the LORD your God is a devouring **fire,** a **jealous** God.

Ezekiel 38:19 KJV

"For in my **jealousy** and in the **fire** of my wrath have I spoken."

Zephaniah 1:18 KJV

...the whole land shall be devoured by the **fire** of his **jealousy.**

Zephaniah 3:8 KJV

...all the earth shall be devoured by the **fire** of his **jealousy.**

[5] Fire of
SICKNESS

Isaiah 10:16

Therefore the Sovereign, the LORD of hosts, will send wasting **sickness** among the stout warriors, and under his glory a **burning** will be **kindled, like the burning of fire.**

[6] Fire of the
GOSPEL

Isaiah 10:17

The light of Israel will become a **fire,** and his Holy One a **flame;** and it will **burn** and devour his thorns in one day.

Isaiah 6:6,7

Then one of the seraphs flew to me, holding a **live coal** that had been taken **from the altar** with a pair of tongs. The seraph touched my mouth with it and said: "Now that this has touched your lips, your guilt has departed and **your sin is blotted out.**"

In the book of Revelation "SUN" is a symbol for the Gospel:

Revelation 1:16-18

...his face was like the sun shining with full force... he placed his right hand on me, saying, "Do not be afraid; **I am the first and the last, and the living one. I was dead,** and see, I am alive forever and ever; and I have the keys of Death and of Hades."

Revelation 12:1

A great portent appeared in heaven: a woman clothed with the **sun**, with the moon under her feet, and on her head a crown of twelve stars.

Revelation 16:8,9

The fourth angel poured his bowl on the **sun,** and it was allowed to scorch people with **fire;** they were scorched by the fierce heat, but they cursed the name of God, who had authority over these plagues, and **they did not repent and give him glory.**

Revelation is a book of symbols. In the preceding verses **"sun"** is symbolic for the **Gospel. [Revelation contains at least 290 different symbols. Revelation Deciphered** is a publication you may obtain. It includes the outlines of all 22 chapters, and a Dictionary of the 290 different symbols.] **Those burned by a** <u>literal</u> **sun [Rev 16:8,9 above] would not be expected to "give Him glory."**

Revelation 21:23

And the city has no need of **sun** or moon to shine on it, for the **glory** of God is its light, and its **lamp** is the **Lamb.**

Malachi 4:2

But for you who revere my name the **sun of righteousness** shall rise, with healing in its wings.

---

[7] Fire of **TRUTH**

"THE TRUTH HURTS"
ONLY THOSE WHO FIGHT IT.

Jeremiah 5:14

Therefore thus says the LORD, the God of hosts: Because they have spoken this word, I am now making **my words** in your mouth **a fire,** and this people wood, and **the fire shall devour them.**

Jeremiah 23:29

Is not **my word** like **fire,** says the LORD…

Jeremiah 20:9

….within me there is something **like a burning fire** shut up **in my bones…**

Psalm 29:7

The **voice** of the LORD flashes forth **flames of fire.**

Luke 24:32

Were not our **hearts burning** within us **while he was talking to us** on the road, while he was opening the **scriptures** to us?"

Isaiah 42:25

So he poured upon him the **heat** of his anger and the fury of war; **it set him on fire** all around, but he did not understand; **it burned him,** but he did not take it to heart.

[8] Fire of DIVISION AMONG FAMILIES

Luke 12:49-53

"I came to bring **fire** to the earth, and how I wish it were already kindled!... Do you think that I have come to bring peace to the earth? No, I tell you, but rather **division!** From now on five in one **household will be divided,** three against two and two against three; they will be divided: father against **son** and son against **father, mother** against daughter and **daughter** against **mother; mother-in-law** against her **daughter-in-law..."**

The **"fire"** of **division** and **discord** among family members and other relatives is caused by:

[a] – **Different life styles** of Christians and non-Christians.
[b] – **Differences in beliefs** of those who rely upon **tradition** as opposed to those who study the Scriptures for themselves with an open mind.
[c] – **Intolerance** of the ideas or actions of others with you.

Attempting to coerce or force others into alternate beliefs or life styles sooner or later results in backlash. **Force** is the **devil's** method. **Freedom of choice** is **God's way.**

[9] Fire of <u>LOVE</u>

When **Johnny Cash** sang **<u>Ring of Fire,</u>** we knew he was singing of **love:** "I fell into a burning ring of fire. I went down down down, and the flames went higher... it burns burns burns, the ring of fire..." Following, in Ezekiel 28, Satan [symbolized by the "king of Tyre"] is thrown OUT of the "fire" rather than being thrown into the "fire."

Ezekiel 28:11-18

...raise a lamentation over the king of Tyre, and say to him, Thus says the Lord God: "You were the signet of **perfection,** full of **wisdom** and perfect in **beauty. You were in Eden,** the garden of God... you were on the holy mountain of God; you walked among the **stones of fire.** You were **blameless** in your ways from the day that you were **created,** until iniquity was found in you... the guardian cherub drove you out from among the **stones of fire. Your heart was proud** because of your beauty... So I brought out **fire from within you; it consumed you..."**

In the preceding Bible text [Eze 28:11-16] it says that Satan ["king of Tyre – the description makes it clear that the "king of Tyre" represents Satan] was once on the **"mountain of God."** As a symbol, "mountain" **represents a** government [See Rev 17:3,9,10; Dan 2:34,35; Zech 4:7; Zech 8:3]. **Lucifer [Satan] was a leader in God's heavenly** government ["mountain of God"]. Living as a part of God's government in heaven is referred to here as being in the midst of "stones of fire." The "fire" **here is obviously** something good! **Even though** "God is love" **[1 John 4:8,16], there is no Bible text which defines this** "fire" as love; **however,** logic **leans heavily in that direction**.

In every mature follower of **Jesus,** His love, like a sacred flame, burns on the altar of the heart.

Speaking symbolically in **Revelation 15:2,3** the saved "play harps" and sing while standing beside the **"sea of glass"** mingled with **"fire."** Why should the saved want to be near **"fire"** if the **"fire"** was something unpleasant?!

[10] ANGELS OF FIRE Not literal fire.

Hebrews 1:7

Of the **angels** he says, **"**Who makes his **angels** winds, and his servants **flames of fire."**

Psalm 104:4 KJV

...who maketh his **angels** spirits; his ministers a **flaming fire.**

[11] Fire of HOLY SPIRIT

Gospel writers **Mark** and **John** quote John the Baptist as saying that **Jesus** would baptize with the **Holy Spirit.** The other two Gospel writers,

Matthew and **Luke,** add that Jesus would baptize with **"fire."**

Mark 1:8

I have baptized you with water; but he will baptize you with the **Holy Spirit."**

Matthew 3:11-16

"I baptize you with water for repentance, but one who is more powerful than I is coming after **me...** He will baptize you with the **Holy Spirit** and **fire.**

John 1:32,33

John testified...He... is the one who baptizes with the **Holy Spirit.**

Luke 3:16,17,22

John answered all of them by saying, "I baptize you with water; but one who is more powerful than I is coming... He will baptize you with the **Holy Spirit** and **fire.**

Symbols of Revelation indicate that **"fire"** represents the **Spirit of Jesus.** Jesus promised to send His **Spirit.**

Revelation 2:18

These are the words of the **Son of God,** who has **eyes** like a **flame of fire.**

Revelation 4:5

...in front of the throne **burn** seven **flaming** torches, which are the seven **spirits of God.**

Revelation 5:6

I saw... **a Lamb...** having... **seven eyes,** which are the **seven spirits** of God sent out into all the earth.

The **"fire"** which came down upon the apostles who spoke in **"tongues"** was <u>outward</u> <u>evidence</u> that they were controlled by His Holy Spirit. This, of course, was **not literal fire,** otherwise it would have burned them, and caught their hair on fire**!**

Acts 2:1-8

When the day of Pentecost had come, they were all together in one place… Divided tongues, as of fire, appeared among them, and a tongue rested on each of them. All of them were filled with the Holy Spirit and began to speak in other languages, as the Spirit gave them ability… Amazed and astonished, they asked, "How is it that we hear, each of us, in our own native language?

[12] GOD AS FIRE
What kind of "fire" is God?

Some people have the idea that no sinner can get close to God and still live. Perhaps they get the idea from**:**

Hebrews 12:29

God is a consuming fire.

Every person who has ever lived [except Jesus] was tainted with sin, including Bible "heroes" [1 John 1:8; Romans 3:10,23]. Yet several individuals have gotten close to God and still lived. **Satan [Lucifer] survived** in God's presence after he rebelled.

Moses got so close to God that his face shone enough to make other people afraid of him [Exodus 34:29-35], and he did not die. Several times **God appeared in the form of an angel,** as in the case of**:**

Gideon [Judges 6:12-14 = "Lord"]
Jacob   [Genesis 32:24-30 =
                "God face to face"]
Abraham [Gen 12:7; 17:1-5 =
                "God Almighty"]
Shadrack, Meshack, Abednego
        [Dan 3]
Adam and Eve   There is evidence
        that God spoke face to face with
        them after they disobeyed
        [Gen 3:8,9].

The fact that **"fire"** did not burn up the **"burning bush"** when **Moses** was there talking with God, indicates that the **"fire"** was <u>not</u> a <u>literal</u> fire. This **"fire"** was merely a symbol of God's presence [Ex 3:1-5]**.**

What kind of "fire" is God?

**Perhaps a combination of the
"fire" of love
"fire" of truth
"fire" of the Gospel
"fire" of His Holy Spirit**

As we consider the many different types of **"fire"** mentioned in the Bible, it becomes evident that **Bible writers seldom referred to <u>literal</u> fire** when they wrote about **"fire."**

BEWARE OF SPIRITUAL ARSONISTS!

<u>REVIEW</u>

To know what type of "fire" a Bible writer referred to, we must always consider the context.

<u>PREVIEW</u>

We have now covered 12 different types of fire. We have six more to go for a total of 18. The last six types of "fire" will be even more interesting.

Is God Really Like That?
Outline No. 7

"Fire" in the Bible
Part II

In Outline No. 6 we covered the first 12 fires:

[1] – Fire of the **TONGUE**
[2] – Fire of **RETURNING GOOD FOR EVIL**
[3] – Fire of **PASSION**
[4] – Fire of **JEALOUSY**
[5] – Fire of **SICKNESS**
[6] – Fire of the **GOSPEL**
[7] – Fire of **TRUTH**
[8] – Fire of **FAMILY DIVISIONS**
[9] – Fire of the **HOLY SPIRIT**
[10] – **ANGELS** of fire
[11] – Fire of **LOVE**
[12] – **GOD** of fire

[13] Fire of <u>HATRED</u> <u>ANGER</u> <u>MURDER</u>

When someone gets extremely angry we say that he is **"really burned"** or **"hot under the collar."** **Anger** or **hatred** in the human heart is referred to in the Bible as **"fire."**

Hosea 7:6,7
For they are **kindled** like an **oven**, their **heart burns** within them; all night their **anger smolders**; in the morning it **blazes** like a **flaming fire**. All of them are **hot** as an **oven**...

Psalm 39:2,3
I held my peace to no avail; my **distress** grew worse, my **heart** became **hot** within me. While I mused, the **fire burned**; then I **spoke** with my tongue...

Jeremiah 20:9
...within me there is something like a **burning fire** shut up in my bones: I am weary with holding it in, and I cannot.

Isaiah 9:17-19
For **wickedness burned like a fire**... the land is burned, and the **people became like fuel** for the **fire; no man spared his brother.**

Psalm 21:8,9
...**your enemies**... those **who hate you**. You will make them like a **fiery furnace** when you appear... fire will consume them.

In Outline No. 6 we learned that **"fire"** in **Satan** would eventually destroy him [Ezekiel 28:16 -- "So I brought out **fire from within you; it consumed you...**"] **Hatred, anger, and murder** in the heart of Satan will eventually destroy him, just as they will destroy all people who have these traits.

What is it that causes men and women to become like a **"fiery furnace"** in such a way that would make them burn up? What will make God's glory unbearable to sinners?

At **creation** man was physically and mentally **perfect**. Since then negative emotions have caused degeneration. The **first negative emotion was the**

guilt of **Adam** and **Eve**. This guilt caused them to cover themselves with fig leaves [Gen 3:7]. **Is it possible** that **rebellion** against God and His laws have caused **natural, physical, and mental changes** which will, in the end, cause sinners to self-destruct?

It has been scientifically proven that fear, guilt, and hatred cause chemical changes to take place in the human body resulting in extreme negative results.

<u>**Spontaneous Human Combustion**</u> is something that has happened many times in the past, and is still happening today – hundreds of cases per year! **Mark Twain** and **Charles Dickens** were two of many authors who wrote about this well-documented phenomenon. **Charles Dickens**, in his 1852 novel Bleak House, **cited 30 cases** [copied from The Anatomy of Drunkeness]. He provided a list of several authorities who considered spontaneous human combustion to be a scientific fact. Because the cause has yet to be explained, many people ignore the undeniable evidence, and claim it does not exist.

Spontaneous human combustion takes place when a human body ignites and **<u>burns</u> <u>from</u> <u>within</u>**, without any external source of fire. The **burning begins from <u>inside</u> a person's body.** Many cases have been observed, but no one can explain <u>why</u> it happens. People are reduced to a   small pile of ashes while curtains, bed sheets,

furniture, or clothes worn by the victim are <u>not</u> burned -- even though it takes over 3,000 degrees Fahrenheit to cremate a body! Cremation takes four hours with the help of 40 gallons of fuel! **SHC** burns from the inside out and, obviously, works differently than cremation.

Hundreds of cases have been reported.   Spontaneous human combustion [SHC] was well known during the 18th and 19th centuries.

No one really knows why SHC happens; however, many cases have occurred in people who are **emotionally distraught**. Many **alcoholics** have experienced SHC. And who is more emotionally distressed than an alcoholic?   Nevertheless, there are **exceptions** to the rule. One time it happened to a **baby** lying in a crib.

In **1959**, in Rockford, Illinois, **Rickey Paul Pruitt, age 4 months**, burned to death in his crib. <u>The crib, bed sheets,</u> and <u>clothes</u> did **<u>not</u> burn at all!**

Some people think that anything they do not understand must come from the devil! **Would a "God of love" allow the devil to burn a little baby to death?** Of course not! In this 21st century men are learning more and more of the relationship between the mind and the body. What affects one affects the other. **Think as Jesus told you to think and you will be healthier.**

The parents of **four year old Amy Kirby**, and her **five year old sister, Alice**, were separated and lived in houses about a mile apart. These two sisters were **very unhappy**, not only because their parents were separated, but because they were separated – one with each parent. On January 5, 1899, in Britain (Halifax), at 11am, **both** sisters burst into flames and died before the flames could be extinguished. **This happened at the same time a mile apart** when no one was near to save them. One neighbor who heard Amy scream said she saw flames three feet tall burning out of Amy's head.

Some consider **SHC** absurd because it is "non-scientific." Some refuse to believe what they cannot explain, regardless of **eye witnesses**; regardless of **proven facts**.

In the year 1788 in **England**, a man walked into a room and saw a **young chambermaid** scrubbing the floor with **fire blazing from her back**. It was not until the man told her that she even knew she was on fire. She was dead before he could put out the flames.

An old **soldier** climbed into a hayloft on February 19, 1888, to sleep off his **drunkenness**. He was completely consumed by fire. The **hay** around him was **not even scorched**.

In **Dallas, Texas**, in **1966**, Olga Stephens, age 75, burned to death sitting in a **parked car**. Witnesses were unable to save her. Firemen reported that no damage was done to the car.

On December 5, **1966**, in Pennsylvania, all that was left of 92 year old Dr. John Bently was his right leg from his knee down, and **a pile of ashes 14 inches across and 5 inches deep.**

The Nigerian Herald of December 27, **1974**, told of how six members of the same family burned to death inside a small wooden room. Nothing else in the room burned, including two cotton mattresses.

The case of **Mary Reeser** of St. Petersburg, Florida, in **1951**, was the **first case to be investigated by modern, scientific methods**. Pathologists, fire officials, arson experts, and even the FBI tried to figure it out, but they could not. **Dr. Wilton M. Krogman,** physical anthropologist at the University of Pennsylvania School of Medicine, and a world-renowned expert on the effects of fire on the human body, said, **"I regard it as the most amazing thing I've ever seen**. As I review it, the short hairs on my neck bristle with vague fear."

Mary's doctor husband had died four years before she moved to St. Petersburg, Florida from Pennsylvania. Not only did she feel lost without her husband, but she was **greatly annoyed** with the sweltering Florida heat. Her plans were to move back to Pennsylvania as soon as possible.

About 8:30 the night before she **(Mary Reeser)** told her doctor son, Richard, that she would take two sleeping pills and retire early so as to get a good night's sleep. At eight o'clock the next morning a neighbor, not wanting to awaken her, proceeded to tie a message on her front door. But **the door knob was hot.** She called for the help of two painters working across the street who found the woman turned into a **pile of ashes, a shrunken head**, and **one foot** that was still wearing a black satin slipper, all together weighing less than **ten pounds.** There was **no fire damage in the apartment.**

Concerning the **shrunken head, Dr. Krogman** said, "…the head is not left complete in ordinary burning cases. Certainly it does not shrivel or… reduce to a smaller size. In the presence of the heat sufficient to destroy soft tissues, the skull would literally explode in many places. I… have never known any exception to this rule. **Never have I seen a skull so shrunken** or a body so completely consumed by heat." [Reader's Digest's Mysteries of the Unexplained, 1982, Pages 78-93]

SHC is something that is quite well known. **ABC-TVs, "That's Incredible"** [January 19 & April 27, 1981] did a special, **"The Man Who Survived Spontaneous Combustion."**

Not all people who die from SHC are alike. True, a large **majority** of them have consumed a lot of **alcoholic** beverages; however, other things sometimes play a part: remorse, melancholy, depression, isolation – like widows or widowers, physically handicapped, physical or mental injury, and/or guilt. Yes, not accepting God's forgiveness has been known to cause a person to self-destruct!

Slightly more women than men are SHC victims. Older people are at greater risk, especially between the ages of 60 and 69, but **it can strike people of any age.**

No one knows what causes a human body to burn from the inside out. The point to be made here is that **people can be consumed from within, just as the Bible indicates, strictly by the laws of nature.** Whether the fires are triggered by a chemical imbalance within, by tormented emotions, by a malfunction of the internal electrical system, or by a **combination**, no human being knows for sure. Atoms are not the smallest things known. **Pyrotrons**, for example, are so tiny that 800,000 trillion of them can fit into the letter o. The enormous energy released in a pyroton collision could generate extremely high temperatures. Perhaps they, along with other unknowns, could cause a chain reaction that would result in SHC. But one thing is sure:

> ### FACT: People can burn to nothing more than a pile of ashes, from the inside out, by natural laws of nature.

[An excellent and most complete book on the subject of Spontaneous Human Combustion can be purchased at your book store: **The Mysterous Fires of Ablaze!** By Larry E. Arnold. It is worth the price.]

The laws of nature are a part of the laws of God. When people rebel against these laws they eventually self-destruct – not necessarily via SHC, but by physical and mental disease. However, this does **not** mean that all who die due to spontaneous human combustion are sinners! **All humanity has degenerated since Creation;** therefore, both the Godly and the ungodly have bodies that malfunction. When Jesus returns, our degenerated bodies will be replaced by new spiritual bodies – like Jesus had after His resurrection. At that time our physical bodies will not malfunction.

Philippians 3:20,21

…we await a Savior, the Lord Jesus Christ, who will change our lowly body to be like his glorious body."

What is it that will "destroy" people when Jesus returns? Note what happens to the **antichrist** when Jesus returns:

2 Thessalonians 2:8 [RSV]

And the lawless one will be revealed. And the Lord Jesus will slay him with the breath of his mouth and destroy him by his appearing and his coming.

2 Thess 2:8 [NRSV]

…will destroy with the breath of his mouth, annihilating him by the manifestation of his coming.

2 Thess 2:8 [Amplified]

…will slay with the breath of his mouth and bring him to an end by the appearance of His coming.

The apostle Paul, in 2 Thessalonians 2:8, expressed himself like the prophet Isaiah:

Isaiah 11:4

…he shall strike the earth with the rod of his mouth, and with the breath of his lips he shall kill the wicked.

The first part of Isaiah 11:4 ["He shall strike the earth with the rod of his mouth."] is obviously symbolic. It could not possibly be taken literally. Why, then, should we take the last part as literal?

> **THINK**: Could it be that our state of mind will make a difference in how our physical bodies react when we see God face to face?

It is possible for people to be in literal fire without being burned. No human being knows how, but the Bible speaks of three men who were thrown into literal fire and walked away without even the smell of smoke [Daniel 3].

Just before the return of Jesus, when the elements of nature will be out of control to a much greater degree than they are today, God will have a way to protect those who have not willfully rebelled against Him or His laws.

Isaiah 43:2,3

When you pass through the waters I will be with you... when you walk through fire you shall not be burned, and the flame shall not consume you. For I am the Lord your God, the Holy One of Israel, your Savior.

The mention of Spontaneous Human Combustion in connection with the final destruction of the unrighteous really bothers some people! Some individuals have the idea that anything they cannot explain must be from the devil!

First of all, just because there is a possibility that the final destruction of some individuals will be the result of SHC, does not mean that all will self-destruct. **"As in the days of Noah,"** when most of the inhabitants of this world were **destroyed by water**, so, many will die when Jesus returns by another nature-out-of-control event. **Literal fire will come from "heaven" – from nature out of control – possibly a comet.** Even now, in our radio and TV news, we are warned of such a possibility. The nature-out-of-control event that caused Noah's flood is discussed in Outline No. 11.

Because we do not understand how something happens does not mean that it does not happen. Because some "experts" tell us that they have "proven" such a thing cannot happen, does not make them right!

Most, but not all, cases of SHC are the result of psychological trauma.

The fact that many who die of SHC are alcoholics does not prove that the alcohol in their bodies is what caused them to burn up, from the inside out, to a small pile of ashes. However, any psychologist will admit that alcoholics are emotionally disturbed – otherwise they would be able to control their drinking.

What happens to the minds and bodies of <u>some</u> people when they are under a great deal of stress – even though the reason for their stress is not obvious – has not been determined nor proven in the minds of those who believe SHC is "impossible." The fact is that there are **hundreds of observed cases of SHC, that have left no more than a small pile of ashes, with no furniture or carpets burned -- not even their clothing!**

Victims of SHC quickly burn, from the inside out, at temperatures hotter than in a cremation! Because some "expert" says he has "proven" that such a thing is impossible, is <u>not</u> proof that it never happened!

Some "religious" people – who obviously have not studied the Bible themselves – claim that SHC is God's way of letting us know that evil people will be forever tormented in a literal burning hell; however, their argument does not make sense. Not only does the Bible <u>not</u> teach such a devilish doctrine, but those who have experienced SHC have burned up to nothing!

It is true that it cannot always be proven that the SHC was caused by severe emotional trauma; however, **the cause is obvious in cases like 9-year old Alain Favier, of Paris, France,** who became extremely angry and died of SHC in the school yard after his cruel classmates had continually teased him because he was fat. Perhaps someday science will show us the scientific reasons for SHC.

REVIEW

[1] At creation man and woman were created perfectly so that they were at ease in the presence of their Creator.

[2] After Adam and Eve disobeyed, negative emotions, including guilt, caused their minds and bodies to begin to degenerate.

[3] At the second coming of Jesus, when it becomes obvious that the unsaved have turned their back upon the opportunity to receive eternal life, their negative emotions <u>may</u>, one way or another, cause them to self-destruct.

[4] The elimination of the unsaved will be from cause to effect. They will have brought eternal death upon themselves by causing God's super natural protection to be withdrawn.

[5] Only our Creator has the ability to keep us from dying. The unsaved will eventually die the death from which there will be no resurrection.

[6] Each individual will, indirectly,
      choose either eternal life or
      eternal death.

PREVIEW

In our next outline we will study
five additional "fires" mentioned in
the Bible. You will find the fire of
Outline No. 18 especially interesting.
It will explain the reason for several
perplexing stories   recorded in the
Old Testament.

A **skeptic** is a person who, when
he sees the handwriting on the
wall, claims it is a forgery. [Morris
Bender]

Is God Really Like That?
Outline No. 8

"Fire" in the Bible
Part III

[14] Fire of Trials and Persecution

Trials and persecution which God ALLOWS is referred to in the Bible as "fire."

Zechariah 13:8,9

In the whole land, says the Lord, two thirds shall be cut off and perish, and one third shall be left alive. And I will put this third into the **fire,** and **refine them** as one refines silver, and **test them** as gold is tested. They will call upon my name, and I will answer.

Isaiah 42:25

So he poured upon him the **heat** of his anger and the might of **battle; it set him on fire** round about, but he did not understand; **it burned him,** but he did not take it to heart.

Please note that in **Isa. 42 & Zech. 13** [above]**,** a conscious reaction came from the people **AFTER** they had been refined or tested by **"fire."**

In the following Bible texts, the **trials** that God **ALLOWS** to come upon us to increase our faith are referred to as **"fire."**

1 Peter 1:6,7

...for a little while you may have to suffer various **trials,** so that the genuineness of your faith, more precious than gold which though perishable is **tested by fire...**

Isaiah 48:10

I have **refined** you, but not like silver; I have **tried you** in the **furnace of affliction.**

Persecution by foreign nations is called "fire."

Jeremiah 15:14

"I will make you **serve your enemies** in a land which you do not know, for in my anger a **fire** is kindled which shall **burn** for ever."

Ezekiel 21:31,32

I will blow upon you with the **fire of my wrath;** and **I will deliver you into the hands of brutal men,** skilled to destroy. **You shall be fuel for the fire;** your blood shall be in the midst of the land...

The **natural results** which people bring upon themselves as they abuse others is referred to as **"fire."**

Habakkuk 2:12,13

Woe to him who builds a town with blood, and founds a city on iniquity! Behold, it is **not from the Lord** of hosts that people labor only for **fire...**

Trials and **persecution** which come to Christians as they work to build up God's Church is referred to as **"fire."**

1 Corinthians 3:9-13

For we are fellow workers for God… each man's work… will be **revealed by fire,** and the **fire will test** what sort of work each one has done.

---

[15] Fire of Judgment Punishment

Bible writers were preoccupied with **fire** as a **punishment** from God. Yes, there will be some **literal fire** at or near the end of time, like there was **literal water** during the time of Noah. Nevertheless, it should be remembered that **most** of the **"fire"** spoken of in the Bible is not literal fire.

Hebrews 10:26,27

For if we sin deliberately after receiving the knowledge of the truth, there no longer remains a sacrifice for sins, but a fearful prospect of **judgment**, and a fury of **fire** which will consume the adversaries.

Isaiah 66:15,16

For behold, the Lord will come in a **fire,** and his chariots like the stormwind, to render his anger in fury, and his rebuke with **flames of fire.** For by **fire** will the Lord execute **judgment,** and **by his sword** upon all flesh; and those slain by the Lord will be many.

The fact that God's judgments involve **"His sword"** shows that the above verses are filled with **symbolism.** According to the book of Revelation, God carries His **"sword"** in His **mouth.**

Revelation 19:15,21

From his **mouth** issues a **sharp sword** with which to smite the nations… (21) And the rest were slain by the **sword** of him who sits upon the horse, **the sword that issues from his mouth…**

Revelation 1:16

…out of his mouth issued a sharp two-edged sword…

Revelation 2:12,16

The words of him who has the **sharp two-edged sword.** (16) I will… war against them with the **sword of my mouth.**

Hebrews 4:12

For the **word of God** is living and active, sharper than any **two-edged sword…**

Ephesians 6:17

…the **sword of the Spirit,** which is the **word of God.**

As we have discovered from careful Bible study during the first seven of these outlines, **God's method** of dealing with sin and sinners is **not by force.** The war between good and evil – between God and Satan – is a **battle of words.** Because God is so much more powerful, **force could never convince the inhabitants of the universe** that God is just, fair, merciful, forgiving, and loving.

What will condemn the nations, as well as individuals, will be their own rebellious and blasphemous words. **Condemnation** of those who rebelled against God and/or His laws will be brought about by their own words. **The choice will have been theirs.**

[16] "Fire" of Wrath

Ezekiel 21:31,32

And I will pour out my **indignation** upon you; I will blow upon you with the **fire of my wrath;** and I will **deliver you into the hand of evil men,** skilful to destroy. **You** shall be **fuel** for the **fire;** your **blood** shall be in the midst of the land; **you will be no more remembered;** for I the Lord have spoken.

In Outline No.3 you read Bible texts which showed that the **"wrath of God"** is when God leaves people to themselves when they insist upon rebelling against Him and His ways of doing things. As you just read in Ezekiel 21:31,32, God merely backs away, refusing to help when enemies seek to destroy or enslave.

[17] "Fire" of Military Destruction

Cities and nations that have been destroyed are said to have experienced **"fire."**

Ezekiel 21:31

I will blow upon you with the **fire** of my wrath; and I will deliver you into the hands of **brutal men, skilful to destroy.**

Obadiah 1:18

The house of Jacob shall be a **fire,** and the house of Joseph a **flame,** and the house of Esau **stubble;** they shall **burn** them and consume them, and there shall be **no survivor** to the house of Esau [Edomites], for the Lord has spoken.

Jeremiah 50:31,32

...your day has come, the time when **I will punish you.** The **proud** one **shall stumble** and fall, with **none to raise him up,** and I will **kindle a fire in his cities,** and it will devour all that is round about him.

The **"fire"** that destroyed **Egypt** was King **Nebuchadnezzar:**

Ezekiel 30:8,10

Then they will know that I am the Lord, when **I set fire to Egypt,** and all her helpers are broken. (10) "Thus says the Lord God: I will put an end to the wealth of Egypt, **by the hand of Nebuchadnezzar."**

[18] "Fire" of Baal

Palestine was once thought of as **"a land flowing with milk and honey"** with a climate like you find in Southern California where almost any kind of fruit can be grown. [See Exodus 3:8,17; 13:5; 33:3; Leviticus 20:24; Num 13:27; 14:8; 16:13,14; Deut 6:3; 8:8; 11:9,15; 27:3; 31:20; Joshua 5:6; 2 Kings 18:32; 1 Chron 31:5; Jeremiah 1:5; 32:22; 41:8; Ezekiel 20:6,15]

Why is "a land flowing with milk and honey" NOT a good description of the land of Palestine **today?** Extensive irrigation is necessary in Palestine today.

FACT: Either several Bible writers were wrong, OR a drastic change has taken place since they wrote!

FACT: March 21 [Passover] and October 24 [Day of Atonement] were special religious holidays to both Israel and the Romans.

An <u>EXTRA</u> <u>SPECIAL</u> <u>DAY</u> to the Jewish people was **MARCH 21** [ancient Nisan 14], the day following **PASSOVER.** This was the anniversary of the first Passover as mentioned in Exodus 12, when the Hebrew slaves escaped from Egypt. However, a startling fact is that **this same day was also a very special and fearful day to the Romans! MARCH 21, "Tubulustrim" to the Romans,** was one of two special holidays at which time two horses were sacrificed. **Why should the Romans, many years after the Exodus Passover, consider March 21 to be important?**

ALSO, <u>OCTOBER 24</u> [Tishri 17] was a special day to **BOTH** ancient Israel and the Romans. According to Jewish tradition, everyone was judged on New Year's Day. However, they had nine more days, until the **Day of Atonement,** before their doom was finally sealed. **Why October 24** was considered **a day of doom to both** ancient Israel <u>and</u> the Romans will become evident as we study the **"fire" of Baal** in Outline No. 9. On this day **["Armilustrim" to the Romans]** the Romans **sacrificed another two horses.**

The ancient **Celtics** celebrated **Halloween** near the end of October. **Why?**

Both pagans and Hebrews (at times) sacrificed their first-born infant sons to **Baal. Why was Baal so feared?** What had Baal done in the past that was so terrible that made people fearful enough, including some Hebrews, to burn their little babies like animal sacrifices?

Astrologers and stargazers often advised kings that **Baal** would help them be victorious in military battle, even **predicting the exact day they should fight.**

Because Israel kept falling back into Baal worship, Hebrew prophets repeatedly warned the Hebrews not to worship the planets – **"the host of heaven."**

<u>**Zephaniah 1:4,5**</u>

...I will cut off from this place the remnant of **Baal** and the name of the idolatrous priests, those who bow down on the roofs to the **host of the heavens...**

2 Kings 17:16,17

And they [Israel] forsook all the commandments of the Lord their God, and made for themselves molten images of two calves; and they made an Asherah, and worshiped all the **host of heaven,** and served **Baal.** And they **burned** their **sons** and **daughters** as offerings...

2 Kings 23:5

...who burned incense to **Baal,** to the sun, and the moon, and the **constellations** and all the **host of the heavens.**

2 Chronicles 33:1-6

Manasseh... reigned fifty-five years in Jerusalem. He did what was evil in the sight of the Lord... For he rebuilt the high places which his father **Hezekiah** had broken down, and erected altars to the **Baals,** and made Asherahs, and worshiped the host of heaven, **and served them...** and he **burned** his **sons** as an offering in the valley of the son of Hinnom... and dealt with **mediums...**

> ## FACT: BAAL was not only worshiped, but greatly feared.

The worship of **Baal,** a part of the **"host of heaven,"** was of major concern to the true prophets. **Why** was it necessary for God's prophets to continually warn Israel and Judah against worshiping **Baal?**

Hezekiah, king of Judah, was about to die [2 Kings 20:1; Isaiah 38:1]. **Isaiah** told him that he would not get well. **Hezekiah,** not willing to take "no" for an answer, cried out in prayer that the Lord was not being fair; that he **deserved** to live longer because he had been a good king [2 Kings 20:2,3; Isa. 38:2,3].

After **Hezekiah** had prayed, the Lord told Isaiah to return and tell the king that **15 years** would be added to his life, **and** that He [the Lord] would deliver **Hezekiah** and **Jerusalem** out of the hand of the king of **Assyria** [Sennacherib – 2 Kings 20:5,6; Isaiah 38:4-6].

Isaiah also told king **Hezekiah** that he would be well enough to go to the Temple in three days. **Hezekiah wanted a sign** that what Isaiah had prophesied would be fulfilled. **So Isaiah gave the king a choice!** The shadow on the sundial was to either go **forward** ten degrees or **backward** ten degrees [2 Kings 20:8-10; Isaiah 38:7,8].

Now, **for such a thing to happen,** something **drastic** had to take place in nature! **What could have happened?** A major clue that something drastic **did** happen in nature:

> ## FACT: Shortly after the time of Isaiah, nations all over the world made calendar reforms.

After **701 BCE** nations all over the world, including Rome, ancient Greece, Israel, Phoenicia, Chaldea, Sumer, China, ancient Egypt, India and others, **all changed their calendars!** All civilizations, **all at the same time,** for some special reason, lengthened their calendars to **365 days** – close to our 365 1/4th days [365.2422 days, 5 hours, 48 minutes, and 45.51 seconds].

365 days is not the exact length of our year. Other calendar changes in various countries of the world, since 701 BCE, were necessary in order to make up for the difference in the 701 calendar and our year -- which is 5 hours and 48 minutes longer than exactly 365 days.

The **Julian calendar** was used in the days of Jesus. Today we use the **Gregorian calendar.** The **change** took place in October 1582 [England waited until Sept 2, 1752. Russia changed in 1918]. The old **Julian calendar** was eleven minutes too long per year. The **Gregorian calendar** added ten days to make up for the loss. Thus Thursday the 4th of October was followed by Friday the 15th. The weekly cycle was not changed.

Before the time of Isaiah there were **360 days** to a year. It took the **360 days to circle the sun,** and **30 days for the moon to circle the earth.** Old Testament prophecies are based on a 360-day year [Daniel 7:25; 12:7; Revelation 11:2,3; 12:6,14; 13:5].

THINK: Something extremely unusual must have happened to the rotation of the earth, and to one or more of the other planets which revolve around our sun! For our earth to take five days longer to travel around the sun could have been caused only by one of two things:

[a] Our earth was slowed down.

or

[b] The orbit of the earth was increased.

FACT: The planet Mars was the cause.

REVIEW

[1] **Palestine** can no longer be called "a land flowing with milk and honey." Something drastically changed in Palestine's climate.

[2] **March 21** and **October 24** were very special days to **both** Hebrews and Romans.

[3] **Baal** was so greatly **feared** that **both** pagans and Hebrews **sacrificed their infants** to Baal!

[4] Hebrew prophets repeatedly warned Israel not to worship Baal. The **Hebrews feared Baal as much as the pagans!**

[5] The **shadow** on **Hezekiah's sundial** went "**back ten degrees**" during a certain day. What earth-shaking event in nature could cause such a phenomenon?

[6] Shortly after the time of the prophet **Isaiah** [after 701 BCE] nations all over the world lengthened their calendars from **360 days** to **365 days!** **Why** did it take over five days longer for the earth to revolve around the sun?

PREVIEW

In Outlines No. 9, 10, and 11 we will discover what Baal was, and why the Hebrews, as well as the rest of the world, were so afraid of Baal.

Is God Really Like That?
Outline No. 9

Baal Worship = Mars Worship

Mars was called different names in different nations:

Baal in ancient Carthage
Baal in ancient Phoenicia
Baal in Hebrew
"Angel of the Lord" in Hebrew
Bel in ancient Chaldea
Mars in ancient Rome
Ares in ancient Greece
Horus in ancient Egypt
Nergal in ancient Assyria
Tyr in ancient Germanic
Indra in ancient Sanskrit and in north India

Gorgon, a feared monster in ancient Greek literature, was **Mars.** Homer wrote of Gorgon in the Iliad. In the Bible, **"Archturus"** – **"Bear"** [Job 9:5-7,9,10] and the dreaded **Leviathan** beast [Job 41:1-43; Isaiah 27:1] both represent the planet **Mars.**

Baal [Mars] is mentioned in the Bible **180 times.** **"Baal"** or **"Bel"** was a part of the names of many people and places, especially kings and queens. For example:

Babel, Tower of
Babylon
Belshazzar = "Bel – or Baal protect the king"

Belteshazzar = Name given to **Daniel** during his Babylonian captivity = "Bel preserve his life."
Balak
Balaam
Jezebel = Ahab's wife = A Phoenician princess. The Phoenician name for the planet Mars was Baal or Bul.
Beelzebub or **Beelzebul**
Baal-tamar = "Baal of the palm tree"
Baal-judah = "lord of fortune" Baale-judah
Jerubbaal = "Let Baal contend against him." The story is interesting. **Gideon** tore down the Altar of Baal. The men of the town told Gideon's father to surrender his son so they could kill him. His father, Joash, replied, "If he [Baal] is a god, let him contend for himself." On that day he [Gideon] was called **Jerubbaal,** that is to say, 'Let Baal contend against him,' because he pulled down his altar" [Judges 6:31,32].

Anyone who has traveled **interstate highways** across the United States [and the rest of the world] has noticed, where the roads have been cut through the tops of mountains, several different types of **layers of rock formations.** For even <u>one</u> such layer to be formed, the land had to be flooded with tremendous amounts of water – oceans of water – stirred up enough, and forceful enough, to cause mountains and valleys to change places!

What caused mountains? What caused all these rock layers? Many Bible students would answer in two words: "Noah's flood." However, **one** flood could **not** lay down **several** layers of **different** solid **rock** formations! **A series of earth-shaking events must have taken place.**

Old Testament prophets predicted several coming judgments which would come by way of destructive forces of nature. It is generally assumed that ancient prophets warned **only** about destruction to take place at the **end** of the world.

THINK: Does it make sense for God to raise up prophets to warn that, unless the people who lived **then** repented, God would, **many centuries later,** bring destruction upon the whole earth? Such an idea lacks credibility!

> **FACT: God would not punish people at the end of the world for sins committed by people thousands of years before!**

Three different types of calamities written about by ancient prophets:

[1] Calamities at an "Appointed Time"

2 Samuel 24:15,16

So the LORD sent a pestilence on **Israel** from that morning until the **appointed time**; and 70,000 of the people died, from Dan to Beersheba. But when the **angel** stretched out his hand toward **Jerusalem** to destroy it, the LORD repented of the evil, and said to the **angel** who was bringing destruction among the people, "It is enough; now stay your hand."

2 Samuel 24:15 – King James

So the Lord sent a pestilence upon **Israel** from the morning even to **the time appointed**...

2 Samuel 24:15 – Amplified Bible

So the Lord sent a pestilence upon **Israel** from the morning even to **the appointed time**...

[2] Past Calamities

2 Samuel 22:8-10 and **Psalm 18:7-19** [following] say about the same thing. These are **eyewitness accounts** of what happened when the planet **Mars [Baal]** came close to the earth. Perhaps you will begin to understand **why even the people of Israel offered their babies as human sacrifices.** Yes, God told them **not** to sacrifice their children; however, the people of Israel were taught that there was **one** God and **only** one God, and that everything either good or bad came directly from God!

2 Samuel 22:8-10

Then the **earth reeled** and **rocked;** the foundations of the **heavens trembled** and quaked, because he was angry. **Smoke** went up **from his nostrils,** and **devouring fire** from his mouth; **glowing coals** flamed forth from him; **He bowed the heavens,** and came down; thick **darkness** was under his feet.

Psalm 18:7-19

Then the **earth reeled** and **rocked;** the foundations also of the **mountains trembled and quaked,** because he was angry. **Smoke** went up from his nostrils, and devouring **fire** from his mouth; **glowing coals** flamed forth from him. He bowed the heavens, and came down; **thick darkness was under his feet.** He rode on a cherub, and flew, he **came swiftly** upon the wings of the **wind.** He made darkness his covering around him, his canopy **thick clouds dark with water.** Out of the **brightness** before him there broke through his clouds **hailstones** and **coals of fire.** The LORD also **thundered** in the heavens and the Most High uttered his voice. And he sent out his **arrows,** and scattered them; he slashed forth **lightning,** and **routed them.** The **channels of the sea were seen,** and the foundations of the world were laid bare at your rebuke, O LORD, at the **blast of the breath of your nostrils.** He reached down from on high, he took me; he **drew me out of mighty waters.** He delivered me from my strong enemy, and from those who hated me; for they were too mighty for me... He brought me out into a broad place; **he delivered me,** because he delighted in me.

2 Samuel 22:8-19 and Psalm 18:7-19 are <u>not</u> symbolic. They were eyewitness descriptions of what was seen. **Remember that Baal [the planet Mars] was considered to be an angry god. The mountains and valleys actually <u>did</u> change places!**

Certain books of the Bible <u>do</u> contain symbolism — books like Daniel, Ezekiel, and Revelation — but the book of Psalms is not one of them. **King David described what actually took place in nature because of the close encounters of the earth and the planet Mars.** Keep in mind that people of the Old Testament believed in only <u>one</u> God. They believed that their "one God" was responsible for <u>everything</u>.

[3] <u>Future</u> Calamities

<u>**Isaiah 24:17-23**</u> [following] helps to show the connection of **Baal worship** and destruction caused by the planet **Mars** as Mars came close to the earth. Note that at the same time the **"host of heaven"** is being **"punished,"** **"the earth staggers"** and the **sun** and the **moon** are affected:

Isaiah 24:17-23

...**the windows of heaven are opened,** and the **fountains** of the **earth tremble.** The earth is utterly broken, the earth is torn asunder, the **earth is violently shaken.** The **earth staggers** like a drunkard, it **sways** like a hut... On that day **the Lord will punish the host of** heaven **in heaven,** and on earth the kings of the earth**...** Then the **moon** will be abashed, and the **sun** ashamed**...**

The destruction spoken of in **Isaiah 30:27-33** [below] is **not** at the **end** of the world. **Why?** Because verse 31 shows that it was to take place **before the fall of Assyria:**

Isaiah 30:27-33

See, the name of the LORD **comes from far away... in thick rising smoke...** his breath is like an **overflowing stream...** the LORD will cause his **majestic voice** to be heard... **a flame of devouring fire,** with a **cloudburst** and **tempest** and **hailstones. The Assyrian will be terror-stricken** at the voice of the LORD, when he strikes with his **rod...** the breath of the LORD, like a **stream of sulfur,** kindles it.

Joel 2:1-11 [following] contains much **symbolism,** and has to be understood accordingly. The words of Joel 2:2: **"Nor will be again after them through the years of all generations,"** show that **this "day of the Lord,"** mentioned in verse one, is **not** the same **"day of the Lord"** that will come at the **end** of the world.

Joel 2:1-11

Sound the trumpet in Zion; sound the alarm on my holy mountain! Let all the inhabitants of the land tremble, for **the day of the Lord is coming, it is near,** a day of **darkness** and gloom, a day of **clouds** and **thick darkness!** Like blackness there is spread upon the

mountains a great and powerful people; **their like has never been from of old, nor will be again after them through the years of all generations.** Fire devours before them, and behind them a **flame burns...** people are in anguish, all faces grow pale... The **earth quakes** before them, the **heavens tremble.** The **sun** and the **moon** are **darkened,** and the **stars** withdraw their shining... For the **day of the Lord** is great and very terrible; who can endure it?

Haggai 2:6,7

For thus says the Lord of hosts: **Once again, in a little while,** I will **shake the heavens** and the **earth** and the **sea** and the **dry land;** and I will **shake all nations,** so that **the treasures of all nations shall come in,** and I will fill this house with splendor, says the Lord of hosts.

Haggai 2:6,7 [above] shows beyond any doubt that all predictions of the prophets for great destruction on the earth were not speaking about the final destruction of this world at the end of time: **"Once again, in a little while..." "So that treasures of all nations shall come in.** And in **Isaiah 24:1,3,6** [following] the predictions, **"scatter its inhabitants"** and **"few men are left,"** show that this is not talking about the final destruction when none will be left:

Isaiah 24:1,3,6

Behold, the Lord will lay waste the earth and make it desolate, and he will **twist its surface** and **scatter its inhabitants...** The earth shall be utterly laid waste... therefore the inhabitants of the earth are **scorched,** and **few men are left.**

___

Catastrophism and the Old Testament, by Donald Wesley Patten, is a book we highly recommend. This informative work gives more than adequate proof of **several earth encounters with the planet Mars** which caused great upheavals in large areas of our world. 13 are listed in his book. You may purchase this volume for **$18.90** [including postage] from Pacific Meridian Pub. Co., 13540 Lake City Way, NE, Seattle, WA 98125. **Also,** you may purchase a more recent work by Donald W. Patten and Samuel R. Windsor, **The Mars-Earth Wars,** which include graphs, charts, maps, and pictures. Price: $34.50 including postage. It is well worth your investment. Years of scientific research is yours in easy to understand language.

By showing how the close encounters of the earth with Mars coincides with Bible stories, **we show that God is not the "killer God" that most people, including Christians, have made Him out to be.** We will understand **why** the people of Israel copied their heathen neighbors and worshiped Mars [Baal].

When Bible writers wrote that **"the earth reeled and rocked"** [Psalm 28:7,8; 2 Samuel 22:8] they did **not** exaggerate! Drastic upheavals in nature, **from**

time to time, caused mountains and valleys to change places. Millions of acres were flooded, depositing layer after layer of sediment and rock each time Mars came close to our earth. **The many layers that we see did not all form at the same time.**

Haggai's prophecy, **"Once again, in a little while, I will shake the heavens and the earth and the sea and the dry land"** [Haggai 2:6; 9-4a.8] was literally fulfilled in the **past,** and, according to **Jesus,** the generation who lives to see Him return will experience the **same type** of earthshaking experience:

Matthew 24:29,30

Immediately after the suffering of those days the **sun** will be darkened, and the **moon** will not give its light; the **stars** will fall from heaven, and the **powers of heaven will be shaken...** and they will see the Son of Man coming on the clouds of heaven with power and great glory.

Mark 13:24,25

But in those days, after that suffering, the **sun** will be darkened, and the **moon** will not give its light, and the **stars** will fall from heaven, and the **powers in the heavens will be shaken.**

According to Donald Patten, a **Mars' flyby** occurred every **54 years** until **701 BCE.** Flybys would **alternate,** one during **October,** the next during **March.** Therefore, there would be **108 years** between **March** flybys, and **108 years** between **October** flybys.

I have on my desk before me a copy of the November 1988 issue of National Geographic. Page 680 describes **22,028 foot high** Mount Kailas in S.W. China as **"the center of the universe for Hindus, Buddhists, and Jains."** To them, one walk around Mount Kailas "washes away the sins of a life." But **108 walks** around Mount Kailas results in great happiness and bliss (nirvana). **Why 108 times around? Bible lands** experienced the most damage **every 108 years** during the **October** flybys. The **Americas** experienced the most damage **every 108 years** during the **March** flybys.

The closer the flyby was to the earth the greater the destruction. The **greatest destruction** to the earth occurred **every 540 years** (every 10th flyby). **The closeness of Mars' flybys** was determined by the position of the planets **Jupiter, Saturn, Neptune,** and **Uranus** in the heavens. The way the planets were lined up determined their gravitational pull upon **Mars,** determining the closeness of Mars' flyby to earth.

Until the last flyby, Mars always made a sunward side flyby, rotating in a clockwise motion. The earth's spin was counterclockwise, resulting in **friction** between the earth's solid crust and the underlying 1,700 mile thick, hot, liquid magma [lava]. **An October flyby** created massive friction from a different direction than

a March flyby. An **October** flyby left the earth with its north **magnetic pole in Antarctica**, while a **March** flyby left the earth with its north **magnetic pole in Canada**. A knowledgeable geologist can recognize these different, ancient, magnetic poles. Geologist, Hulot Gauthier, said [in 2002], that there are signs the North Pole is about to flip to the South Pole, due to the way molten iron is flowing in the Earth's core.

Mars' flybys recharged the earth's magnetic field every 54 years. The earth loses its magnetic field strength at a known and continuous rate, at about 4 ½ % a year, or about 50% loss every 1,350 years. **Today** the earth's magnetic field strength measures at the **.307 Gauss** level. Following the last Mar's flyby in **701 BCE** it measured at the **1.2 Gauss** level, or about four times its present value.

At the present time, earth's magnetic field strength is not being generated by anything on earth. Yet "the earth requires an umbrella, such as its geomagnetic sheath, to ward off the alpha and beta particles in the solar wind. If this umbrella folds, life soon will cease on our planet on every continent…" [Donald Patten, Catastrophism and the Old Testament]

Mars' flybys generated massive amounts of **friction** between the bottom of the solid crust and the top of the hot, liquid mantle. **Because there have been no flybys since 701 BCE, the earth's magnetic field has decreased.** This fact makes the prediction of Jesus that **"the powers of the heavens will be shaken"** [Matthew 24:29; Mark 13:25] **before He returns** the second time, <u>very</u> <u>interesting</u>, and possibly significant. Some may consider our present reduced geometric field strength an indication that Jesus will soon return.

Learning the results of what happened to our earth as Mars periodically caused great upheavals in nature**,** helps us to conclude that **our earth experienced crustal skids during the last few <u>thousand</u> years, rather than continental drifts"** over **"millions"** of years!

A Mars' Flyby Caused

[a] Crustal skids on the hot liquid mantle.
[b] A reversal of earth's magnetic field.
[c] An increase in the earth's magnetic field.
[d] Changes on the earth's surface. Mountains, valleys, water, and dry land changed places. Gravity pulled the crust of the earth upward.
[e] Spin axis shifts
[f] Volcanoes
[g] Floods

[h] <u>Flux</u> <u>tube</u> [see 10-3a.4 for flux tube] displays between earth and Mars. Bible writers were not the only ones to periodically warn of approaching destruction. **Ancient writings** of the Assyrians, Greeks, Persians, Romans, and Chinese predicted oncoming dangers. **Astrologers, stargazers, mathematicians, seers,** and **prophets** all made their predictions. **Some were right in their predictions, and some were wrong. Kings wanted to know,** "Should I go to war, and upon which day?" **This is where God's faithful prophets had an advantage.**

God could, at any time, either supernaturally change the natural course of nature, or He could [and often did] warn His people against being in certain places at the wrong time.

> **<u>FACT</u>: In any situation God has a controlling hand – a veto! He has the power to change the course of nature at any time.**

The <u>reason</u> we study Mars' flybys is to more fully understand why <u>today's</u> <u>earth</u> is <u>drastically</u> <u>different</u> than in <u>Bible</u> times. The world at the time of creation was much more pleasant than our present world.

Also, our study will show us that God is <u>not</u> the killer God that so many people, including Christians, make Him out to be. Whenever a nation disregards God's instructions, **God partially withdraws His protection,** and **allows** nature to take its course; He **allows** evil men to work their evil. As we look around us in the world today, we notice that **countries that attempt to follow God's laws usually have the least problems.** Countries like **Russia** who have openly rejected God, have more problems!

Both the **heathen** and **Israel** worshiped and feared the planet **Mars** to the extent that they even offered little children as human sacrifices to **Baal.** Following are facts and questions which indicate that something affected our earth in a most dramatic and destructive way:

[a] **Palestine** can no longer be called a **"land flowing with milk and honey."**

[b] **March 21** and **October 24** were important religious holidays to **both** Hebrews and Romans.

[c] What caused the shadow on Hezekiah's sun dial to move backward "ten degrees" in one day?

[d] Shortly after the time of Isaiah (after **701 BC**) all nations made drastic **calendar reforms. Why?** [See Earth–Mars Wars 9-4b.7]

The "Sun Stood Still"

Joshua 10:5-14

Then the five kings of the **Amorites...** went up with all their armies and encamped against **Gibeon...** And the men of Gibeon sent to **Joshua...** saying... "help us..." So Joshua went up from **Gilgal,** he and all the people of war with him... And the Lord said to Joshua, **"Do not fear them, for I have given them into your hands; there shall not a man of them stand before you."** So Joshua came upon them suddenly, having marched all night from Gilgal. And **the Lord threw them into a panic** before **Israel, who slew them with a great slaughter at Gibeon...** And they fled before Israel... the **Lord threw down great stones from heaven** upon them... there were **more who died of hailstones than the men of Israel killed** with the sword. Then **spoke Joshua to the Lord** in the day when the Lord gave the **Amorites** over to the men of Israel; and he said in the sight of Israel, **"Sun, stand thou still at Gibeon,** and the **moon** in the valley of Ajalon. And **the sun stood still,** and the **moon stayed,** until the nation took vengeance on their enemies. Is it not written in the book of *Jashar? The sun stayed in the midst of heaven, and did not hasten to go down for **about** a whole day. There has been no day like it before or since, when the Lord hearkened to the voice of a man; for the **Lord fought for Israel. [*This book is not in the**

Please note that there were **three categories of Amorites** mentioned in Joshua 10:

[1] Amorites killed by Israeli **soldiers.**

[2] **Amorites who escaped** [Josh 10:16,20]

[3] **Amorites killed by the forces of nature.**

Consider the order of events:

[1] **God: "I have given them into your hands."**

[2] **Lord "threw them into a panic."**

[3] **Israel slew them with a great slaughter.**

[4] **They were running away from Israel when**

[5] **"The Lord threw down great stones."**

[6] **Joshua commanded the sun to stand still.**

Please note that the enemy was running away **before** the **hailstones** fell, **and** both the running away and the hailstones came **before** Joshua commanded the sun to stand still.

Few Bible students would suggest that God Himself stationed Himself above the earth, miraculously created ice balls or fire balls, and then enjoyed target practice! If that is **really** what God did, then we have to admit He did not have perfect aim, since many of them escaped!

Our earth spins at about 1,000 miles per hour. Can you imagine what would have happened to buildings, animals, and people if the world suddenly stopped spinning!

Normally the solid crust of the earth and the liquid mantle below spin together. In this case, the daylight was lengthened by four to six hours [The literal reading of the Hebrew manuscript is, **the sun "did not hasten to go down as a perfect day."** The Hebrews referred to any portion of a day as a "day."]. The earth's crust wanted to follow **Mars** because of Mar's gravitational pull, instead of continuing to spin with the mantle. The result was that **the crust slowed down.** The earth tilted or twisted, resulting in the sun being seen longer.

It is quite **possible** that **Joshua** was inspired to command the sun to stand still -- even though the sun did <u>not</u> stand still. The sun does not revolve around the earth. The earth spins on its axis to cause daylight and darkness; nevertheless, even today we speak of the "sunrise" and "sunset."

The Bible records the **final four Mars' flybys,** and **five of the last six.** Two more of these flybys will be covered in **Outline No. 10,** and another in **Outline No. 11.**

Is God Really Like That?
Outline No. 10

185,000 Assyrians Die
"Angel of the Lord"

An understanding of what **really** happened when the **Assyrian army** was defeated can be gained only after reading **all** that the book of **Isaiah** says concerning Israel's miraculous deliverance:

Isaiah 10:12,16,17

When the Lord has finished all his work on Mt. Zion and on Jerusalem, he will **punish** the arrogant boasting of the **king of Assyria** and his haughty pride... Therefore the Sovereign, the lord of hosts, will send **wasting sickness among his stout warriors,** and under his glory **a burning will be kindled,** like the burning of fire. The light of Israel will become a fire, and his Holy One a flame, and it will burn and devour his thorns and briers on **one day.**

Isaiah 24:1.19.20

Now the LORD is about to lay waste the earth and make it desolate, and he will **twist its surface** and scatter its inhabitants. The earth is utterly broken, the earth is torn asunder, the earth is **violently** shaken. The **earth staggers** like a drunkard, it **sways like a hut**...

Isaiah 30:27-33

See, the name of the **LORD comes from far away, burning** with his anger; and in **thick rising smoke;** his lips are full of indignation, and his tongue like a **devouring stream** that reaches up to the neck... And the Lord will cause his **majestic voice** to be heard... and a **flame of devouring fire**, with **cloudburst** and **tempest** and **hailstones.** The **Assyrian will be terror-stricken** at the voice of the LORD, when he strikes with his rod For **his burning place has long been prepared;** truly it is made ready for the king, its **pyre made deep and wide**, with **fire** and wood in abundance; the breath of the LORD, like a stream of **sulfur**, kindles it.

Isaiah 31:4-9

...the **LORD** of hosts **will come down to fight** upon Mt. Zion and upon its hill. Like birds hovering overhead, so the LORD of hosts will protect **Jerusalem;** he will protect and deliver it, he will spare and rescue it... Then **the Assyrian shall fall by a sword, not of mortals; and a sword, not of humans**, shall devour him; **he shall flee from the sword,** and his young men shall be put to forced labor. His rock shall pass away in terror, and **his officers desert the standard in panic,"** says the LORD, whose **fire is in Zion**, and whose **furnace is in Jerusalem.**

Isaiah 37:5-7

[Also 2 Kings 19:5-7]

When the servants of **King Hezekiah** came to **Isaiah,** Isaiah said to them, "Say to your master, 'Thus says the LORD: Do not be afraid because of the words that you have heard, with which the servants of the **king of Assyria** have reviled me. I myself will put a spirit in him, so that **he shall hear a rumor, and return to his own land; I will cause him to fall by the sword in his own land.'"

Isaiah 37:33-38

[Also 2 Chron 32:20,21]

Therefore thus says the LORD concerning the **king of Assyria:** He shall not come into this city... By the way that he came, by the same he shall return; **he shall not come into this city,** says the LORD. For **I will defend this city to save it,** for my own sake and for the sake of my servant, David.

Then the **angel of the LORD** set out and **struck down one hundred eighty-five thousand** in the camp of the **Assyrians;** when the morning dawned, they were all dead bodies. **Then King Sennacherib of Assyria left, went home,** and lived at **Nineveh.** As he was worshiping in the house of his god Nisrock, **his sons,** Adammelech and Sharezer **killed him with the sword,** and they escaped into the land of Ararat. His son Esar-haddon succeeded him.

The book of **Isaiah** is **not written in chronological order;** nevertheless, consider a brief outline of what is recorded:

Isaiah 10:12 – Lord will punish the king of Assyria.

Isaiah 10:16 – **"wasting sickness"** sent among Assyrians **"like burning fire"**

Isaiah 10:17 – **"in one day" "fire"** was to devour

Isaiah 24:1 – Lord will **"twist"** surface of the earth

Isaiah 24:19 – Earth **"violently shaken"**

Isaiah 20 – Earth **"staggers"** and **"sways"**

Isaiah 30:27-33 – The **"name of the Lord" "comes from afar" "thick rising smoke" "a flame of fire" "over flowing stream" "cloudburst" "hailstones" "tempest"**

Isaiah 30:31 – Assyrians **"terror stricken"**

Isaiah 30:33 – **"his burning place has long been prepared"**

Isaiah 30:33 – **"breath of the Lord"** like**"brimstone"**

Isaiah 31:4,5 – Lord will **"come down" "like birds hovering"** will deliver... Jerusalem

Isaiah 31:8 – **"Assyrians shall fall from a** sword" "not of man" **"officers desert/flee in panic"**

Isaiah 37:7 – King of Assyria will **"hear a rumor" "return to his own land" "I will make him fall by the sword in his own land."**

Isaiah 37:33 – **Assyrian king** not to go near Jerusalem

Isaiah 37:25 – "I will defend this city to save it."

Isaiah 37:36 – **"angel of the Lord"** slew **185,000**

Isaiah 37: 37,38 – King **Sennacherib** returned to Nineveh and was **killed by his sons.**

Remember that Bible writers wrote as if God actually <u>did</u> things which He merely <u>allowed</u>. The following phrases must be considered in <u>this</u> light:

"The Lord will punish..." "I will make him fall by the sword in his own land." God did not <u>force</u> the Assyrian king to go into his house **at Nineveh so his sons could kill him!"**

Isaiah described the destruction: "hailstones" "burning" "thick rising smoke" "devouring fire" "overflowing stream" "cloud-burst" "tempest" This is a strange way to describe the work of **"the angel of the Lord."** The surface of the earth was to **"twist," "stagger," "shake violently," and "sway."**
Did a <u>**literal angel**</u> kill 185,000 soldiers, or did they die of some **terrible disease** as Isaiah predicted [Isa. 10:16]? Did the Assyrians die by a **"sword"** in the hand of an **"angel"** as Isaiah predicted [Isa. 31:8]**, or did they die because some catastrophe of nature,** which caused the earth to "twist," "stagger," and "shake **violently,"** accompanied by **"smoke," "devouring fire," "tempests," "cloudbursts,"** and **"HAIL-STONES"?!**

Just how literal did Isaiah intend to be? Or was Isaiah confused as to the cause and final outcome? Did Isaiah predict a terrible disease in **<u>Chapter 10,</u>** an earthshaking disturbance of nature in **<u>Chapter 30,</u>** and then receive a new and different revelation by the time he got around to writing **<u>Chapter 37,</u>** where he described the **"angel of the Lord" killing 185,000 Assyrian soldiers with a "sword"?!**

Shortly after the "angel of the Lord" killed 185,000 soldiers [Isa. 37:26], Isaiah wrote about the shadow on **Hezekiah's sundial** reversing itself. **"So the sun turned back on the dial the ten steps by which it had declined"** [Isa. 38:8].

By piecing together **historical records,** we know that the Assyrian army was destroyed during its invasion of Judah somewhere around **700 BC.** What happened shortly after Isaiah died – shortly after 701 BC? **Nations all over the world added to their calendars five days – from 360 days a year to 365 days a year!**

> ### THINK: What caused the orbit of the earth to be pushed or pulled outward an extra 67,000 miles?

701 BCE was the date of the **last Mars' flyby.** According to Donald Patten in his book, **Catastrophism and the Old Testament,** every time before 701 BCE **Mars** always arrived at the intersection <u>first</u> during the spring flybys. **The only time the <u>earth</u> arrived <u>first</u> was in 701 BCE,** resulting in a **permanent change** in Mars' orbit. **701 BCE** is the date of the **last major catastrophe** to affect the whole earth.

1 Chronicles 21:16

And **David** lifted up his eyes and **saw the angel of the Lord standing between earth and heaven,** and **in his hand a drawn sword stretched out over Jerusalem.**

If we take this **"angel"** to be a <u>literal</u> angel, then we must conclude that angels are much larger than we ever imagined. To describe an angel as **"standing between earth and heaven"** indicates an extremely tall being! If we believe this **"angel"** was a <u>literal</u> angel, we must assume that angels are the cause of fire, tempests, earthquakes, and hailstones! **If this is so, why is it that meteorologists can predict when a hurricane will hit land?** Is it logical and reasonable

to believe that <u>literal</u> angels have the power to "twist" and "violently shake" the earth?

The description of an angel large enough to be **"standing between earth and heaven,** having a sword big enough to stretch over the city of Jerusalem, should cause one to consider other explanations. **What was it that people saw** while looking at "an angel of the Lord" which held an extremely large sword," causing tremendous damage and killing thousands of people?

In 1978, **Voyager II** sent back to earth pictures of the planet **Jupiter** and its satellite **Io** [Eye'-oh] which greatly surprised everyone. Pictures show a **constant flow of <u>electrons</u> flowing <u>between Jupiter and Io</u>** with an estimated strength of 5,000,000 amperes – 400,000 volts, equivalent of five million 100-watt bulbs. This <u>**flux** tube</u> between **Jupiter** and **Io** is **<u>260,000 miles long.</u>** Donald Patten's book, <u>Catastrophism and the Old Testament,</u> gives adequate evidence why the **same type of flux tube** existed between **earth** and the planet **Mars** during the Mars' flybys. Such a **flux tube** probably formed when the earth and Mars were about 100,000 miles apart. [See Don Patten books: 9-5b.4]

The **celestial lightning** of the **flux tube** was **attracted to iron** <u>in the same way lightning is attracted to little lightning rods</u> on top of buildings today. The **Hebrews,** not being as prepared for war as their enemies, **benefited in two ways:**

[1] Their weapons were <u>not</u> made of iron; therefore, they did <u>not</u> attract the lightning as did the more advanced equipment of their enemies.

[2] God, through His prophets, when Israel obeyed, warned the Hebrews not to be in the wrong place at the wrong time!

Josephus, a Jewish soldier and historian, wrote about the **Mars' flyby** that took place when the Israeli army was ready to fight the Philistine army:

"**God** disturbed their enemies with an **earthquake,** and **moved the ground** under them to such a degree, that he caused it to **tremble,** and made them **shake,** inasmuch that by its trembling, he made some unable to keep their feet, and **made them fall down,** and by opening up the **chasms,** he caused that others should be hurried down into them; after which he caused such a **noise** of **thunder** to come among them, and made **fiery lightning** shine so terribly round about them, that it was ready to **burn their faces,** and so suddenly **shook their weapons out of their hands;** that he **made them fly and return home naked.**" [<u>Antiquities</u> <u>of</u> <u>the</u> <u>Jews</u>, **Book VI, Chapter 2, Page 2]** [See <u>Earth</u>-<u>Mars</u> <u>Wars</u> 9-4b.6]

King David Numbers Israel

<u>I Chron. 21:1-30</u>

[Also <u>2 Sam. 24:1-25</u>]
Satan stood up against Israel, and he **incited David to number Israel. (2)** So David said to **Joab** and the commanders of his army, "Go, number Israel, from Beersheba to Dan, and bring me a report that I may know their number." **(3)** But **Joab said,** "Why then should my lord require this? **Why should we bring guilt upon Israel?" (4)** But the king's word prevailed against Joab. So Joab departed and went throughout all Israel, and came to Jerusalem. **(5)** And Joab gave the sum of the numbering of the people to David. In all **Israel** there were **1,100,000** men who drew the sword, and in **Judah 470,000** who drew the sword. **(6)** But he did not include Levi and Benjamin in the numbering, for the king's command was abhorrent to Joab. **(7)** But **God was displeased** with this thing, and **he smote Israel. (8)** And **David said to God, "I have sinned greatly... I have done foolishly." (9)** And the Lord spoke to **Gad, David's seer,** saying, **(10) "Go and say to David, 'Thus says the Lord, <u>Three</u> <u>things</u> <u>I</u> offer y<u>o</u>u; <u>choose</u> <u>one</u> of them... (11)** So **Gad** came to

David and said, "Thus says the Lord, 'Take which you will: **(12)** either **three years of famine;** or **three months of devastation by your foes,** while the sword of your enemies overtakes you; or else **three days of the sword of the Lord, pestilence** upon your land, and the **angel of the Lord destroying throughout all the territory of Israel.' Now decide** which answer I shall return to **him who sent me." (13)** Then **David said to Gad, "I** am in great distress; let me fall into the hand of the Lord, for **his mercy is great;** but let me not fall into the hand of man." **(14)** So **the Lord sent a pestilence upon Israel;** and there fell 70,000 men of Israel. **(15)** And **God sent an angel to Jerusalem to destroy it;** but when he was about to destroy it**, the Lord repented of the evil...** (16) David... saw the angel of the Lord **standing between earth and heaven,** and in his hand a drawn sword stretched out over Jerusalem... (26) And David built there an altar to the Lord presenting **burnt offerings** and **peace offerings,** and called upon the Lord, and he answered him with fire from heaven upon the altar of burnt offering. (27) Then the Lord commanded the angel; and he put his sword back into its sheath.

David yielded to Satanic influences [1 Chron 21:1], and **deliberately did what he believed was wrong, by** numbering the adult men of Israel [1 Chron 21:3,8,17]. **Evidently David knew a catastrophe was due at the "appointed time"** [2 Sam 24:15] and was possibly concerned about the loss of military power, not leaving the responsibility of loss of life to God.

Ignoring the objections of **Joab,** the leader of his army, David went to almost ten months of trouble in taking a census the <u>first</u> time [2 Sam 24:8 9-2a#1]. To know how many men were killed, David had to number Israel a <u>second</u> time.

David's **conscience** tormented him, admitting that he had "sinned greatly." **By deliberately doing something that was contrary to God's desire, David gave Satan a license to <u>deceive</u> him into thinking that it was <u>God</u> who was directly responsible for the loss of 70,000 lives. "The Lord <u>repented</u> of the <u>evil</u>"!!!** [1 Chronicles 21:15]

Question **Number** **One:** Which one would **YOU** have chosen?! Any person with common sense would have chosen **"3 days of pestilence"** over either **"3 years of famine"** or **"3 months of slaughter." "Him who sent me"** [2 Sam 24:1; 1 Chron 21:12] knew beforehand which of the three choices David would make!

Question Number Two: What kind of a "God of love" would force David to make such a choice, and then kill **"70,000"** able-bodied men [besides women and children] for one of King David's sins? David himself said, **"It is I who have sinned. But what have these sheep done?"**

Question Number Three: Why was the solution to the problem of getting God calmed down, **the offering of animal sacrifices;** animal sacrifices which major prophets claimed were not God's idea? [Review Outline No. 5] **Baal–Mars** worshipers sacrificed **bulls** on **their** altars!

David built his altar on **Mt. Moriah,** the highest point in the area. This is where Abraham tried to offer his son, Isaac, as a human sacrifice. It is where Solomon built his temple. Today it is the site of the Moslem's sacred "Dome of the Rock."

Why could the Hebrews not tell, by looking, exactly what they were **seeing?** Because they were **blinded by tradition.** A Mars' flyby only happened in their half of the world

every 108 years; therefore, there were no eye witnesses of the last flyby. **More importantly,** the Hebrews were taught that there was only one God; that **every** event, good or bad, **came directly from God!** This is **why they mistook the "angel of the Lord"** as a literal angel.

Mars had two small moons, **Deimos** and **Phobos,** which **looked like bull's horns** to some ancient observers. This is **why** the **bull** was **sacred** to many heathen nations.

The **bull** has his way in **India** even today! **THINK: Why** did Solomon offer 22,000 **bulls** at the dedication of his Temple?! Because the **Romans** thought these two Mars moons looked like horses, they **sacrificed two horses** on their two most important holidays of the year: March 21 and October 24 -- **the days also celebrated by the Hebrews!!**

> **FACT: Getting Mars mixed up with the "angel of God" has helped to promote the satanic ideas of a harsh, unforgiving, and get-even God.**

Because few people have even <u>heard</u> of the planet Mars coming close to the earth every 54 years [every 108 years in each hemisphere], it is sometimes difficult for individuals to even consider the idea.

Certain Bible texts cannot be explained unless this earth experienced more than one event when the oceans and mountains changed places.

Nevertheless, such world changes really did take place. One evidence that a large comet or planet came close to the earth is what is referred to as the **"ring of fire" – a chain of volcanoes** around the circle of the earth.

Is God Really Like That?
Outline No. 11

Noah's Flood

Was there <u>really</u> a worldwide flood? Did **Noah** <u>really</u> build a boat large enough to save himself, his family, the animals, and the birds?

[When ** comes at the <u>end</u> of a word, check the **Glossary** on page 11-39]

Those who do not accept the authenticity of the Bible make light of the idea of a flood that covered the whole world. Yet, the more we study the more we discover the <u>natural</u> causes of Noah's flood.

> **FACT:** **All** ancient civilizations passed down stories of a world-wide flood, even though the details of the story vary.

The **Epic of Gilgamesh**. Gilgamesh was an ancient Babylonian king who wrote hundreds of years before Moses wrote Genesis. The epic, written 3,000 to 4,000 years ago [Some say it was written as far back as 2600 BCE], inscribed upon clay tablets and found in Assurbanipal's Library, is an account of Noah's ["Utnapishtim"] flood written long before the Bible account. It is written in the first person singular ["I"] as if written by Noah himself. **Several ideas expressed in this epic are false** – like the idea that there are several gods [**Planets were worshiped as intelligent "gods."**]. Nevertheless, the ideas about the ark and its construction have been proven true scientifically.

The **Sumerian**** flood story, as told in the **Epic of Gilgamesh** [written on clay tablets many years before Genesis was written], represents about 200 lines of poetry, including sections where God supposedly spoke to Noah. As you read, keep in mind that this king [Gilgamesh] highly overrated himself, thinking that he himself was half man and half god! As you read the following, it will become obvious that **his "days" were much longer than our days.** This Gilgamesh text came out of ancient Mesopotamia; discovered in the library of King Ashurbanipal [668-627 B.C.].

Epic of Gilgamesh

"In those days the world teemed, the people multiplied, the world bellowed like a wild bull, and the great god was aroused by the clamour. **Enlil** [Sumerian word for **Baal = Mars**] heard the clamour and he said to the gods in council [planets were thought of as gods], 'The uproar of mankind is intolerable and sleep is no longer possible by reason of the babel.' So the gods in their hearts were moved to let loose the **deluge;** but my lord, **Ea,** warned me in a dream. He whispered their words to **my house of reeds,** 'Reed-house, reed-house! Wall, O Wall, hearken reed-house, wall reflect;... tear down your house and **build yourself a boat,** abandon possessions and look for life, despise worldly goods and save your soul alive. Tear down your house, I say, and **build a boat.** These are the **measurements...** let her beam equal her length, let her deck be **roofed...** then take into the boat the seed of all living creatures... the children brought **pitch** and the men whatever necessary. On the 5th day I laid the **keel** and the **ribs,** then I made fast the **planking.** The ground space was one acre, each side of the deck measured **120 cubits,** making a square. I built **6 decks below, 7 in all,** I divided them into **9 sections** with **bulkheads** between. I drove in wedges where necessary, I saw to the punt-poles, and laid in **supplies.** The carriers brought **oil** in baskets, I poured **pitch** into the furnace and **asphalt** and **oil;** more oil was consumed in **caulking...** I loaded into her all that I had of gold and of living things, **my family,** my kin, the **beasts** of the field both wild and tame, and all the **craftsmen.** I sent them on board, for **the time** that Shamash had ordained was **already filled** when he said, 'In the evening, when the rider of the storm sends down the destroying rain, enter the boat and batten her down. **The time was fulfilled** [The fixed time arrived], the evening came, the rider of the storm sent down the rain. I

looked out at the weather and it was terrible, so I boarded the boat and battened her down. All was now complete, the battening and the caulking; so I handed the tiller to **Puzur-Amurri** the steersman, with the navigation and the care of the whole boat. With the first light of dawn a **black cloud** came from the **horizon;** it **thundered** within where Adad, lord of the storm was riding...Then the **gods of the abyss** rose up... the **7 judges of hell,** the Annunaki, raised their **torches, lighting the land** with their livid **flame.** A stupor of despair went up to heaven when the god of the storm **turned daylight into darkness,** when he smashed the land like a cup. One whole day the tempest raged gathering fury as it went, it poured over the people like the tides of battle; a man could not see his brother nor the people be seen from heaven. **Even the gods were terrified** at the flood, **they fled to the highest heaven...** For **6 days and 6 nights** the winds blew, torrent and tempest and flood overwhelmed the world**...** I looked at the face of the world and there was silence, **all mankind was turned to clay.** The surface of the sea stretched as flat as a rooftop; I opened a hatch and the light fell on my face. Then I bowed low, I sat down and I wept, the tears streamed down my face, for on every side was the waste of water. I looked for land in vain, but 14 leagues distant [approximately 42 miles] there appeared a **mountain,** and there the **boat grounded;** on the **mountain of Nisir** the boat held fast, she held fast and did not budge**...** When the 7th day dawned

I loosed a **dove** and let her go. She flew away, but finding no resting place she returned. Then I took a **swallow,** and she flew away, but finding no resting place she returned. I loosed a **raven,** she saw that the waters had retreated, she ate, she flew around, she cawed, and she did not come back. Then I threw everything open to the four winds, I made a **sacrifice...** Let all the gods gather around the sacrifice, except **Enlil [= Baal = Mars].** He shall not approach this offering, for without reflection **he brought the flood;** he consigned my people to destruction. [See The Epic of Gilgamesh by N.K. Sanders, 1964, England & Baltimore]

Gilgamesh was known as the **Lord of wisdom,** who knew everything; who carried back word of the time before the Flood.

According to this **Epic of Gilgamesh,** Noah was not taken by surprise:

"The time was fulfilled"
or
"The fixed time arrived."

The water, wind, and fire came together. The tempest lasted a relatively short time even though it rained for a longer period.

Ancient **Hindu** sacred writings refer to Noah as the **great Nu,** as does the **Egyptian Book of the Dead.**

Noah's Flood in the Bible

Genesis chapters 6, 7, & 8 speaks of Noah's flood. God instructed Noah to make his boat **waterproof** [Gen 6:14] with a **roof** [Gen. 6:16]. The **size** of the boat was to be **300 "cubits"** long, **50 "cubits"** wide, and **30 "cubits"** high, with **3 floors** [Gen.6:15,16].

Rain fell for **40 days** [Gen 7:12]. It took **150 days** for the water to recede enough for Noah and his family to leave the ark [Gen 7:4; 8:3], which came to rest upon the **"mountains of Ararat"** in Turkey.

New Testament writers considered Noah's flood to be **a literal fact.** They quoted **Jesus** Himself speaking of this earth-shaking event:

Matthew 24:37-39

[Jesus speaking]
As were the days of **Noah,** so will be the coming of the Son of man. For as in those days before the **flood...**

Luke 17:26,27

[Jesus speaking]
As it was in the days of **Noah...** so will it be on the day when the Son of man is revealed.

2 Peter 2:5

...he did not spare the ancient world, but preserved **Noah,** a herald of righteousness, with seven other persons, when he brought a **flood** upon the world of the ungodly...

A 1989 **map,** published by the **Turkish Ministry of Tourism,** shows **"Nuh'un Gemisi" ["Noah's Boat"]** listed as an historic site two miles from the Turkish-Iranian border. Now under state control, the **Turkish Ministry of Culture** has made the area a **National Park.** There is a **visitor's center** – a building with tables to seat 40 or 50 guests. My name is included in the first seven names on the visitor's sign in book.

Could it possibly be that the Turks have properly pinpointed the exact location of **Noah's Ark** on their latest map at an **elevation** of only **6,300 feet?** The answer, backed up by **scientific proof,** is **YES!** **I, personally, have been there and have actually walked upon the remains of Noah's Ark!**

If it were not for uninspired **tradition** and a few deliberate **hoaxes,** the location of Noah's Ark would have been known by the whole world years ago. **At times the obvious escapes us because our minds have been clouded by tradition or hearsay. Many Christians are so anxious to "prove the Bible true" that they will believe, as fact, any alleged "eyewitness" account, supposedly seen many years ago.**

What about all the reports of Ark sightings on Mt. Ararat?

All we have are unsubstantiated **rumors** of sightings – "sightings" from a long distance away which take a great deal of imagination! One

such "sighting" in the 1980's proved to be, close-up, nothing more than a solid rock! All expeditions to Mt. Ararat have always failed to produce **any** tangible evidence. Some Ark hunters have brought back pieces of unexplained "wood" they claim "must have been" part of Noah's Ark at one time! They bring back just enough "evidence" to get people to donate more money to finance their next expedition. And those who supposedly have **"seen"** Noah's Ark on Mt. Ararat, **for some strange reason, ALWAYS FORGET TO SNAP A CLOSE-UP PICTURE!!** Hundreds of expeditions to Mt. Ararat failed to produce **any** genuine evidence – only a few pieces of petrified wood which naïve Christians look upon with awe.

Why do we know for sure that **all stories of Noah's Ark seen on Mt. Ararat cannot possibly be true?** First of all, we know that there was only one Noah's Ark. Noah's Ark has been "seen" on lakes, ledges, under glaciers, in one piece, and in several pieces! And most puzzling of all, no one bothered to produce a photograph!! Really now, if YOU were the one who risked your life climbing Mt. Ararat after spending thousands of dollars for transportation and equipment, wouldn't you bother to take a picture? **The only genuine pictures taken of the remains of Noah's Ark are the ones that have been taken at the Ark site at Al Judi in Turkey!**

I own a copy of a letter written by an 80 year old man living in the U.S., dated June 21, 1989, who **<u>admitted in writing</u>** that the so-called "eyewitness" account he had written in **1939,** was nothing more than a **hoax!** His hoax, by the way, has been copied and recopied many times during the past **65** years! His letter reads in part:

> "One day she told me the story that the ark still existed and it was thawing out from a glacier on Mount Ararat. Well, I wrote up the story and published it in the March 1939 issue of NEW EDEN and used the pseudonym of Valadamir Roskovitsky which I devised from a Russian I knew named Vladamir Rossosheim. This was in the March 1939 issue. The story went wild worldwide, and I got letters from as far as India, Australia, and New Zealand. It has been retold in at least a dozen books and still going today. I hang my head in shame that I have caused so many to spend so much money chasing a willo-the-wisp. I must have cost folks a quarter million dollars all told. Sorry." [Signed F.M. Gurley]

Some are so tied to **traditional beliefs** that they believe that proof of the Ark at a 6,300 foot level, 17 miles south, southwest of Mt. Ararat, proves the Bible wrong! **Noah's Ark,** being discovered at **6,300 feet elevation** rather than 16,000 feet, is no less of a testimony to the accuracy of the Bible. The Bible has been proven true no matter where the Ark has been found. Hundreds of expeditions to Mt. Ararat failed to produce **<u>any</u>** genuine evidence.

Some "Ark hunters" are extremely reluctant to accept certain proven facts because they have traveled year after year to Mt. Ararat looking for **Noah's Ark,** supposedly buried and perfectly preserved under many feet of solid ice – all at the expense of the "faithful" who have donated thousands of dollars to "prove the Bible right."

No criticism should be made of Ark hunters who, in the **<u>past,</u>** have accepted donations for Ark expeditions to Mt. Ararat; however, people who <u>continue</u> to financially support the "Ark hunters" who refuse to consider and/or accept **proven facts** concerning the remains of Noah's Ark, are giving to men rather than to God.

According to the **Epic of Gilgamesh** [the oldest account of Noah's flood] the Ark landed on **Mt. Nissir.** Until about 50 years ago the village near the Ark site, now called **Uzengili** [ooze-en'-gil-lee], was named **Nasar** on the Turkish maps.

Berosus: "A portion of the ship which came to rest in Armenia still remains in the mountains of the Korduaians [Kurds] of Armenia, and some of the people, scraping off pieces of bitumen from the ship, bring them back and use them as talismans."

The Assyrian king, **Ashumasrpal II, 883-859 BCE,** claimed to know the resting place of the Ark. He said it was **Nisir.**

During the month that **Israel** was declared to be a legal nation by the United Nations [May 15, 1948], an **earthquake** took place 17 miles south of Mt. Ararat, causing land on both sides of a **boat-shaped formation** to drop away. Shortly after this earthquake a **Kurdish farmer** [Ali Oglu Reshit Sarihan, age 22 at the time], claimed that the remains of Noah's Ark were in his field, 500 yards from the village of **Uzengili** [ooze-en'-gil-lee], formally named **Nasar.** [Nasar means "to present a sacrifice."] **Nasar was on "Mahser" slope =** "The Last Judgment" or **Mahsur slope =** "Raised from the Dead" or "Resurrection Day." He, "Reshit," was the Turk who discovered Noah's Ark. It was in his field in which he tended sheep. However, an earthquake on November 25, 1978 pushed the Ark out of the ground even further.

At that time, just before the earthquake, it seemed like heaven was trying to tell the earth's inhabitants that something extra special was taking place! **This earthquake was preceded by the sky turning silver!** Everyone was out in the streets looking up at this strange sight just before the earthquake hit. For this reason there were few injuries – all were outside at the time.

What was even more strange was the people living in ***Dogubayazit [dough-u-by'-a-zit]**** just ten miles away, were not aware of any earthquake; yet they, also, saw the sky that appeared to turn to silver! ***[The town in which I stayed at the Ararat Hotel, when visiting the Ark site.]**

The **Koran** reads that Noah's Ark landed on **Mt. Judi** [Houd 11:44]. Today there are **three** places in Eastern Turkey named **"Mt. Judi." One** of these three has the village of **Uzengili** [Nasar] on its hillside. Meanings of the names of several other locations near the Ark site add proof that this **is** the place where Noah's Ark came to rest.

Having **"faith"** that Noah's Ark is hidden, perfectly preserved, below snow and ice on Mt. Ararat, is merely having "faith" in **tradition.** All the tradition in the world will not cause Noah's Ark to be found on Mt. Ararat, rather than on one of the other mountains in the **Ararat chain.**

Genesis 8:4

...the ark came to rest upon the **mountains** of Ararat.

The use of the name, **"Ararat,"** began in the **11ᵗʰ century AD.** Jeremiah 51:27 refers to **"Ararat"** as a **"kingdom."** The **"mountains of Ararat"** of the Bible are what we now refer to as **Armenia** [90,000 square miles]. Mt. Ararat and Little Ararat cover only 600 square miles. The mountains of Ararat are just north of ancient Assyria and Nineveh. **Mt. Ararat, <u>as</u> <u>it</u> <u>is</u> <u>today</u>, did not exist at the time of the flood. Geology shows Mt. Ararat to be a relatively young volcanic cone.**

Advanced scientific technology has made it possible for us to know **<u>for</u> <u>sure</u>** that the remains of Noah's Ark have been found.

In June of 1986 an explorer, **David F. Fasold, proved scientifically** with a new, state of the art, subsurface, ground penetrating radar scanner, the existence of a **man-made ship** the **same length as the Noah's Ark of the Bible** – using the **Egyptian cubit** measurement.

David F. Fasold was the one who conducted the **<u>first</u>** radar survey of the remains of Noah's **Ark,** which showed clearly its decks and walls. However, Fasold was <u>not</u> the <u>only</u> one who did a radar survey. In August of 1986, a couple of months after Fasold, **Dr. John Baumgardner,** a card-carrying scientist – a geophysicist from New Mexico's Los Alamos National Laboratory, independently brought his own radar scanner to the same site. The results of his survey are on record. Independently he **duplicated** what David Fasold had already shown. A detailed description of this proof can be viewed on a **video, <u>The</u> <u>Discovery</u> <u>of</u> <u>Noah's</u> <u>Ark</u>** [Distributed at the Ark Site Visitor Center in Turkey]. You may purchase this highly recommended video by writing to **American Media, Box 4646, Westlake Village, California 91359** [$36. includes shipping]

Yes, two different survey teams measured the Ark at different times. David Fasold's measurement was **515 feet long.** Dr. John Baumgardner's measurement was **515.7 feet long.** The Bible says the Ark was **"300 cubits"** long [Gen 6:16] – **<u>not</u>** "450 feet" as it says in the New International Version. The writers of the NIV used the Hebrew cubit in their figuring. We know from radar results that the Egyptian cubit was used – the same cubit used in building the Great Pyramid of Giza. [300 cubits x 20.6 inches = 6,180 inches, divided by 12 = 515 feet.] Because Moses, the original author of much of the book of Genesis, was born and educated in Egypt in physics, geometry, astronomy, medicine, and chemistry, it is only logical that he would think in terms of the Egyptian cubit, just as a person raised in the U.S. today would think in terms of **feet** rather than **meters.**

The **width of the Ark,** as determined by the survey teams, was about 137.5 feet, which is different than the "50 cubits" recorded in the Bible. Why? There is no simple answer. David Fasold, in his book, **The Ark of Noah,** goes into great detail as to how the Bible measurements are correct when figured by cubic cubits, measuring the volume. The "50 cubits" wide and "30 cubits" high of the Bible [Gen 6:15] added together make the actual width as shown by the radar survey [137.5 feet wide]. Even though the "300 cubits" of the Bible is the correct <u>length</u> measurement, shown by the radar surveys, the actual <u>width</u> is <u>more</u> than "50 cubits."

A literal width of only 86 feet ["50 cubits" **x** 20.6 divided by 12] would be proportionately too narrow for a **515 foot long ship** that would be able to keep from breaking in two or capsizing in strong winds.

Some **"experts,"** who refuse to even look at or study the remains of Noah's **Ark,** refer to the knowledge that wooden ships over 300 feet long will not keep from breaking in two when traveling on rough seas.

However, ships, when reinforced and strapped in iron, hold up well.

Iron was used in the building of Noah's Ark. Iron reinforcements were **necessary** in the construction of Noah's Ark. Ship builders have demonstrated that about 300 feet is the limit for the fiber stress of wood used in the construction of a ship. Noah built the Ark out of natural materials at hand. No one knows how many of the details were included in God's instructions to Noah. Whether or not God specifically instructed Noah in **every** detail – down to the type of metal bracing and waterproof covering – we do not know. What we **do** know are some of the **results** – proven by the radar scans.

> **FACT: Iron was used long before the so-called "iron age."**

Genesis 4:19-22

Lamech took two wives... Adah... Zillah... Zillah bore **Tubal-cain;** he was the forger of all instruments of **bronze** and **iron.**

Tubal-cain was the 7th generation in the line of Cain.

After **Cain** killed his brother, **Abel,** "the Lord set a mark upon Cain, lest any finding him should kill him [Gen 4:15]. **This mark was <u>not</u> a mark of punishment, but <u>a</u> <u>mark</u> <u>of</u> <u>protection</u>!** It was immediately recognizable by all. What was this mark? **Could it be that Cain was "red" like his father, Adam? Lamech** killed a man in self-defense [Gen 4:23,24] seven generations after Cain. Evidently he was afraid that people would try to kill him. **Why?** Did he still have the "**mark**"? Is it possible that the mark was his red hair or skin color? **Abel** was not the easiest brother to get along with. The root meaning of his name means vain in act or word.

A **sickle** of **wrought iron**** was found at the base of the **Sphinx.** An **iron blade** was found in masonry of the **Great Pyramid. Angular brackets** recovered from the Ark site, analyzed by the Los Alamos National Laboratory, were 91.84% wrought iron. Because there was no nickel in the iron found in Noah's Ark, we know it was not brought in by a meteor from outer space. **Iron amulets**** have been found with silver heads in Egypt, dating back to 3000 BCE..

Today, Noah's Ark clearly shows an **abundance of iron,** not only in evenly spaced fittings, but in **flakes** within the cement-like mixture covering the ark. Today one can see **iron rivets** from Noah's Ark on display in Cornesville, Tennesse.

All the evidence shows clearly that the **outside** of Noah's Ark was **not** made of **wood** of any kind —only the inside was divided with planks, support poles, beams, room dividers, and floorboards. And these were probably made of cedar or cypress wood.

But how about Genesis 6:14?

Genesis 6:14 King James
"Make thee an ark of **gopher wood;** rooms shall thou make in the ark, and shall **pitch** it within and without with **pitch.**"

Oxford New International Scofield Study Bible
"...and **coat it** with **pitch** inside and out."

New English Bible
"Make yourself an ark with **ribs** of **cypress;** cover it with **reeds...**"

Catholic Douay Version
"Make yourself an ark of **timber planks...**"

New World Translation
"...you must **cover** it inside and out with **tar**"

The meaning of the Hebrew word ["kaphar"] translated as "gopher" in the KJV means simply "cover." The idea that the **framework** ["ribs"] of the Ark was made of "**timber planks**" has been proven correct. What we have today are the decayed remains of a **huge ship** made of **timbers, planks, beams,** and **floorboards** covered with an endurable, waterproof covering that served to protect Noah and his family, and to preserve it for us to see.

The Hebrew word does **not** mean wood or pitch. It means simply **to cover.** A literal translation reads something like this: **"Cover it inside and outside with cover."**

When people, even translators, get a preconceived idea in their heads only because of tradition, they are tempted to translate words according to what they think the Bible writer meant rather than translate them according to the actual meaning of the Hebrew or Greek.

[Other places in the Bible where translators have done the same thing is adding the word **"unknown"** before tongues in 1 Cor. 14:2. The word **"begotten"** in John 3:16. The word **"is"** before inspired in 2 Timothy 3:16.]

Noah used iron nails, spikes, pins, clamps, and/or brackets to hold it together and reinforce the wooden structure of the Ark. Recovered **iron** objects **dug up** at the Ark site are **82 to 94% wrought iron.**** **5,400 iron readings** from the radar scans appear in lines that crisscross, producing outlines of squares and rectangles **at evenly spaced intervals.** The **iron** readings are **not in a random pattern.** None are in clusters. Also, **no iron readings appeared outside the boat-shape of the Ark.** All iron readings were confined to the 43,000 square foot area of the Ark itself.

Ancient bulkheads [partitions separating compartments] have slowly rotted away for thousands of years since the flood, and have been replaced by silt, sand, and dirt; however, we find much of the replacement material in the **same form and shape** of what was originally there! How can we detect the original form and shape if the timbers have decomposed? We can tell because of the **oxygenated iron.** Even though the iron fittings, iron nails, iron spikes, and/or iron reinforcements have corroded, the oxygenated iron still responds to the subsurface radar scanner.

The **Koran** quotes God as saying, "We carried Noah in a vessel built with **planks** and **nails.**"

When **Dr. John Baumgardner,** a geophysicist at the Los Alamos research Lab in New Mexico, was asked about the results of the subsurface radar scans on the remains of Noah's Ark, replied, **"Yes, yes, there's a likelihood that it's either nails or spikes we're seeing."**

Anyone who gets permission from the Turks to walk on the remains of Noah's Ark, as **I did,** can take pictures of the upper deck **support beams** protruding from the **side columns.** Diagnostic equipment used on the Ark site by David Fasold and John Baumgardner clearly showed outlines of beams, inner crossbeams, and collapsed decks. Yet, **some areas have not collapsed.** Void spaces can be detected, especially at the upper end; the bow. We encourage the Turks to carefully excavate as quickly as possible.

The Turkish Ministry of Culture has now made the remains of Noah's Ark a national park.

Exactly what is it that a person **sees** who travels to the Ark site in Turkey, 17 miles south, southwest of Mt. Ararat? After he arrives at the new **Welcome Center** built by the Turks, he looks down upon a formation [in a non-volcanic area] that is roughly **boat-shaped.** The **earthquakes** in May of 1948 and Nov 25, 1978, caused the land mass around the remains of Noah's Ark to fall away, leaving the boat-shape that can be seen today.

The **"pitch"** that was used to waterproof the Ark is still abundant **today** in that general area of the world. **Bitumen** or **asphalt** wells still bubble up from beneath the earth's surface at or near the **Dead Sea,** and at the city of **Hit** on the **Euphrates River,** above Babylon. This **"pitch"** ["kopher"] of Genesis 6:14 – **"bitumen," "tar,"** or **"asphalt"** – however you want to translate it – is **a liquid when it comes out of the ground, but hardens when exposed to the air.** Noah used a weather resistant, cement-like sealer to cover the "wood," "reeds," "planks," and/or "ribs" of Genesis 6:14, and treated it **"inside and out"** to make it waterproof. Noah is quoted in the **Epic of Gilgamesh** as saying, "I smeared it with **pitch** inside, and **bitumen** without." "I poured **24,000 gallons** of bitumen into the **kiln."**** **Scientific evidence** proves beyond a doubt that what we have 17 miles south of Mt. Ararat is **not a pile of clay,** but decomposed **wood on the inside,** and **cement on the outside.** **Iron remains** make it possible for us to know the size and details of the Ark's construction, including its **rooms, partitions,** and **main divisions.**

The **Epic of Gilgamesh** [11-1b & 11-2a], written hundreds of years before Moses wrote Genesis, says that Noah ["Utnapishtim"] was told to tear down his **reed house** and build himself a boat. A **raft** made of **reeds** could not have punctured, filled with water, or sunk. The **Hindu Vedas**

[Indian sacred writings from the 2nd millennium BC] described the Ark as the **raft** of "Manu" ["Great Nu"]. **A three-storied structure was probably built upon a boat-shaped reed raft.**

Josephus: Noah was to make an ark of four stories high. [Josephus in *Antiquities of the Jews,* Book 1, ch. 3]

Persian traditions claimed Noah's Ark was called **Varuna's House of Clay.** "Vara" means "an underground fortress of a tomb." Around 800 BC the **Assyrians** called it **Varuna's House of Clay.**

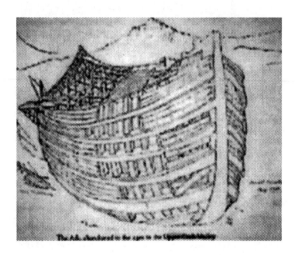

They entered it at the surface. It was **3 stories deep in the ground,** thus an underground fortress came to be known as a "vara." **King Varuna is Noah. Josephus:** Noah was to make an ark of four stories high. [Josephus in *Antiquities of the Jews,* Book 1, ch. 3]

MOON POOL

Another significant discovery, pinpointed by David Fasold's testing equipment, is the existence of a **hull pool ["moon pool"].** These are often found in fishing boats which allow fishing from the center of the boat. On the forward, center section of the Ark is a rectangular **moon pool 201 feet long and 26 feet wide.** Water extended up into the hull. **This served to relieve the stress on the hull [the backbone of the Ark], and to reduce buoyancy.** It served to slow down the forward speed of the Ark in the presence of strong winds, tides, or tidal waves. The **moon pool** also served as a **drain,** especially to wash out the manure from hundreds of birds and animals. Another advantage of the **moon pool** was to **push stale air out** and **suck fresh air in** − like a **giant piston;** the natural result of water surging in and out when in rough waters. **Windows** or **vents** were at or near the **top** of the Ark. Through this moon pool **fish** could be caught for animal food.

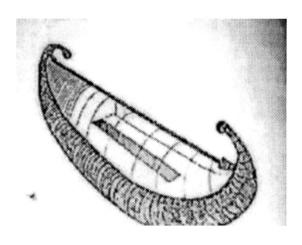

Also, it was through the **moon pool** that huge **anchors** were dropped and controlled. In and around the Turkish city of **Kazan** [car-zan], **5,700 feet elevation**, 14 miles from the Ark site, a **dozen anchor stones** [drogue stones] have been discovered. [See me standing beside an anchor stone below.] These **anchor stones** average **10 feet tall, 5 feet wide, 15 inches thick,** weighing about **8,000 lbs.** Each anchor stone has a **3 to 4 inch hole** near the top where the anchor stone is thickest. These anchor stones are **smooth on both sides.** The edges of the holes were made smooth to ease the wear and tear on the ropes. Of course, these anchor stones weighed much less in the water. The **Koran** makes an interesting statement: **"In the name of Allah it will cast anchor."** [Sura 11:44].

The huge drogue stones used on ancient ships have been found on a plateau several miles away, possibly dropped there when the ship started to go aground. Elevation of these stones = 5,500 ft.

Christians regarded the **anchor stones** as **holy stones.** Most of these anchor stones had only eight crosses.

The following text shows that **drogue stones** were used even in New Testament times for the same reason Noah used them:

Acts 27:17

"And fearing that we might run on the rocks, they let out **four anchors from the stern,** and prayed for the day to come."

Drogue stones needed for a ship the size of the Ark could total some 15 tons. Genesis says the Ark came to rest on the mountainS of Ararat. It does not say it *grounded* but came to rest as the drogues came in contact with the bottom.

The finding of Noah's Ark on a mountain in Turkey shows:

[1] Noah was a real person.
[2] There really was a world-wide flood just as the Bible, Jesus, and archaeological evidence indicates.
[3] It implies the existence of an intelligent Creator.

**FACT: The discovery
of Noah's Ark
causes great frustration
in the minds
of evolutionists.
It questions their
credibility.**

It is true that no bronze plaque has been found crediting the building of Noah's Ark to Noah and his sons. But how can anyone explain, rationally, any other reason for a 515 foot long ship, perfectly and symmetrically built, 6,300 feet above sea level on an 11 degree slope, **2,000 miles from the nearest ocean** – 2,000 miles from the Arctic Ocean, and 2,000 miles from the Indian Ocean – a most unlikely place for a huge ship!

**FACT: A huge, ancient ship
has been found
on a mountain near
Mt. Ararat in Turkey –
a ship four or five
thousand years old,
built by highly
intelligent individuals.**

It is <u>not</u> true that Noah was from an age when people were only half civilized. Those who accept the Bible as true, understand that man

was perfect when God created him in the beginning – he was already preprogrammed! His IQ was "out of this world!" He had perfect memory, and was a genuine genius. **He used 100% of his brain power; we, today, use only 10 to 15%.** Some ancient records indicate men were twice as tall as men today.

Samuel R. Windsor, a marine engineer and business partner of a naval architect, who has been to the Ark site in Turkey, and has carefully studied the results of the radar surveys, is of the opinion that this Ark was built by a **genius.** He believes the mathematical design of the Ark will eventually prove to be **a marvel of marine engineering,** rather than the work of unlearned, uncivilized men. Christians, Jews, and Moslems who accept the Genesis account as true, find it easy to believe that man has degenerated <u>after</u> being created perfectly, **not vice versa.**

"The oldest structures of antiquity that contain the two ratios of both **pi**** and **phi** are seen **in Noah's Ark <u>and</u> the Great Pyramid.** I believe that **Imhotep,** the Shepherd King, who was <u>not</u> Egyptian, and who was the designer and architect during the reign of Cheops, was **Shem.**" [*The Ark of Noah* p.128, by David Fasold, 1988, WYNWOOD Press, N.Y., New York]

We are living in an interesting age when anti-Biblical ideas are pressured upon people in all walks of life. Influential, powerful, and wealthy individuals and organizations will do almost anything in their attempts to prove the Bible false. **A scientist who admits that he or she believes in Noah and a world-wide flood, may lose his job and reputation!** Nevertheless, the recorded, **scientifically proven facts speak loudly for themselves.**

Another secret revealed to Gilgamesh was the result of eating the plant of life and longevity: ***"The Old Man will Be Made Young"***. This plant was found growing inside the hulk of the Ark, covered with thorns. This famous youth plant, Genclik Koku, in which the roots grow deep, will give "everlasting life;" the old will be made young!

Josephus: "Unless physically dug up and transplanted elsewhere, **this plant would be found only at the Ark site!"**

The **reason** a flood was **allowed** was the total wickedness and rebellion of the human race as a whole:

Genesis 6:5-8

The Lord saw that the wickedness of man was great in the earth, and that every imagination of the thoughts of his heart was only evil continually. **[6]** And **the Lord was sorry that he had made man on the earth,** and it grieved him to his heart. **[7]** So the Lord said, **"I will blot out man** whom I have created... man and beast and creeping things and **birds** of the air, for **I am sorry that I have made them."** **[8]** But **Noah** found favor in the eyes of the Lord.

From early on, man got the <u>wrong idea</u> that it was the <u>true</u> Lord God who caused all evil [as well as the good]. The <u>counterfeit</u> lord [Studied in Outlines 19 thru 24], appearing as an "angel of light," deceived most people in "prehistoric" times before Noah's flood, just as he has deceived the majority today.

The idea that the wickedness and rebellion of mankind caught our **Creator** by surprise disagrees with the views of New Testament writers. The true Lord God knew the end result of the deceptions of the counterfeit lord god, and He even devised a plan, before the creation of man, to save everyone who would be willing to be saved:

Matthew 25:34

Then the King will say to those at his right hand, "Come, O blessed of My Father, inherit the kingdom **prepared for you from the foundation of the world."**

Ephesians 1:4,5

Even as he chose us in him **before the foundation of the world...** He destined us in love to be his sons through Jesus...

1 Peter 1:19,20

...with the precious blood of Christ, like that of a lamb without blemish or spot. **He was destined before the foundation of the world...**

No person or group ever caught God by surprise! Why would God be "sorry that He had made man" [Gen 6:6,7] if He:

[a] Knew beforehand they would rebel?

[b] Already had a plan to save them?

The **reason** for God **allowing** the flood was the total rebellion of the world in general. The same principle works today for nations, as well as for individuals. The nations of the world who think and act contrary to the laws of their Creator, suffer the most; **from cause to effect.** God allows the nations to do it "their way" if they **insist** upon disregarding revealed Truth. **We would have reason to be concerned if our nation passed laws which were against the laws of God.**

People who lived in Noah's day did not catch God by surprise. God's patience did not run out. **God did not lose control of His emotions and murder millions of people!** In fact, God predicted the coming of the flood **120 years in advance:**

Genesis 6:3

The Living Bible

Then Jehovah said, "My spirit must not forever be disgraced by man, wholly evil as he is. I will give him **120 years** to mend his ways."

At times we hear someone say, "Yes, there was a big flood, but it did _not_ cover the _entire_ world."

Then why was Noah given 120 years to build an ark? Would not God have made it easier on Noah to merely instruct him where to travel in order to avoid the flood waters?

Also, if Noah's flood was not a world-wide flood, then the following Bible texts do not make sense:

Genesis 9:15

"I will remember my covenant which is between me and you and every living creature of all flesh; and **the waters shall never again become a flood to destroy all flesh.**"

Psalm 104:5-9

"...the waters stood above the mountains. At your rebuke they fled... You have set a bound that they may not pass over; **that they turn not again to cover the earth.**"

Since the time of Noah's flood there have been many floods – but none were world-wide floods [Review Outline No. 9-4b to 9-7b]

According to the oldest written records, "written" on clay tablets, there was a cataclysmic event, unequaled in the history of the world, that resulted in a world-wide flood, and the almost total extinction of mankind. You can see these records for yourself [Even though you will not be able to read them in English!] in the **British museum** and in the **University of Pennsylvania Museum.**

Records of Noah's flood have been discovered in almost every area of the world. Stories of a world-wide flood, a boat, and the seed of mankind preserved, have been found in over 200 different countries. Many times Truth is not accepted because it seems so unbelievable.

The **Toltec Indians** of ancient **Mexico** said the first world lasted 1716 years after which it was destroyed by a great flood that covered the highest mountains. Only one family named Coxcox survived.

The **Hawaii** legend: After the first man [Kunivhonna] the world became wicked. The only good man was Nu-u. He made a great canoe with a house on it, and filled it with animals. Water killed all the people. Only Nu-u and his family were saved.

The **Chinese** considered the Flood a world-wide event; not a local flood. One **Chinese** tradition claims a tremendous world wide flood occurred around 2300 B.C.; that all **Chinese** are direct descendants of **Nu-wah.** The **Chinese** boast of an unbroken line of history for over 4,500 years. **Another Chinese** flood story goes like this: Fuhi, his wife, three sons, and three daughters escaped a great flood. They were the only people alive on the earth. After the flood they repopulated the world.

Evidences of a world-wide flood appear all over the world. For example, **Lake Titicaca** in the city of **Tiahuanaco,** between Peru and Bolivia, **elevation 12,500 feet,** was built at sea level before Noah's Flood. **Its inhabitants drowned!** It was constructed of stone blocks weighing 100 to 200 tons each, that had been transported from 30 to 90 miles. Gateways, 30 ft. long and 15 ft. high, had been hewn from solid stone. This feat would not have been possible at 12,000 ft.

Hans Schindler, in his publication, *The Calendar of Tiahuanaco,* shows a calendar in rock surfaces [petroglyphs], obviously one that precedes the time of Noah's Flood, where an orbiting satellite made 447 revolutions around the earth in **a year of only 290 days!**

Isaiah 24:1

Behold, the Lord makes the earth empty, and makes it waste, and **turns it upside down,** and scatters abroad the inhabitants thereof.

Isa 24:1 NRSV

Now the Lord is about to lay waste the earth and make it desolate, and **he will twist it desolate,** and he will scatter its inhabitants.

Psalm 107:33,35

He turns rivers into a desert... He turns a desert into pools of water...

Psalm 66:6

He turned the sea into dry land.

Acts 2:20

The **sun** shall be turned to darkness and the **moon** to blood, before the coming of the Lord's great and glorious day.

Isaiah 24:20

The earth staggers like a drunkard, it sways like a hut.

Psalm 46:1,2

God is our refuge and strength... Therefore we will not fear... though the mountains shake in the heart of the sea.

Isaiah 29:5,6

And **in an instant, suddenly,** you will be visited by the Lord of hosts with thunder and **earthquake** and great noise, with **whirlwind** and **tempest**, and the **flame of a devouring fire.**

Immanuel Velikovsky, in his book, ***Worlds in Collision,*** wrote that there was a **series** of catastrophes during the 8th and 7th centuries BC [Review Outlines Nos. 8-3 to 10-5]

"A blast from the planet Mars fell upon the camp of the Assyrians and annihilated it."

One celestial chart shows west and east are reversed! In one cave were painted stars in the heavens which would make no sense unless the **"world had been turned upside down"** [Isaiah 24:1]. Modern astronomy does not admit, or even consider the possibility that at some historical time east and west as well as south and north were reversed. At one time, after the thick cloud cover revealed the sky, people were surprised that the sun rose in the east!

"The priests asserted that since Egypt became a kingdom, **four times** in this period **the sun rose contrary to the usual;** twice it rose where it now sets, and twice it set where it now rises." [Ibid. p. 105]

Pomponius Mela, a Latin author of the first century, wrote: "The Egyptians pride themselves on being the most ancient people in the world. In their authentic annals... one may read that since they have been in existence, the course of the stars has changed directions four times, and that the sun has set twice in that part of the sky where it rises today." [Ibid. p.106]

In the Papyrus Ipuwer: "The land turns over as does a potter's wheel, and the earth turned upside down." [Ibid. p.107]

In the **tomb of Senmut,** the architect of Queen Hatshepsut, a panel on the ceiling shows the celestial sphere... in the reversed orientation of the southern sky... Orion, the most conspicuous constellation of the southern sky, appeared to be moving eastward, in the wrong direction." [Ibid. p.108]

"**Zeus** [Jupiter} changed the course of the sun, causing it to rise in the east and not in the west." [Ibid. p.110]

Third century... **Egypt:** "The inhabitants of this country [3rd century] say that they have it from their ancestors that the sun now sets where it formerly rose." [Ibid. p.112]

In Tractate Sanhedrin of the **Talmud** it is said: **"Seven days before the deluge,** the Holy One changed the primeval order and **the sun rose in the west and set in the east."** [Ibid. p.113]

"The **Koran** speaks of the Lord of two easts and of two wests." [Ibid. p.114]

"The **Talmud** and other ancient rabbinical sources tell of great disturbances in the solar movement **at the time of the Exodus** and

the **Passage of the Sea** and the **Lawgiving.** In old Midrashim it is repeatedly narrated that **four times the sun was forced out of its course in the few weeks between the day of the Exodus and the day of the Lawgiving."** [Ibid.p.116]

The **Papyrus Ipuwer:** "The earth turned over like a potter's wheel, and the earth is upside down," was written by an **eyewitness** of the **plagues** and the **Exodus...** The south becomes north, and the earth turns over." [Ibid. p.117]

"The earth was removed to an orbit farther from the sun." [Ibid. p.120] Before the flood there were **290 days to a year.** Following the flood there were **360 days to the year.** After 701 BC calendars all over the world were changed, coming closer to our present **365+ days.** [Review Outlines Nos. 8 thru 10] On a manuscript of Timaeus: "A calendar of a solar year of 360 days was introduced by the Hykos after the fall of the Middle Kingdom. The calendar year of the Middle Kingdom apparently had fewer days." [Ibid.124]

"Because of various simultaneous changes in the movement of the earth and moon, and because observation of the sky was hindered when it was hidden in smoke and clouds, the calendar could not be correctly computed; the changed length of the year, the month, and the day required prolonged, unobstructed observation... The month of the Exodus, which was in the spring, became the first month of the year." [Ibid. pp.122,123]

The "Shadow of Death"

Isaiah 9:2

The people who **walked in darkness** have seen a great light; those who lived in a land of **deep darkness...**"

Psalm 23:4

Even though I walk through the valley of the **shadow of death,** I fear no evil; for Thou art with me.

"After the destruction of the fourth sun, the world plunged in darkness during the space of twenty-five years." [Ibed. 128]

"*Nihongi,* a chronicle of **Japan** from the earliest period, refers to a time when there was **continuous darkness** and **no difference of day and night.**" [Ibid. 1 130]

Except for Caleb and Joshua, everyone who left Egypt died in the desert. No green thing ever grew without the sunshine. What they had to eat was the **"manna from heaven"** which fell through the clouds every morning:

Psalm 78:23,24

Yet he commanded the skies above, and opened the doors of heaven; he rained down on the **manna to eat,** and gave them the **grain** of heaven.

This grain manna which came down from the clouds **tasted good** and **smelled good.** They were able to gather it, and **bake** it over the fire. The planet god whom the whole world credited with this "heavenly ambrosia," was Jupiter. Jupiter as well as the planet Mars were worshiped as **Baal** during different periods of time. **In countries all over the world** this heavenly manna was eaten. The cows, horses, and sheep also were saved from starvation because they, also, freely ate.

Immediately after Noah's Flood, there were only 360 days to a year, and 30 days to a month. **Before the flood** there were fewer days in a year. Following close encounters with the planet **Mars,** the year was lengthened to 365+ days. Through the centuries there have been several calendar changes in all countries of the world, each being preceded by a close encounter with **Mars.**

A **series** of catastrophes occurred that changed the **axis** and **orbit** of the **earth,** and the orbit of the **moon;** that have repeatedly reduced civilization on this earth to ruins. And something like what has happened in the past, **probably** will happen again before Jesus returns:

Matthew 24:29-31

Immediately after the suffering of those days the **sun will be darkened,** and the **moon will not give its light;** and **the powers of**

heaven will be shaken. Then the sign of the Son of Man will appear in heaven... And he will send out his **angels** with a **loud** trumpet call, and they will gather his elect from the four winds, from one end of heaven to the other.

The visitation of the planet **Mars** resulted in **pole shifts**, which, in turn, created more than one **"ice age"** located in different areas of the poles. We are talking about thousands of years; not millions of years as the evolutionists try to make us believe.

> **FACT**: The Discovery of Noah's Ark and Proof there Really Was a World-wide Flood = the Biggest Stumbling Block for Evolutionists.

How could all races and all five colors descend from only Noah and his wife?

First of all, Noah's three sons married different women. Obviously there would have been sons and daughters marrying their sisters, brothers, and cousins. People had degenerated since Adam and Eve; therefore, people were not as healthy as those who descended from the "father and mother of all living" [Noah and his wife]. Following the Flood people did not live nearly as long.

Genesis 5:32

And Noah was 500 years old; and Noah begat Shem, Ham, and Japheth.
NRSV--After Noah was 500 years old, Noah became the father of Shem. Ham, and Japheth.

Noah's three sons were not triplets. **Ham** was the youngest [Gen 9:24]. **Shem** was younger than **Japheth** [according to some translations: Gen 10:21] but listed first because he was considered the most important of the three, as **Abraham** was listed first of the four sons of Terah even though he was the youngest of the four. **Shem outlived Abraham by 35 years. Abraham** after Sarah's death had **six more sons** by his new wife, **Katura.** She was **Hagar,** Sarah's **maid,** with whom Abraham had **Ishmael.**

How could only 4 men manage a ship the size of the Ark? How could 8 people handle all the chores necessary to sustain life? How could Ham, Shem, and Japheth, the fruit of the union of Noah and one wife, regardless of a variation in types of wives, be the progenitors of all the racial variations and colors of mankind in the new world after the Flood?"
Polygamy was practiced before Noah's Flood. **Lamech** is an example of someone who had two wives [Gen 4:19-22].

Evidently polygamy was accepted and also practiced <u>after</u> Noah's Flood. **David** had 16 wives before Bathsheba. **Solomon** had many wives plus an additional 300 concubines. **So polygamy was practiced before and after the Flood.**

Terah, the father of Abraham, possibly had more than one wife to enable Abraham [Abram] to marry his "half-sister, Sarah (Sari).

If Noah had but one wife, would not she have been venerated early on as next to Eve, **the mother of all living?!** Noah's wife is never mentioned by name. In fact, in the line of Seth no woman since Eve is mentioned by name until Sari (Sarah), Abram's (Abraham's) wife.

Noah's wife, who accompanied him into the Ark, need not have been the mother of Noah's three sons who entered the **Ark.**

It is <u>possible</u> that she was the mother of Ham, and the sister of Tubal-cain was Naamah" [Gen 4:22]. Why did the Bible writers record, by name, the line of Cain/Noah without recording the name of the wife of Noah? Was Naamah one of Noah's wives; the only one who accompanied him into the Ark?

Noah had three sons, but probably not with one wife. Only one wife accompanied him into the Ark.

As probably was the custom in those days, Noah must have chosen wives for his sons, each of whom possessed traits that collectively would produce a gene pool that would insure survival. Perhaps this is one of the reasons why people did not live nearly as long after the flood. Today, for good reasons, it is against the law to marry a sister, or even a cousin.

If Noah's sons were not different in color and other racial variations, how could different colors exist today – since all came from the one line of Noah?

There are **other reasons** why different races have various colors of skin. Living in hot climates for several generations can and will change skin color.

Noah saw the need to preserve mankind in the strength, adaptability, and diversity of characteristics that existed in mankind in general before the Flood. He could accomplish this by having more than one wife. One of Noah's wives, named Waliya, called him "madjnun" (insane) and stayed behind with her son Kanacan, whom the Arabs call Yam. This Arab tradition is referred to in the Houd 11:41-43.

The Bible declares that there were only eight people saved in Noah's Ark. **Other ancient sources claim there** were more than eight altogether, including hired help. According to these ancient sources:

The **Koran** explicitly mentions members of Noah's family who would not board: "Noah cried out to his son, who stood apart: 'Embark with us, my child,' he said. 'Do not stay with the unbelievers!' He replied: 'I shall seek refuge in a mountain, which will protect me from the Flood'... Noah's son was drowned [Sura Houd 40]. But the sons that did board are spoken of as representing nations or distinct lines... "Blessing upon thee and on the nations with thee." [Houd 50]

"Tablet XI, column 1 of the Sin-leqi-unninni version [line 85] says that even "the children of all the craftsmen I drove aboard." Noah was to bring his men servants, maid servants, and their young. **Berosus**** records that Xisouthros [Noah] was to embark with his kin and closest friends.

The Babylonians refer to **Buzur** and **Uragal** who helped in handling the anchor lines for the anchor stones. The tomb of **Noah's sister** in Syria and the tomb of **Noah's mother** in Iran (Marand), indicate there **may** have been more than eight. According to Mesopotamian accounts, Noah appointed **Buzur-Kurgala** the sailor to be in charge. According to a Babylonian text: "And **Uragal** parted the anchor cable."

It is believed by some that Naamah, sister of Tubal-cain, was the mother of Ham; that black headed people are the descendants of Cain. **Ham,** of course, came through the Flood. **Ham's son, Mizraim,** was not that far removed that he didn't know the truth. It was **Mizraim's brother's son, Nimrod,** through **Cush,** who really turned people back to **idolatry** as the world had been before. The Hamitic, or descendants of the line of Cain, ruled the earth. Mizraim, son of Ham [Gen 10:6] was the first king of Egypt.

Cause of the Flood

The worldwide flood at the time of Noah fits into the pattern of the **Mars' flybys,** except that the destruction at the time of Noah's Flood in **2484 BCE** was **greater** and **more far-reaching. The Mars' flyby at the time of Noah's Flood was the closest it has ever come to earth.**

Berosus appears quite positive about the astronomical event that caused the Flood and about a future event: "Berosus, interpreter of Belus, affirms all that the earth inherits will be consigned to flame when the five planets assemble in Cancer, so arranged in a row that a straight line may pass through their spheres. When the same gathering takes place in Capricorn, then we are in danger of the Deluge."

More than one historic record indicates that **Noah** was **not taken by surprise.** The <u>Talmud</u> [Historic Jewish laws and commentaries] makes interesting statements about Noah's flood which involve the **stars** or **planets:**

> "The **flood** was produced by the union of the male waters, which are above the firmament [sky], and the female waters issuing from the earth. **The upper waters rushed through space left when God removed two stars** out of the constellation **Pleiades...** There were other changes among the **celestial** heavenly spheres during the year of the flood." [<u>Legends of the Jews</u> by Louis Ginzberg, Jewish Publication Society of America, 1920 Volume 1, Page 180]

Noah's flood began **October 24, 2484 BCE,** wrote **Donald Wesley Patten,** on the 17th day of the 2nd month of the Old Hebrew <u>civil</u> calendar, **named after the planet Mars** ["Marchesvan" or the month of Mars]. It has been calculated that the planet **Mars** came closer to the earth on October 24, 2484 BCE than at any other time during its flybys. **Why?** Because it was the only time **Jupiter, Saturn, Neptune,** and **Uranus** were **all lined up** to cause the extra gravitational pull.

> "**Mars must have had an icy satellite** [Glacis] which pierced the Earth's <u>Roche</u> Limit, at 11,000 miles, and **fragmented...** Thus two planets each experienced a massive flood on the same day...

Mars sprayed with one million cubic miles of icy fragments... earth with twelve million." [<u>Catastrophism and the Old Testament</u>, pp. 34,35 Donald Patten] [See **9-4b.5** for books, prices]

QUESTION: Is there <u>evidence</u> that Mars was showered with **a "million square miles of ice?** Close-up pictures of the planet **Mars** from **Viking I** and **Viking II** show dry, 300 mile long, river beds! **Dry canals indicate ancient floods.** But **Mars' gravitational force is not strong enough** to retain water vapor! The extreme cold on Mars must have frozen the rivers. The **U.S. "Spirit" landed successfully on Mars 01-03-04** and took **pictures of ice on the high mountains!**

During **March 2004** it was decided definitely that **there was, at one time, much water on Mars.**

<u>Mars</u> <u>looked</u> <u>like</u> <u>a</u> <u>comet</u> <u>with</u> <u>a</u> <u>glorious</u> <u>tail</u> for some time after receiving its "million square miles of ice." Dry river beds that are now on Mars used to be a big mystery – and they still are a big mystery to many. But not to those who understand the close encounters of Earth and Mars, especially on **October 24, 2484 BCE.**

<u>**Mars Landing Missions**</u>

Nov 2, 1971 – Mars 2 [USSR]
    crashed
Dec 2, 1971 – Mars 3 [USSR]

landed
**Sept 3, 1976 – Viking 2 [US]
landed**
Dec 3, 1999 – Mars Polar Lander
[US] crashed.
Deep Space 2 Probes [US] crashed
Dec 25, 2003 – Beagle 2 [ESA] lost
Jan 3, 2004 -- Spirit [US] landed

The **Epic of Gilgamesh, Josephus,** the **Koran,** and **Berosus, Babylonians, Greeks,** and **Chinese** <u>all</u> claim that the planet **Mars** was what caused Noah's Flood. To the **Chinese** Mars was **Ying Huo.** To the **Romans** Mars was **Baal.** To the **Babylonians** Mars was **Nergal,** "the most violent among the gods," "lord of the storm who brings defeat," "unpredictable planet," "raging firegod." To the **Greeks** Mars was **Ares.**

Mars had two small moons, **Deimos** and **Phobos,** which **looked like bull's horns** to some ancient observers. This is <u>why</u> the <u>bull</u> was <u>sacred</u> to many heathen nations. The **bull** has his way in **India** even **today!** <u>**THINK:**</u> **Why did Solomon offer <u>22,000 bulls</u> at the dedication of his Temple?!** Because the <u>Romans</u> thought these two Mars moons looked like horses, <u>**they**</u> **sacrificed two horses** on their two most important holidays of the year: March 21 and October 24 -- the days also celebrated by the Hebrews!!

What were the <u>sources</u> of enough water to cover the whole earth at one time?

<u>**Genesis 7:11**</u>

"…all of the **fountains of the great deep** burst forth, and the **windows of the heavens** were opened."

Several sources say the flood was caused by the planet **Mars** [Baal]. Whenever a huge comet or planet came close to our earth, the tremendous pull of **gravity** caused the land masses to rise to the extent that great mountain ranges were formed – like the Himalayas, including Mt. Everest [29,028 foot evaluation = 5 miles]. Not only were great land masses raised up into mountains, but **water beneath the earth's crust was released. The "fountains of the great deep burst forth."**

<u>**Genesis 1:6-10**</u>

And God said, "Let there be a firmament [expanse] in the midst of the waters, and let it **separate the waters from the waters."** So God made the firmament and **separated the waters that were under the firmament from the waters that were above the firmament.** And it was so. God called the firmament Sky… And God said, **"Let the waters under the sky be gathered together into one place, and let the dry land appear."** And it was so. God called the **dry land Earth,** and the **waters** that were gathered together he called **Seas.**

<u>**Psalm 24:1,2**</u>

The **earth** is the Lord's… for he has founded it <u>on</u> the **seas,** and established it on the **rivers.**

Psalm 136:3-6

O give thanks to the **Lord of lords...** who spread out the earth <u>on</u> the **waters."**

Noah's flood was not merely some rain storm! The preceding Bible texts tell us that in order to produce dry land, God had to secure the excess water that was "under the firmament" below the surface of our planet earth. **The result of the division was "dry land" and "seas."** Today, 3/4th of our earth is covered with water! Not so before the gravitational pull of the planet **Mars** rearranged the order that was established at Creation.

At Creation our world surface was mostly land. Now our world surface is mostly water!

Before Creation it did not rain on the earth [**Gen 2:5**], and many believe that no rain came until after the flood – after which a rainbow appeared in the sky. Regardless, **where did the 40 days of rain originate?** Please refer back to <u>Genesis 7:11</u>.

"<u>and</u> the windows of the heavens were opened."

Evidently something very unusual happened. The **40 days of continuous rain had to come from a unique source.**

<u>Genesis 1:6-10</u>   tells us that, at Creation, God **divided** the waters that were <u>above</u> the firmament [atmosphere] from those <u>below</u> the firmament. What happened to the water that went up?

You probably have already heard of the "water canopy" theory believed by many; however, someone has figured that a water vapor canopy of more than 20 inches would result in too high a temperature on our earth's surface. Such a small amount of water would hardly explain rain for "40 days and 40 nights."

There <u>is</u> evidence that there was, at the time of Creation, **a water vapor canopy** that resulted in a **greenhouse effect** before the flood. We know that there must have been warm climates all over the earth because of the abundance of vegetation all over our planet – even at the north and south poles. **For example,** even the highest mountains today, like **Mt. Everest** [29,000 ft. = 5 miles], have fossils of sea creatures on their peaks! Scientists of the 19th century found skeletons of marine animals, fish that swam in the ocean, and shells of **mollusks.** Obviously, the **Himalayas** had risen from beneath the sea! The water vapor canopy is probably one of the reasons people lived so much longer before the flood than after the flood. Instead of living 900+ years as they did during the first ten generations, the lifespan was reduced to a mere 500 to 200 years or less, during the first five generations following the flood.

Nevertheless, it does not take too much mental energy to figure out that the **waters from above** probably came, not only from the water vapor canopy, but from ice connected to the planet **Mars** or one of its satellites – as suggested by Donald Patten.

Dry riverbeds now seen on Mars indicate much water was there at one time.

So, where did all the water go following the flood?

Three things happened when the planet Mars came in close proximity to our earth:

[1]   Land masses, because of the gravitational pulls, were raised to form **mountains**. When Noah and his family stepped out of the Ark, the world they saw was nothing like they had ever seen before. Rugged mountain peaks faced them on all sides.

[2]   The **"fountains of the deep"** which God confined beneath our earth crust, were **released**, causing, along with the water from above, the flooding of the whole earth. The **Epic of Gilgamesh** says, **"And when the storm came to an end and the terrible waterspouts ceased,** I opened the windows… like seaweed the corpses floated."

[3] The **gravitational pull caused our earth to spin out of its axis** and a **pole shift** to occur, causing **extreme cold** temperatures at the north and south poles. The earth may have rolled as much as 27 degrees at the time of the Flood. This is why large animals were quick-frozen with undigested food still in their stomachs. It also shows that before the flood there was enough green vegetation to feed thousands of large animals, **even at the north and south poles! Coal beds** are also the result of much vegetation destroyed and compressed.

When the **plates** in the crust of the earth became, to some extent, as they were before earth's close encounter with **Mars,** and the **huge mountains** remained as they became, and the **oceans** became more spread out and deeper, the earth appeared as we see it today [3/4th water]. If we could see how many miles deep the oceans really are, we would be amazed.

Darwin recorded in his ***Journal of Researchs*** [03-30-1835 entry] that "the shores of the Atlantic had been driven back some 700 miles, and at some time in the past the bed of the ocean had risen and formed a chain of mountains more than 7,000 feet high."

Before Noah's flood most of the earth was land on top of the water beneath [Ps 24:1 = the earth was made on the seas; Ps 136:6 = the earth was made <u>above</u> the waters]. Today most of the land is beneath the water.

Why were so many people deceived into worshiping the planet Mars?

"Bel [Mars]... sent a great deluge which destroyed my people" – Epic of Gilgamesh.

<u>Berossus,</u> a Chaldean priest of **Bel [Mars],** who lived around 300 BCE, said the flood was caused by **Bel** – the planet **Mars. "**...when the five planets assemble in **Cancer,** so arranged in a row...When the same gathering takes place in **Capri-corn,** then we are in danger of the Deluge."

<u>Berossus</u> also wrote that pilgrimages were made to the Ark site for at least 2,000 years after the flood. "A portion of the ship which came to rest in Armenia still remains in the mountains of the Korduaians [Kurds} of Armenia, and some of the people, scraping off pieces of bitumen from the ship, bring them back and use them as talismans."
Other ancient literature refers to **Mars** as **"the storm god."** Nicholas of Damascus was quoted by **Josephus** as saying [around 50 AD] that the timbers were preserved for many years, and that a portion of the boat still remained. The remains of iron fittings, iron nails, iron spikes, and/or iron supports are found in definite lineal and geometrical patterns

today.

When people continually turn their backs upon the laws and attitudes of the true Lord God, they separate themselves from Him and His supernatural protection. **It is then that the counterfeit lord Satan is allowed to deceive.** To them, the planet Mars was the "war god." whom they credited with intelligence! <u>Before</u> Noah's flood **much of the world's population actually worshiped the planet Mars [Baal].** After the flood, because people knew the **"war god" Mars** was the cause of the destruction, they worshiped the planet **Mars** that **came close to this earth every 54 years** as one of their many "gods" [Review Outlines No. 9-3a to 9-7, and Outline No. 10]. When people, even today, turn their backs upon the wisdom and instruction of God, it becomes easy to follow the crowd. Every instruction God has given to us is for our own good.

How can we, <u>today</u>, be kept from being deceived like ancient Israel? Well, first of all, we <u>can</u> tell the difference between a planet and an intelligent being! However, **Satan, "the angel of light"** [2 Cor. 11:14], is deceiving people **today** by **<u>using different methods</u>.** Today our problem is falling for <u>counterfeit philosophy,</u> <u>evolutionists,</u> and <u>counterfeit religious leaders</u> who teach that our **"God of love"** is a "killer God" who <u>breaks His own</u>

law – **a "God of love"** who will take a person who does not live up to all of His rules, and **torment** him or her for **"millions of years"**! A deity who would do such a thing is not **"a God of love,"** but a devil!

FACT: God never acts like the devil! "God is love," and He always acts that way. Always!

We can be absolutely sure that any supernatural being who does not reflect **love** and **fairness** in his actions, is not a holy angel or the **genuine** Lord God. The counterfeit "angel of light" is still at work today.

How could Noah fit so many animals into the Ark?

Genesis 8:19

"And **every animal**, every creeping thing, and every bird, everything that moves on the earth, went out of the ark **by families** [KJV: "after their kinds"]."

Genesis 1:20-25

And God said, "Let the waters bring forth swarms of living creatures, and let birds fly above the earth... So God created the great **sea monsters**... every winged bird of every kind... "Be fruitful and multiply and **fill the waters** in the **seas**... Let the earth bring forth living creatures and creeping things and **wild animals**... And it was so. God made the **wild animals** of the earth of **every kind,** and the **cattle** of **every kind...**"

---

[1] First of all, we do not have to be concerned with the **"sea monsters"** [Including Dinosaurs] nor anything that lived in the ocean. Flood or no flood, it was possible for them to survive.

[2] Two of every "unclean" animal [male and female] were to be saved in the Ark; along with seven pair of the "clean" animals: Genesis 7:2. [There were not many "clean" animals. **"Clean"** and **"unclean"** are listed in Lev. 5, 11, and Deut. 14. People were allowed to eat only the **"clean."**]

[3] Noah was told to load **"kinds"** or **"families"** of the various types of animals.

Of course, no one knows exactly how many different **"kinds"** were taken on Noah's Ark; however, there were not as many as people think. The horse, zebra, and donkeys can all interbreed, even though there are some problems today when they do. **Perhaps** it was not necessary to take too many **"kinds"** of dogs or cats. Neither do we know if lions and tigers were meat eaters before the flood. Certainly

snakes could easily survive on water and upon things floating in the water. Some animals, of course, hibernated.

[4] The size of Noah's Ark is **515' long, 137.5' wide,** and **51.5' high = 3,646,683 cubic feet,** or 2/3rds the size of the Titanic. Someone has figured the Ark could fit over 600 railroad cars on the three decks, with much room to spare for food and water.

[5] Personally, I do not see why Sea Monsters [Now known as Dinosaurs] had to be taken into the Ark to survive. We know that Sea Monsters spend most of their time under water, coming to the surface for air only after long periods of time. **Regardless**, the **eggs** of the largest dinosaurs were no bigger than a football! According to the Bible, the Sea Monsters [Dinosaurs as they are referred to today] were created during creation week – <u>not</u> millions of years before creation, as some evolutionists try to make us believe – as is stated in public school text books. **Dinosaur bones have been dug up in the same area as human bones, and on the same level!**

How Could Noah and Helpers See Inside a Dark Ark?

Most do not realize that those who lived <u>before</u> Noah's Flood were much more intelligent than people are today! Adam was perfect when created.

Adam was created perfect in every way; he was preprogrammed! And there is genuine historical evidence that, before Noah's Flood, they became evil enough to even engage in **nuclear war!** They flew airplanes and used electric lighting! Their surgical procedures were more advanced than even ours today. Noah and his family were members of a highly civilized race.

<u>Genesis 6:16</u>
A **light** shall you make to the ark, and to a cubit shall you finish it upward; and the door of the ark shall you set in the side of it; with lower, second, and third stories shall you make it. [The Sacred Scriptures, Bethel Edition]

"In this account we find two indications that lead us to believe that **electricity may have played a vital role in the operation of the ark.** One reference I found in Genesis 8:6, where the Hebrew word *challon* or 'opening' is used, referring to the window through which Noah released the birds. The other reference [Gen.16:6]; however, utilizes a different word -- *toshar* – which is translated as '**window**' but **does not mean window** or opening at all! Where it is used (22 times in the O.T.) its meaning is given as '**a brightness, a brilliance, the light of the noonday sun.**' Its cognates refer to something that 'glistens, glitters, or shines.' Many Jewish scholars of the traditional school identify *tsohar* as '**a light which has its origins in a shining crystal**" [*Secrets of the Lost Races* by Rene Noorbergen pp.45,46]

"An ancient Jewish manuscript entitled 'The Queen of Sheba and Her Only Son Men-yelek, translated by Sir E.A.Wallis Budge, contains this statement: "Now the **House of Solomon the King** was **illuminated as by day,** for in his wisdom he had made shining pearls which were like unto the sun, the moon and the stars **in the roof of his house**" [Noorbergen p. 46].

"The Sumerian** text also mentions that in the preparation of Ziusudra's (Noah's) 'huge boat,' the hero (Noah) brought 'his rays [of the sun] into the boat, in order to give it light" [Noorbergen p. 47].

For sure we know that the pre-flood knowledge of electricity was also understood by some of the descendants of Noah after the flood. Several high voltage **electric batteries 2,000 years old,** as well as **spark plugs,** have been found in Iraq.

DINOSAURS TODAY

According to your Bible, dinosaurs were created along with all the other animals, on the <u>same</u> <u>day</u> as Adam and Eve were created:

Genesis 1:21-31

So God created the great <u>**sea monsters**</u>... "Be fruitful and multiply and fill the waters in the seas... God made the <u>**wild animals**</u> of the earth <u>of</u> <u>**every**</u> <u>**kind**</u>... Then God said, "Let us make **man** in our image... male and female... God saw everything that he had made, and indeed, it was very good... the 6th day.

Job 40:15-19

Look at **Be'he-moth,** which I made just as I made you; it eats grass like an ox. Its **strength** is in its loins, and its **power** in the muscles of its belly. It makes its <u>**tail stiff like a cedar;**</u> the sinews of its thighs are knit together. Its **bones** are **tubes of bronze,** its **limbs like bars of iron.** It is the first of the great acts of God, **only its Maker can approach it with the sword.**

Psalm 74:13,14

You divided the sea by your might; you broke the heads of the **dragons** in the waters. You crushed the heads of **Le-vi'a-than.**

Job 41:1-26

"Can you draw out **Le-vi'a-than** with a fishhook... Lay hands on it; think of the battle; you will not do it again! Any hope of capturing it will be disappointed; were not even the gods overwhelmed at the sight of it? No one is so fierce as to dare stir it up... Who can confront it and be safe—under the whole heaven, who?... From its mouth go **flaming torches;** sparks of **fire leap out.** Out of its nostrils comes smoke, as from a boiling pot and burning rushes. Its breath kindles coals, and a **flame comes out of its mouth.** In its neck abides strength... When it raises itself up the gods are afraid... Though the sword reaches it, it does not avail, nor does the spear, the dart, or the javelin.

Descriptions in the Bible of animals that seem to fit what we know as dinosaurs, are not called dinosaurs. Why?

Because it was not until **1841** that anyone called them dinosaurs. Sir Richard Owen of the British museum, named them **"dinosaur"** from Greek words meaning, **"terrible lizard."**

The **Hebrew word** translated 30 times in the KJV Bible as **"dragon,"** comes from *tannin, tannim, tannoth*. **Strong's Concordance** lists **"dinosaur"** as one of the meanings of **"tannin/m."** The Hebrew word for **sea monsters** [*tannin*] in **Gen 1:21** is usually translated as **"dragon."**

It seems obvious that how the Bible describes **sea monsters, dragons, Leviathans,** is a description of what we know as various types of dinosaurs.

Behemoth: "It is the first of the great acts of God – only its maker can approach it." This seems to indicate that this could have been the largest animal of Creation. **A few translations say that the** Behemoth **is the same as a hippopotamus or elephant;** however, no hippo or elephant has a **"tail stiff like a cedar,"** potamus or elephant; however, no

hippo or elephant has a **"tail stiff like a cedar."**

Evidently the **behemoth,** according to the Bible's description, **has no enemies that he fears.** And certainly the hippo and elephant are not the largest animals.

At **Creation** all animals were vegetarians. **Isaiah looked forward to a time when all animals will be vegetarians:**

Isaiah 11:6,7

The **wolf** shall live with the **lamb,** the **leopard** shall lie down with the **kid,** the **calf** and the **lion** and the fatling together, and a little child shall lead them. The **cow** and the **bear** shall **graze,** their young shall lie down together; and the **lion** shall **eat straw** like the **ox.**

Genesis 1:30,31

And to **every beast** of the earth... I have given **every green plant for food.**

All animals, including man, were given a vegetarian diet at Creation. The time that animals began to eat each other, we do not know. However, it was not until **after the flood** that **people** were given permission to eat flesh:

Genesis 9:1-4

God blessed Noah and his sons... Every moving thing that lives shall be food for you; and just as I gave you the green plants, I give you everything. Only, **you shall not eat flesh with its** life, that is, its **blood.**

One of the results of people eating flesh, was the shortening of their lives. Instead of living 900+ years before the flood, people within only five generations following the flood, lived only 500 to 200 years or less. Health laws were given to the Israelites later on which specified only certain **"clean meats"** they could eat. Today we know scientifically **why blood and fat was forbidden.** That was the beginning of kosher meat. Today we know that blood in red meat is 40% saturated fat.

To Bible students, one thing is certain. Dinosaurs were <u>not</u> created <u>before</u> man, and they did <u>not</u> become extinct <u>before</u> the Genesis Creation. This we know <u>for</u> <u>sure</u>! After the flood it was man vs. dinosaurs for survival.

Scientists from the University of Montana found T. rex bones [Tyrannosaurus rex] that were not totally fossilized. **Sections of the bones contained blood cells and hemoglobin.** Obviously these bones were not "millions of years old" as evolutionists claim, and as is written in public school text books.

Every once in a while these days, we hear of what look like the 65 ft. long **Brontosaurus,** with its relatively small head, long neck, and long tail showing itself in various large bodies of water around the world. Some, but not many, have survived 6,000+ years since Noah's Flood.

Thousands of clay pots and rocks have been dug up with drawings and paintings of dinosaurs on them, with long necks and long tails. Also, **dinosaur bones and human bones have been uncovered together!** Cave walls depict the same. **Indians carved pictures of dinosaurs on walls of the Grand Canyon. How did they know what they looked like?**

St. George, the Patron saint of England and Portugal, slew a dragon in 275 A.D. **Alexander the Great** reported his soldiers were scared by great dragons that lived in caves, when they were in what is now India. **I, personally,** have seen dragons on the walls of the ruins of Babylon. Obviously, they must have known what they looked like in 600 BC. There are many legends of people being killed by dragons = dinosaurs.

There is an interesting story in Daniel 14:22-42 in the Catholic Douay version of how the prophet Daniel killed a great dragon that people worshiped.

Some dinosaurs have sharp, pointed teeth suitable for eating flesh. The giant panda, also, has sharp teeth, and eats bamboo. Many **bears** have sharp teeth, yet most of them are mostly vegetarians. The Bible does not tell us <u>when</u> animals began eating flesh. We know that they did <u>not</u> at Creation. Neither do we know when people began eating flesh. All we know for sure is that people were given permission to eat flesh <u>after</u> they left Noah's Ark.

No one knows how many super large dinosaurs Noah took into the Ark – if any. We do know <u>some</u> dinosaurs were as small as sheep. I personally believe it would not have been practical to take dinosaurs that weighed many tons into the Ark. After the flood there was not the hundreds of pounds of vegetation available to daily feed the super large dinosaurs. Nevertheless, many of the extremely large sea monsters <u>did</u> survive the flood. We even see some of them today in the largest bodies of water, and in unpopulated areas.

For many years huge **sea monsters** have been seen in and around **Monterey Bay, California.** Evidently various types of sea monsters find the mile deep **Submarine Canyon** [deep enough to hide the Grand Canyon] a good place to hide and eat. Some have elephant-like legs. Monterrey Bay's **"Old Man of the Sea,"** seen by many over the years, has a long, snake-like body over 100 feet long. At times its long human-like head stood out of the water eight feet – a head topped with flowing **red hair.** Another **crocodile-like monster** is long, multi-humped, four feet wide, with v-shaped teeth. Another monster with an **elephant-like trunk,** with reddish eyes protruding from each side of its head was seen so regularly people nicknamed it **Bobo.**

Near Monterey Bay some unknown creature escaped when it bent a three-foot iron hook! Also, in the same area, a giant 66 foot long **squid** was found, estimated to have weighed 84,000 pounds when alive. There have been numerous reports of 100 foot long squid-like creatures.

The largest sea monster known to have been seen at Monterey Bay was a **great blue whale** – "the largest mammal ever to have inhabited the earth." These creatures reach 100 feet and approximately **300,000 pounds.**

In **1971** on a St. Augustine, Florida, beach, a partially decomposed, **200-foot, 12,000 pound sea monster** ["Octopus Giganteus Verrill"] appeared. The largest known octopus was only 20 feet long.

<u>Proof</u> Dinosaurs Lived On Earth Since Noah's Flood

Pottery has been found with the **first Pharaoh of Egypt** [King Nar-mer] and **a long necked dinosaur** painted on them.
From the **11th century** comes a Viking Woodcut showing a **dragon swallowing a man.**

There are **thousands of dragon**

legends from **countries all over the world** of **people killing dinosaurs.**

A Chinese **man named "Yu," after the flood, surveyed** the land of **China** and **divided it** into sections. He built **channels** to drain the water off to the sea. He drove off or killed the **snakes** and **dragons** to make farm land.

Marduk, a god of Babylon, **killed a dragon** in **600 B.C.**

Captin Peter M'Quhaet and his crew saw a **60 foot sea monster** swim under their boat August 1848.

In 1850 a whaling ship, the Monogahel, out of New Bedford, killed a **103 foot sea monster.** It had **two blow holes**, four swim fins, an alligator-like head, and 94 very sharp teeth in his huge head.

On April 26, 1907, Arthur Henry Roston [chief officer on his ship] saw, off the Irish coast near Cork, a **long-necked sea monster.**

In 1571 Spanish conquistadors (conquerors) told about strange stones [20 in all world wide] from Ica, **Peru,** with strange creatures carved on them. Called **Nasca Burial Stones** today. Dated 500 B.C. to 500 A.D., these various drawings showed **brain surgery,** and replacing **artificial limbs** on people. **500 of the stones also showed dinosaurs** on them! That was over **2,000 years ago!**

In the Congo and Zaire, **Africa,** there is the Likouala swamp of **55,000 square miles.** During the past 200 years there have been several reports of **dinosaur** sightings.

Before the Dark Ages people reported many sightings of sea monsters while traveling over the high seas to the Americas.

Near Ica, Peru, there is a dry desert where have been found **2,000 year old pottery** with **circles** painted on the skins of dinosaurs.

Yes, there are dinosaurs living on earth today!

Easter Eggs

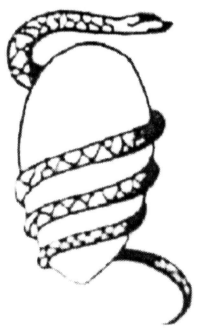

2,000 years before the Christian era the Egg of Ishtar [Venus] figured in rites where sacred bread was offered to the gods.

Noah's Ark was the original Egg of Easter. "Hot Cross Buns" and cakes for the **"Queen of Heaven"** were associated with this Egg.

The Egyptian word for the Ark [Kutu] was the same as **coffin.** Evidently Noah's Ark looked like a floating egg, especially when it began to deteriorate and crack from hundreds of years of exposure to the elements. Out of this cracked, hatched "Egg" came the seeds of mankind.

The sacred Egg of paganism is the Egg in which the world was shut up..

The Ark was also referred to as **"Typhon's Egg."** David Fasold believed Typhon was Shem. The cross [*T*] was a symbol of Tammuz.

Sacred eggs were hung in the temples in Egypt. Dyed and painted eggs are used in China and Japan. Now you know the origin of the **"Easter Egg hunt."**

The **pillar of fire** that accompanied Israel in the wilderness after they left Egypt – the one that kept changing directions – probably looked like a serpent. At one time **Moses** had them look at the image of a serpent so they would not die! Regardless, Israel followed the example of other nations and, at times, often prayed and offered sacrifices to various heathen gods – like the planet Mars.

Review

[1] A description of Noah's Flood and its cause was written in the **Epic of Gilgamesh** hundreds of years before the Bible was written.

[2] The **Bible account** of Noah's Flood is recorded in Genesis chapters 6, 7, and 8. New Testament writers, along with **Jesus,** considered Noah's Flood a literal fact.

[3] Uninspired **tradition,** along with several deliberate hoaxes, have influenced seekers of Noah's Ark to search in the wrong places – on Mt. Ararat.

[4] Those who have returned claiming they had found the Ark on Mt. Ararat always forget to snap a close-up picture!!

[5] Ancient sources testify that Noah's Ark has been seen: **Gilgamesh,** the **Koran,** the **Talmud, Josephus, Berosus, David Fasold, Babylonians, Chinese,** and **Greeks.**

[6] The Bible does not say Noah's Ark landed on Mt. Ararat, but on the **mountains** of Ararat [Genesis 8:4].

[7] Subsurface radar surveys were completed by David Fasold and Dr. John Baumgardner, at different times, resulting with proof of a huge 515 foot long boat, four or five thousand years old, on a hill 17 miles south of Mt. Ararat.

[8] **Iron** was used in the construction of Noah's Ark.

[9] **"Gopher"** is not the name of any kind of wood. The word simply means **"cover."** The outside of the Ark was/is made of a water-proof cement which has served to preserve it for thousands of years.

[10] The **Turkish Ministry of Culture** has made the remains of Noah's Ark a **national park.** There is a **Welcome Center** there now.

[11] In the bottom of Noah's Ark is a 201 foot long, 26 foot wide **moon pool** which helped to control the Ark in rough waters, eliminate manure, and circulate fresh air.

[12] **Twelve anchor stones** [drogue stones] were found a short distance [14 miles] from where the Ark grounded.

[13] People were **not half civilized** during Noah's time, but were highly civilized with much higher **IQs** than people have today. Adam and Eve were created perfectly; with minds preprogrammed.

[14] Flood waters <u>did</u> cover the entire world. Evidence in all countries of the world show proof of this fact.

[15] Evidence shows that oceans and mountains were formed, and did change places on more than one occasion.

[16] **Polygamy** was practiced before and after the Flood; therefore, it is <u>possible</u> that Noah had more than one wife before the Flood, which helps to explain how five races and colors could come from Noah.

[17] The natural cause of Noah's Flood, <u>and</u> several other catastrophes, have to do with close encounters with Mars and Venus.

[18] Enough water to cover the entire world came from below the earth's surface, and from the sky. The water source from the sky had to be more than the water canopy that was around our globe.

[19] Before Noah's Flood most of the earth's surface was land; following Noah's Flood most of the earth's surface was water – as it is today.

[20] Most people on earth worshiped the god planets because these planets so often came close enough to disrupt the earth..

[21] It was not necessary to fit as many animals into the Ark as most people think. **Families,** or **kinds** were taken in.

[22] **Dinosaurs** were not created separately before the Genesis creation, nor did they become extinct before the Genesis creation. All through history, in nations around the world, there have been thousands of stories of the conflict between dinosaurs and people.

[23] **Dinosaurs** are still living in isolated parts of this world, and in a few large bodies of water.

[24] The **Easter Egg** had its beginning when people saw the remains of Noah's Ark. Also, people were confused by what they saw of "snakes" and "bull's horns" in the sky and around plants and their satellites. They credited such with intelligence!

GLOSSARY

Amulets = Anything worn about the person as protection against accident or evil; a charm. These have been found with silver heads in Egypt dating back to 3,000 BC where archaeologists have found an iron pin with a gold head.

Apis = Sacred bull of Venus when Venus was a comet. Turned into a cow because of the manna from heaven.

Ares = **Mars**

Athene = **Venus**

BCE = **Before Christian Era**

Berosus – **"Bel is his shepherd"**
Chaldean priest of Bel [Mars] Chaldean-Babylonian historian, scribe, astronomer, and seer of the 3rd century BC

Bow of boat = **Front end of Ark.**

Bituminous = **A petroleum product also translated as asphalt, tar, pitch**

Coffin = **kutu** = Egyptian name for Ark

Cubit = **Egyptian** = 20.6 inches
Hebrew = 18 inches

Dogubayazit = **Dough-you-bye'-a-zit**
Dog = "east" or East U-by'-a-zit A town half way between the Ark site and the anchor stones.

Drogue Stone = **Anchor stone**

Gopher = **"to cover"** = *kaphar*
Not "wood" of any kind.

Hull pool = **Moon pool** = The 201 x 26 foot opening in the bottom of the Ark through which the water entered.

Ishtar = **Venus** =
Babylonian/Assyrian
Goddess of war, love, fertility.
Phoenician: Astarte or Ashtoreth
"The fearful dragon."
"Queen of Heaven"

Jove = Jupiter
Jupiter = **Planet** = Roman name
Zeus = Greek name

Kiln = An oven or furnace for baking, burning, or drying bricks, lime, pottery, cement

Kutu = **coffin** = Egyptian name for Ark

Leviathan = A gigantic unidentified water beast mentioned one time in the Bible.

Mars = **Planet** = Roman name
Nergal = Chaldean name
Ares = Greek "raging flame-god"

Mazzaroth = Venus [Job 38:32.33]

Moon pool = See Hull pool

Nasar = **"To make a sacrifice or a presentation"**

Nargal = Mars

Nergal = Mars
Nisir = See **Nasar**

pi = Used to determine the ratio of
   the circumference of a circle to
   its diameter.
   The ratio itself **(3.14159...)**
   Used on both Noah's Ark &
   Great Pyramid of Giza
Plato = **Greek philosopher**
   Friend of Socrates 427?-347?
   BC

Stern of boat = **Back end of Ark.**
Sumerian [soo-**mir'**-e-an] =
   Pertaining to ancient **Sumer**
   – an ancient non-Semitic people
   formerly occupying a part of
   lower Babylonia from 3300 to
   1800 B.C. language written in
   cuneiform on rocks and clay
   tablets.
   First civilization after the flood.

Tammuz = God of agriculture
   Brother and husband of Ishtar
   Worshiped in Babylon,
   Assyria,Phoenicia, Palestine,
   The cult eventually adopted by
   the Jews.
Typhon = Comet in days of Exodus
   "globe of fire" = "Shem"

Utnapishtim = **Gilgamesh** = **Noah**

Venus = **Iris** = Egyptian name
   Ishtar = Babylonian name
   Athene = Greek name
   Became the **"Morning Star."**
   Was **a comet** for 8 centuries after

the Exodus, before it became a
planet.

Wrought iron = **commercially pure**
   Wrought iron is "commercially
   pure iron, prepared from pig
   iron, and easily forged and
   welded into various shapes."
   Pig iron is "crude iron poured
   from a blast furnace."

Zeus = **Jupiter** Greek supreme
   deity
   Jupiter = Roman name

New Visitor's Center

Boat Shape

Paul Sweitzer and anchor stone

Side columns from which upper deck support
beams protrude

Standing on remains of Noah's Ark

tormented with **fire** and **brimstone** in the presence of the holy angels and in the presence of the **Lamb.**"

Is God Really Like That?
Outline No. 12

Congratulations Satan!

As intelligent and fair-minded individuals, we like to give credit where credit is due. And the **devil** certainly deserves congratulations for his success in one big phase of his war with Jesus. Satan actually has millions of Christians believing that God would torture people in ways humans would not think of doing! **Congratulations Satan!** You have done an excellent job in deceiving preachers and laity alike. Hundreds of years of preaching the doctrines of eternal torment has made skeptics and infidels by the millions. It has driven many into insanity and atheism.

Well-meaning preachers have taken prophetic symbols and have tried to make them literal, teaching a God of love in one breath, and a cruel God of hate and revenge in the next.
For example:

Revelation 14:9,10

And another **angel**, a third, followed them, saying with a loud voice, "If any one worships the **beast** and **its image,** and receives a **mark in his forehead** or **on his hand,** he also shall **drink** the **wine** of God's wrath, **poured** unmixed into the **cup** of his anger, and he shall be tormented with **fire** and **brimstone** in the presence of the holy angels and in the presence of the **Lamb.**"

What does the average **"scholar"** do with this text? He considers **"angel," "beast," "its image," "mark on his forehead," "on his hand," "cup," "drink," "wine," "poured,"** and **"Lamb"** to be <u>symbolic</u> – which they **are.** Then he/she takes the other two key words in this text, and says they are **literal!** **"Fire** and **brimstone,"** he/she says, **"are literal,** not symbolic! "Eleven key words are symbolic," he says, "fire and brimstone are not." **Should we congratulate the devil, or should we question the intelligence of the clergy?**

By the way, it is mostly the less educated faction of the clergy today who are still whooping it up about hell fire, smoke, and brimstone [sulfur].

The apostle **Paul,** the **best educated** and most scholarly of all the apostles, who wrote almost half of the N.T., **never once mentioned a burning hell!**

Many preachers <u>know</u> that it does not make sense to teach that a **"God of love"** will torture people **"forever"** in some fire trap they have yet to locate. But, like poor Jonah, they would rather see millions driven to insanity and atheism than to <u>admit</u> they might be wrong! They urge that the infliction of endless misery upon the wicked would show God's hatred of sin. **What blasphemy! Cruelty is satanic. God is love. Jesus said:**

Luke 6:27

Love your enemies, do good to those who hate you.

How could **Jesus** tell **us** to love **our** enemies, and to do good to those who hate **us,** if **He** hates **His** enemies, and plans on torturing them, either mentally or physically, for all eternity?

Hitler More Loving Than God?!!!

During World War II **Hitler** and his henchmen murdered millions of Jewish people – some of them by fire. **Hitler was condemned by an outraged world,** yet millions of **Christians are now teaching** their children that our **"God of love" is,** even at the present time, **doing something much more horrible** than was ever done by Hitler! At least Hitler killed his prisoners in the end! **Was Hitler really more loving than God?!**

The apostle **Paul** wrote – the apostle who **never** wrote about a burning hell:

Romans 6:23

For the wages of sin is **death,** but the free gift of God is **eternal life** in Christ Jesus our Lord.

Life is life regardless of whether it is lived in happiness or in misery. **Paul**

did **not** write that the wages of sin are **eternal life in hell! If** the wages of sin will be eternal torture, then **Jesus** never suffered what all the lost will suffer! **Heaven's idea is to do away with sin and sinners – not to make them immortal!**

1 Corinthians 15:3-6,17,18

Christ died for our sins... he was raised on the third day... he appeared to more than 500 brethren at one time, most of whom are still alive, though **some have fallen asleep... If Christ has not been raised,** your faith is futile and you are still in your sins. Then those who have **fallen asleep** in Christ have **perished.**

Paul did **not** say that those who had died had gone to heaven or any other place, only that they had **"fallen asleep."** Then **Paul** pointed out that **if** Jesus had **not** been raised from the grave, then those who had died ["fallen asleep"] had **"perished."**

In the city of Nain, **Jesus** stopped a funeral procession. The only son of a widow had died. Jesus raised him to life! If this widow's son had been in heaven or "hell," would not **Jesus** have called him from one place or another? If he was in heaven at the time, he certainly made a fast trip back!

Luke 7:11-15

"Young man, I say to you, arise."

John 11:39,43,44

Jesus said, "Take away the stone." **Martha,** the sister of the **dead man,** said to him, "Lord, by this time there will be an odor, for he has been **dead four days.**" ...he [Jesus] cried with a loud voice, **"Lazarus, come out."** The **dead man** came out, his hands and feet bound with bandages, and his face wrapped with a cloth. Jesus said to them, "Unbind him, and let him go."

Jesus told **Lazarus** to **"come out,"** not "come down." Was Jesus a little mixed up?

Revelation 20:13,14

And the sea gave up the dead in it, **Death** and **Hades** gave up the dead in them, and all were **judged** by what they had done. Then **Death** and **Hades** were thrown into the lake of fire.

If **hell** is a place of eternal fire and torment, as some **traditions** proclaim, then why, in Rev. 20 above, were people in such a place **before** they had been judged? It would be like sending a man to the electric chair before he had been given a trial! Note that **"Hades"** was thrown into **"the lake of fire"** – which means we better make a careful study of this important subject **for ourselves** before we attempt to judge God's character.

As you continue to study, be fair to yourself. **Some of the things your Bible teaches may surprise you.** Wait until we have covered the subject fully [Including the "Soul," "Spirit," "Hell," the Occult, the End of Sin and Sinners, and the "Rich Man and Lazarus"] before coming to any definite conclusions.

The ABCs of Death

[1] **The wages of sin = death – not eternal life in torment** [Rom. 6:23].

[2] **Paul: "death = a sleep"** [1 Cor 15::6] **Luke**: "death = a sleep" [Acts 7:60] **David**: "death = a sleep" [Ps. 13:3] **Job**: "death = a sleep" [Job 14:12] **Jesus**: "death = a sleep" [John 11]

John 11:11-14

Thus he [Jesus] spoke... to them [disciples], **"Our friend Lazarus has fallen asleep,** but I go to awake him out of **sleep.**" The disciples said to him, "Lord, if he has fallen asleep, he will recover." Now Jesus had spoken of his **death,** but they thought that he meant taking rest in sleep. **Then Jesus told them plainly, "Lazarus is dead."**

---

[3] **People & animals go to the same place at death:**

Ecclesiastes 3:19,20

For the **fate** of the sons of **men** and the fate of **beasts** is the **same;** as one dies, so dies the other. They all have the **same breath,** and **man has no advantage** over the beasts; for all is vanity. **All go to one place;** all are from the dust, and all turn to dust again.

[4] People know nothing while dead:

Ecclesiastes 9:5,6,10

For the living know that they will die, but the **dead know nothing,** and they have no more reward; but the **memory** of them is lost. **Their love** and their **hate** and their **envy** have **already perished,** and they have no more forever any share in all that is done under the sun. Whatsoever your hand finds to do, do it with your might; for there is **no work** or **thought** or **knowledge** or **wisdom** in **sheol** [the grave], to which you are going.

Psalm 146:4

When his **breath** departs he returns to his earth; on that very day his **plans perish.**

[5] The dead do not remember God:

Psalm 115:17

The **dead do not praise the Lord,** nor do **any** that go down into **silence.**

Psalm 6:5

For in **death** there is **no remembrance** of thee; in **sheol** [the grave] who can give thee praise?

Isaiah 38:18

For **sheol** [grave] cannot thank thee, **death** cannot celebrate thee; they that go down into the pit **cannot hope** for thy salvation.

[6] Righteous people who did not go to heaven:

Acts 2:29,34

I say to you confidently of the patriarch **David** that he both **died** and was **buried,** and his **tomb** is with us to this day... For **David did not ascend** into the heavens...

Hebrews 11:4-13, 39, 40

Abel... Enoch... Noah... Abraham... Sarah... all these, though they were commended for **their faith,** did not receive what was promised, since God had provided something better, so that they would not, apart from us, be made perfect.

[7] People will not be rewarded until Jesus returns to earth;

Matthew 16:27

For the Son of man is to come with his angels in the glory of his Father, and **then** he will repay **every man** for what he has done.

1 Corinthians 15:22,23

For as in Adam all die, so also in Christ shall **all be made alive.** But each in his own order: Christ the first fruits, then **at his coming** those who belong to Christ.

1 Thessalonians 4:15-17

For this we declare to you by the word of the Lord, that we who are alive, who are left until the coming of the Lord, shall <u>not</u> precede those who have **fallen asleep.** For the Lord himself will descend from heaven with a cry of command… And the **dead in Christ will rise first;** then <u>we</u> who are alive, who are left, **shall be caught up together <u>with</u> them** in the clouds to meet the Lord in the air; and so we shall always be with the Lord.

Why would Jesus, at His second coming, call people back to life **IF** they were already alive in heaven? As we have just read from the writings of the apostle **Paul**, the righteous who are still alive when Jesus returns, and the righteous **dead** who will be raised to new life at the second coming, **all go to heaven together at the same time!**

Please note that the **righteous** are in their **graves** or **tombs** until Jesus' second coming:

John 5:28,29

"The hour is coming when **all** who are in the **tombs <u>will</u> <u>hear</u> <u>his</u> <u>voice</u>** and come forth, those who have done <u>good</u>, to the **resurrection** of life, and those who have done evil, to the resurrection of judgment."

---

[8] <u>No</u> <u>one</u> <u>receives</u> <u>immortality</u> <u>until</u> <u>the</u> <u>second</u> <u>coming</u> <u>of</u> <u>Jesus</u>:

1 Corinthians 15:51-53

"Lo! I tell you a mystery. We shall not all **sleep**, but we shall be **changed**, **in a moment,** in the twinkling of an eye, **at the last trumpet.** For the trumpet will sound, and the **dead** will be **raised imperishable**, and we shall be changed. For this perishable nature must put on the **imperishable**, and this **<u>MORTAL</u> nature must <u>PUT ON IMMORTALITY</u>."**

---

[9] <u>We</u> <u>will</u> <u>not</u> <u>be</u> <u>together</u> <u>with</u> <u>Jesus</u> <u>until</u> <u>He</u> <u>returns</u> <u>at</u> <u>His</u> <u>second</u> <u>coming</u>:

John 14:3

And if I go and prepare a place for you, I will come again, and will take you to myself, that where I am you may be also.

Jesus said that He would **"come again"** so that we could be together. **Does it make sense** to take a long journey to be with the ones we love if we are **already** with them? **No,** the righteous do not go to heaven, and do not receive immortality, until the resurrection at the second coming of Jesus.

Did not Jesus promise the thief on the cross that the thief would go to heaven that very day?

Luke 23:43

And he [Jesus] said to him [the thief], "Truly, I say to you, today you will be with me in Paradise."

It is only by **comparing Scripture** that some problems can be solved. According to this text in Luke 23:43, Jesus promised the thief, **"today you will be with me in Paradise."** The **problem**: How could Jesus be with the thief in heaven that day [Friday] when **Jesus Himself did not go to heaven that day!!!**

John 20:17

Jesus said to her [Mary], "Do not hold me, because I have not yet ascended to the Father."

It was **Sunday morning** ["the first day of the week"] when Jesus told Mary that He had not yet ascended to heaven. **What is the solution for what seems to be a contradiction?**

The solution: All punctuation was added many years after the writing of the original Bible manuscripts. Possibly the **comma** should have been placed **after** "today" rather than before. This would make the text read in such a way that the Bible would not contradict itself. Thus the passage possibly should read, **"Truly, I say to you today, you will be with me in Paradise."**

Deuteronomy 18:10-12

There shall not be found among you any one who... practices divination, a soothsayer... or a sorcerer, or a charmer, or a **medium,** or a wizzard, or a **necromancer.** For whoever does these things is **an abomination to the Lord.**

"Necromancy," according to Webster, is revealing the future by pretended communication with the spirits of the dead.

> **FACT: According to the Bible, all fortune tellers are an abomination to the Lord.**

REVIEW

The reason for this course of study about God is to show, from the Bible, that He is not the temperamental two-faced God that too many people, including many Christians, have made Him out to be.

The idea that God would create us without our consent, and then torment us "for ever" for not obeying all of His rules, is impossible, if God is really a "God of love" as the apostle John claimed [1 John 4:8,16].

PREVIEW

Our Bible-based studies covered in the next few outlines are not the easiest to understand. Yet, with a little concentration, you will soon realize that God really is a "God of love." He is the One whom you can trust in this life and with eternal life.

<u>All</u> your questions will <u>not</u> be answered until you have completed this series within a series. Topics to be studied:

The Bible Hell
Soul
Spirit
The Occult and Satanism
UFOs and their occupants
Lazarus and the Rich Man
End of Sin and Sinners

12-8

Is God Really Like That?
Outline No. 13

The Bible Hell

When the average person, Christian or non-Christian, thinks of **"HELL,"** he or she usually thinks of a terrible place of fiery torment. **Why?** Because this is what he has been taught since being a little baby! Some, not knowing the difference, believe that **"HADES"** is where the devil lives! When you complete this outline you will know better.

sheol = hell = grave

In the **Hebrew Old Testament** there is **one word** and only one word from which we get our English word, **"hell."** That word is **"sheol,"** which simply means **grave.** **Sheol** appears **65 times** in the KJV Old Testament; however, it has been translated three different ways:

> 31 times as "hell"
> 31 times as "grave"
> 3 times as "pit"

The following Bible text is an **example** of how the Hebrew word, **"sheol,"** always means **"grave,"** regardless of how it has been translated:

Psalm 49:14 – RSV

Like **sheep** they are appointed for **Sheol; Death** shall be their shepherd; straight to the **grave** they descend, and their form shall waste away; **Sheol** shall be their home.

Instead of **sheol,** the <u>King James Version</u> translated it as **grave.** Instead of **sheol,** the <u>Catholic Douay Version</u> translated it as **hell.**

IF we would interpret **sheol** as **"hell"** in the preceding Bible text [Ps. 49:14] in the same way that "eternal fire" preachers do other texts, then we would have poor **sheep** going to a **"burning hell."** No, <u>both</u> sheep and people go to the **grave** when they die and are buried.

hades = hell = grave

In the **Greek** New Testament there are <u>**three**</u> words from which we get our English word **"hell."** They are:

[1] <u>**Hades**</u> = **same as the OT sheol = grave.**
   Hades – used eleven times in the N.T.
   <u>Matt</u> 11:23; 16:18
   <u>Luke</u> 10:15; 16:23
   <u>Acts</u> 2:27; 2:31   <u>1 Cor</u> 15:55
   <u>Rev</u> 1:18; 6:8; 20:13; 20:14

[2] <u>**Gehenna**</u> [gee-hen'-nah] = **place of burning** or **Valley of Hinnom**
   Gehenna – used twelve times in the N.T.

Matt 5:22, 29, 30; 10:28;
Matt 18:9; 23:15,33;
Mark 9:43,45,47;
Luke 12:5; James 3:6

[3] <u>Tartarus</u> = "to cast down to" or
                      "place of darkness"
**Tartarus – used one time in
the N.T.**
<u>2 Peter 2:4</u>

Once in a while we hear people say
that **Jesus** spent a short time in **hell,**
thinking that Jesus went to a place of
burning. **Jesus** simply went to the
grave = the Hades hell:

<u>Psalm 16:10 – King James</u>

For thou wilt not leave my soul in
hell…

<u>Psalm 16:10 – Revised Standard</u>

For thou will not give me up to
Sheol…

<u>Acts 2:27 – King James</u>

Because thou will not leave my
soul in **hell…**

<u>Acts 2:27 – Revised Standard</u>

For thou will not abandon my soul
to **Hades…**

Gehenna hell

One of the three **Greek** words that are
translated as **"hell"** in the **King James
Version** is **"gehenna"** [gee-hen'-
nah], meaning **"place of burning"** or
"Valley of Hinnom."

This **"Valley of Hinnom"** was a
deep, narrow gorge located just
south of Jerusalem where, after the
introduction of the fire gods of Ahaz,
the **idolatrous Jews offered their
children as human sacrifices to
Moloch.** Because of this sin, Jeremiah
[Jer. 7:32,33] predicted that the Lord
would make the valley of the son of
Hinnom a "valley of slaughter" where
corpses of the Israelites would be
buried until there was no more place
for them, and the remaining bodies
would be food for the birds and beasts.
This led to the valley being regarded
as a place of judgment of the wicked.
Today the fires are not burning!

In this **"Valley of Hinnom"** the
bodies of dead animals and the refuse
of the city were cast. **Fires burned
continuously,** and worms infested
the carcasses of the animals. **What
the fire did not destroy the worms
consumed. This was a type of
complete destruction.**

<u>1 Peter 3:18-20</u>

"He [Jesus] was put to death in
the flesh, but made alive in the
spirit, "in which he went and
preached ["made a proclamation"
= NRSV] to the spirits in prison,
who formerly did not obey, <u>when
**God's patience waited in the days
of Noah, during the building of
the ark,** in which a few, that is,
eight persons, were saved through
water."

People who have not studied **all** that
their Bibles tell them about **death,** can
easily misunderstand the above text.

To whom did Jesus preach – or make a proclamation? The answer is in **verse 20: "**who formerly did not obey, when God's patience waited in the days of Noah, during the building of the ark**…"**

The people who died in Noah's flood were the ones God "preached to" through Noah. They had the same thing happen to them as the people of Capernaum: <u>Matt 11:23</u> – "Capernaum**…** You shall be brought down to **Hades" [KJV = "hell"].** **Hades** and **Sheol** are the Greek and Hebrew words for "grave." When Jesus went to the **KJV "hell,"** and the **KJV "Sheol,"** Jesus merely went to the grave.

<u>Acts 2:27</u>

"For you will not abandon my soul to **Hades [KJV = "hell"],** nor let thy Holy One see corruption." <u>Ps 16:10</u> – "For you do not give me up to **Sheol" [KJV = "hell"].**

<u>Rev 1:18</u>

"I have the keys of Death and **Hades" [KJV = "hell"].** By claiming to have the keys of death and hades, Jesus claimed that the resurrection of the dead would become a literal fact because of His creative power.

<u>If</u> Jesus <u>did</u> go and preach to <u>literal</u>, conscious dead people, it means that <u>Heb. 9:27,28</u> is wrong:: "And just as it is appointed for men to **<u>die once</u>, and after that the judgment,** so Christ**…** will appear a second time, **not to deal with sin** but to save those who are eagerly waiting for him**."**

Five people in the Bible, including Jesus, referred to death as "<u>sleep</u>:

<u>John 11:11-14 = Jesus</u>

Thus he **[Jesus]** spoke**…** to them [disciples], "Our friend **Lazarus has fallen asleep,** but I go to awake him out of **sleep."** The disciples said to him, "Lord, if he has fallen asleep, he will recover." Now Jesus had spoken of his **death,** but they thought that he meant taking rest in sleep. **Then Jesus told them plainly, "Lazarus is dead."**

<u>1 Cor 15:6 = Paul</u>

Then he [**Jesus**] appeared to more than 500 brethren at one time, most of whom are still alive, though some have **fallen asleep.**

<u>Acts 7:59,60 = Luke</u>

As they were stoning **Stephen,** he prayed, "Lord Jesus, receive my spirit**…** And when he had said this, **he fell asleep.**

<u>Psalm 13:3 = David</u>

O Lord**…** lighten my eyes, lest I **sleep** the **sleep of death.**

<u>Job 14:12 = Job</u>

So man lies down and rises not again; till the heavens are no more he will not awake, or be roused out of his **sleep.**

The dead know nothing at all:

<u>Psalm 115:17</u>

The dead do not praise the Lord, nor do any that go down into silence.

<u>Psalm 6:5</u>

For in **death** there is **no remembrance** of thee; in **sheol** [the grave] who can give thee praise?

Isaiah 38:18

For **sheol** [grave] cannot thank thee, **death** cannot celebrate thee; they that go down into the pit **cannot hope** for thy salvation.

Tartarus

The **third Greek** word translated as **"hell"** in the New Testament [used just one time] is **"tartarus"** ["to cast down to" or "place of darkness"]. 2 Peter 2:4 speaks of evil angels being cast into **"hell"** [tar-tar'-us"] until the judgment. This pictures **"hell"** as a place of darkness or gloom, which is **a fit representation of the darkness that enshrouded Satan and his angels when they were separated from God and heaven.** Revelation 12:7-9 is evidence that Peter was speaking of the darkness of this world. The text says that Satan and his angels were cast down to **this earth:**

Revelation 12:7-9

Now war arose in heaven [no one was killed], **Michael and his angels** fighting against the **dragon;** and the **dragon and his angels** fought, but they were **defeated** and there was **no longer any place for them in heaven.** And the great **dragon** was thrown down, that ancient **serpent,** who is called the **Devil** and **Satan,** the **deceiver of the whole world** - he was **thrown down to the earth,** and his angels were thrown down <u>with</u> him.

Only in a **parable** does the Bible speak of punishment in **"hades"** [Luke 16:23]. This parable will be studied in detail in another outline. One reference in a parable is <u>not</u> sufficient evidence to teach that Jesus or anyone else went to a place of burning at death, especially when the rest of the Bible teaches otherwise.

The **righteous dead** will come out of **"hades"** [the grave] at the second coming of Jesus:

1 Thessalonians 4:15-18

For this we declare to you by the word of the Lord, that we who are alive, who are left until the coming of the Lord, shall not precede those who have fallen asleep. For the Lord himself will descend from heaven with a cry of command, with the archangel's call, and with the sound of the trumpet of God. And **the dead in Christ will rise first;** then we who are alive, who are left, shall be caught up together with them in the clouds to meet the Lord in the air; and so we shall always be with the Lord. Therefore comfort one another with these words.

I Corinthians 15:51-53

Lo! I tell you a mystery. We shall not all sleep, but we shall all be changed, in a moment, in the twinkling of an eye, **at the last trumpet.** For the trumpet will sound, and **the dead will be raised** imperishable, and we shall be changed. For this perishable nature must put on the imperishable, and this mortal nature must put on **immortality.**

Revelation 20:6

Blessed and holy is he who shares in the **first resurrection!** Over such the second death has no power, but they shall be priests of God and of Christ, and they shall reign with him a thousand years.

According to the apostle **John** [who wrote both the Gospel of John and Revelation] there will be **two different resurrections:**

John 5:28,29

...the hour is coming when <u>all</u> who are in the tombs will hear his voice and come forth, those who have done **good,** to the **resurrection of life,** and those who have done **evil,** to the **resurrection of judgment.**

The **<u>un</u>righteous dead** will not come out of **"hades"** [the grave] until **<u>after</u>** the "one thousand years" of Rev. 20, at the **end** of the **Millennium:**

Revelation 20:5

The rest of the dead did not come to life until the thousand years were ended.

Once in a while we find a Christian who does not accept the idea that God [Jesus] created human beings in one day as stated in the book of Genesis. Yet these same Christians actually believe that God will raise them to life at the resurrection! **What happened? Did God learn <u>how</u> since the Genesis creation,** to create new life in one day, so that He could do it at the resurrection? The point is that **a person cannot believe one**

without believing the other! If He will be able to raise the dead to life at the time of the first and second resurrections, then He was able to create man and woman in one day - just as Genesis said He did!

FACT: Everyone who dies, either good or bad, goes to a "hell."

Yes, <u>all</u> who die go to the same place - to the "hades hell" = the grave = "sheol" in the Hebrew Old Testament:

Ecclesiastes 3:19,20

For the fate of the sons of **men** and the fate of **beasts** is the same; as one dies, so dies the other. They all have the same breath, and man has no advantage over the beasts; **all go to one place;** all are from the dust, and all turn to dust again.

However, <u>all</u> the dead do not come <u>out</u> of the grave at the same time. The righteous come out of their graves at the **first resurrection.** The unrighteous must wait until the **second resurrection** of **Revelation 20:5.** It is extremely important to understand that there is **no fire** or torture in the **grave** - in **sheol** - in **hades.**

The **"burning hell"** we hear so much about is the **"GEHENNA HELL."** However, **<u>no</u> one,** good <u>or</u> bad, is burning in **any** type of "hell" at the present time! **After** the "one thousand years" ["Millennium"] of Revelation 20, the "wicked" and the "unrighteous" will be **destroyed** in the **"gehenna hell."** This "burning" will be studied in detail in our study, **"The <u>End</u> <u>of</u> <u>Sin</u> <u>and</u> <u>Sinners</u>."**

<u>FACT</u>: The Bible "hell" is a place where <u>both</u> body <u>and</u> "soul" are destroyed.

It is **tradition** and **<u>only</u> tradition** that has taught us about an **"immortal soul."** Those who have studied the Bible for themselves know that the Bible does **not teach that anyone continues to live in <u>any</u>** form after he or she dies. **<u>Tradition</u>** teaches it. Non-Christian religions teach it. But the **Bible** does **<u>not</u>** teach that man lives on in another conscious form after death.

<u>Matthew 10:28 – Jesus speaking</u>

And do not fear those who kill the body but cannot kill the soul; rather fear him who can destroy **<u>both</u>** body **<u>and</u>** soul in hell.

<u>Ezekiel 18:4</u>

Behold, all souls are mine; the soul of the father as well as the soul of the son is mine: **the soul that sins shall die.**

<u>Psalm 33:19</u>

...deliver their soul from death...

<u>James 5:20</u>

...save his soul from death...

Jesus and **Bible writers** taught that the **"soul" <u>can</u>** die, and that it **<u>will</u>** die! Therefore, the human **"soul"** cannot be immortal. The apostle **Paul** said that **<u>only</u> God** is **immortal**:

<u>1 Timothy 6:15,16</u>

...the King of kings and Lord of lords, who **<u>alone</u>** has **immortality.**

<u>REVIEW</u>

[1] - The one Hebrew word for **"hell"** ["sheol"] means "grave" in every case. **Sheep and people go to the same place at death.**

[2] - There are three different Greek words used in the New Testament which have been translated as "hell." They are "Hades," "Gehenna," and "Tartarus."

[3] – The New Testament equivalent of the Old Testament "hell" **["sheol"]** is **"hades."** It means **"grave."**

[4] – **Everyone who dies, both good <u>or</u> bad, goes to "hell"** – the **"hades hell"** = the grave.

[5] – **Jesus went to "hell"** – to the **"hades hell"** – the grave.

[6] – There is **no fire in "hades."**

[7] – **"Gehenna" is the "burning hell"** of the New Testament which takes place in the **future**. No <u>one</u> is burning in "hell" <u>now</u>.

[8] – **Both the body and "soul" <u>can</u> and <u>will</u> be destroyed** of those who do not qualify for eternal life.

PREVIEW

It will take quite a bit of study before you complete your search of what happens to all people when they die. Tradition has created terrible fear in the minds of <u>billions</u> of people who have been deceived by the lies of Satan and his human followers.

Rather than just **tradition,** you will be studying what **Jesus** and the **Bible** writers said about death. It is only by comparing Scripture that anyone can come to intelligent conclusions.

The most important reason for our study is to learn and accept the fact that **"God is love,"** as the apostle John wrote, and that He always **<u>acts</u>** that way. **Always!**

Be assured that when you complete your Bible study of the **soul, spirit, the occult, the end of sin and sinners,** and the parable of **the Rich Man and Lazarus,** you will have a deep and genuine desire to know and meet your **Creator** and **Friend.**

Be patient! Consider one topic at a time, and **do not jump to any conclusions one way or the other,** until you have read **<u>everything</u>** your Bible says about death and the hereafter.

Is God Really Like That? Outline No. 14

Soul and Spirit

Back in the days of the **Egyptians** and the **Babylonians** many were taught that man was divided into two distinct and separate parts: the **"body"** and the **"soul."** They were taught that the **"soul"** portion of man could never cease to exist; that at death it left the body to become part of another form of life. Because it was not until the past few hundred years that the average person could study God's theology for himself, the heathen ideas filtered down into the Christian Church.

This is why most Christians today have been taught, from childhood, by parents, priests, and/or preachers that the "soul" separates itself from the physical body at death and travels to either heaven or hell. But as we study the Bible for ourselves, we discover that **it is not the "soul" which "returns to God," but the spirit:**

Ecclesiastes 12:7
And the dust returns to the earth as it was, and the **spirit returns to God** who gave it.

When the Bible speaks of the **"soul"** it refers to the **whole person** as a complete unit – in the same way someone today might refer to his **"50 head of cattle." For example:**

Acts 2:41
So those who had received his word were baptized, and there were added that day about **three thousand souls.**

Proverbs 25:25
Like cold water to a **thirsty soul,** so is good news from a far country.

We know for sure that the **"3,000 souls"** that were baptized and added to the Christian Church that day **had bodies!** Yet they are referred to as **"souls."** And how could a **"soul"** need or drink **water** if it had no body?!

In many verses where the King James Version uses the word **"soul,"** the NKJV and the RSV used the word **"person." For example:**

Ezekiel 13:19
KJV: to slay the **souls**
RSV: putting to death **persons**
NKJV: killing **people**

Genesis 2:7
KJV: man became a living **soul**
RSV: man became a living **being**
NKJV: man became a living **being**

Leviticus 5:2

KJV: if **a soul** touch
RSV: if **any one** touch
NKJV: if **a person** touches

Leviticus 17:12

KJV: No **soul**… shall eat blood
RSV: No **person**… shall eat blood
NKJV: No **one**… shall eat blood

Leviticus 18:27

KJV: he shall save his **soul**
RSV: he shall save his **life**
NKJV: he preserves **himself**

Matthew 16:26

KJV: lose his own **soul**
RSV: forfeits his **life**

Psalm 116:4

KJV: O Lord… deliver my **soul**
RSV: O Lord… save my **life**

Nowhere in the Bible does it say that the **"soul"** goes anywhere! The first time **"soul"** is mentioned in the Bible shows that man does not **have** a soul; he **is** a soul:

Genesis 2:7

Then the Lord God formed man of **dust** from the ground, and breathed into his nostrils the **breath of life;** and man became a
KJV: living **soul.**
RSV: living **being.**

1 Corinthians 15:45

Thus it is written [Genesis 2:7], "The first Adam was made a
KJV: living **soul."**
RSV: living **being."**

The **solution** to the question of a **"living soul"** boils down to simple arithmetic:

$$\begin{array}{l} \textbf{Dust} \\ \textbf{+ \underline{Breath of life}} \\ \textbf{= A living soul [or "being."]} \end{array}$$

When the **"breath of life"** leaves the body at death there ceases to <u>be</u> a **"living soul"** [or **"being"**] because a **"living soul"** is a **combination** of the **"dust"** and the **"breath of life."**

We put **electricity** into a **light bulb** to create **light.** When we separate the electricity from the light bulb where did the light go? It goes to the same place the **"soul"** goes when it is separated from the **"dust." There is no light; there is no "living soul."**

When we take the **nails** out of a **box** and lay the pieces of wood in a pile, **where did the box go?** There is no more box! <u>Before</u> someone put the nails and boards together in the first place, there was no box.

When God separated the body of **Adam** from the "breath of life [at Adam's death] there was no more Adam – he returned to "dust." **God had the knowledge to create man in the beginning, and He will use the same knowledge to re-create man at the great resurrection.**

FACT: Man does not
<u>have</u> a soul;
he <u>is</u> a soul.

God did not **give** man an immortal soul. He **made** him a **living** soul. According to your Bible, **only** God has immortality:

1 Timothy 6:15,16

…the King of kings and Lord of lords, who **alone** has immortality.

When will those who qualify for eternal life become immortal? According to the apostle **Paul,** immortality will be given at the resurrection at the second coming of Jesus:

1 Corinthians 15:51-53

Lo! I tell you a mystery. We shall not all **sleep,** but we shall **all be changed, in a moment,** in the twinkling of an eye, **at the last trumpet.** For the trumpet will sound, and the **dead** will be **raised imperishable,** and we shall be **changed.** For this perishable nature must put on the imperishable, and this **mortal** nature must put on **immortality.**

The word "soul" in the Old Testament has been translated from **one** Hebrew word **["nephesh"] 471 times** [in every case but two = Job 30:15; Isaiah 57:16]; however, this same Hebrew word ["nephesh"] has **also** been translated [in the King James Version] as:

"dead" 5 times [!]
"dead body" 7 times
"life" "lives" 118 times
"person" 29 times
"mind" 15 times
"heart" 15 times
"creature" 9 times
"man" 4 times
"beast" 3 times

Important facts about this Hebrew word for **SOUL** ["nephesh"]:

[1]

It can stand for many English words:
soul – life – person – beast
dead – dead body – creature – mind

[2]

It is used to describe something which can be killed, or to designate even a dead person.

[3]

It is used with the adjective "living":

Revelation 16:3

"every **living** soul died"

Genesis 2:7

"man became a **living** soul"

It would have been unnecessary to use **"living"** with **"soul"** if the Hebrew word itself meant an immortal, never-dying entity or being.

Following are **EXAMPLES** of how this Hebrew word for **soul** ["nephesh"] is used in the Old Testament. Keep in mind that the translators had to decide <u>which</u> word fit <u>best</u>. **Each** of the English words in **bold type** in the following eight Bible texts have been translated from this one Hebrew word:

Ezekiel 18:4

...the **soul** [nephesh] that sins shall die.

Leviticus 21:11

He shall not go in to any **dead body** [nephesh]...

Numbers 31:19

...whoever of you has killed any **person** [nephesh] ...

Leviticus 19:28

You shall not make any cuttings in your flesh on account of the **dead** [nephesh]...

Leviticus 24:18

He who kills a **beast** [nephesh] shall make it good, **life** [nephesh] for **life** [nephesh].

Genesis 1:20

Let the waters bring forth swarms of living **creatures** [nephesh]...

Genesis 1:30

And to every beast... bird... anything that has the **breath of life** [nephesh], I have given every green plant for food.

Does not the Bible tell us that <u>some</u> part of us goes back to God at death?

Ecclesiastes 12:7

Then shall the **dust** return to the earth as it was: and the **SPIRIT** returns to God who gave it."

As we continue this study of the **Soul and Spirit,** we will understand that this **"spirit"** is the same **"breath of life"** that God gave to man at creation. Your Bible does <u>not</u> teach that a conscious **"spirit"** capable of thinking, makes its way toward the starry heavens at death.

Remember that **God was here on earth when He created man in the first place, that God is omnipresent** [everywhere at once], and that, in one sense, is here on earth now.

There is **no scriptural proof** that the **"breath of life"** or the **"spirit"** which goes back to God is a <u>conscious</u> element. The thinking part of man [the mind] is dependent upon the body for life. **Man is a whole unit** of which one portion cannot **consciously** exist of itself.

The word **"SPIRIT"** in the Old Testament is translated from <u>one</u> **Hebrew word ["ruach"] 232 times** in every Bible text except two [Job 26:4; Prov 20:27]. This Hebrew word is not only translated [in the King James Version] 232 times as **"spirit,"** but **also** as:

"wind" 117 times
"breath" 33 times
"blast" 4 times

As we look at some **EXAMPLES** of how the Hebrew word **"SPIRIT"** **["ruach"]** is used in the Old Testament, remember that the translators had to decide which meaning best fit in each Bible verse. **"SPIRIT," "WIND,"** and **"BREATH" all come from one Hebrew word** ["ruach"]. This helps us to understand that the **"spirit"** that returns to God at death is none other than the **"breath of life"** that caused **Adam** to become a **"living soul."**

Psalm 146:4

When his **breath** [ruach] departs he returns to his earth; on that very day his
KJV: thoughts perish.
RSV: plans perish.

Ecclesiastes 12:7

And the dust returns to the earth as it was, and the **spirit** [ruach] returns to God who gave it.

Genesis 8:1

God made a **wind** [ruach] blow over the earth, and the waters subsided...

In the preceding three Bible texts, **SPIRIT, BREATH, and WIND** all were translated from one Hebrew word **["ruach"]. "Spirit"** and the **"breath of life"** are one and the same. **The "spirit" does not have the ability to think apart from the body any more than wind or breath!**

> ### FACT: The "spirit" and the "breath of life" are the same.

In the New Testament **several words** refer to man:

"Body" 145 times from "sarx"
"Flesh" 147 times from "sarx"
"Soul" 58 times from "psuche"
"Life" 40 times from "psuche"
"Spirit" 151 times from "pnuema"

There is nothing in the meanings of the preceding Greek words that could indicate some consciousness existing independently from the body. **In Hebrew tradition man is regarded as a unity.** As a farmer might say he has **90 head of cattle,** so the Hebrews could refer to man as either **flesh, body, soul,** or **spirit,** depending upon the point of view from which the person was to be considered.

The apostle **Paul's "works of the flesh"** refer to man as a whole:

Galatians 5:19-21

Now the **works of the flesh** are plain: immorality, licentiousness, **idolatry, sorcery,** enmity, strife, **jealousy, anger, selfishness...**

Several of the preceding **"works of the flesh"** have nothing to do with the **"flesh"** as we think of flesh. Paul was using the word **"flesh"** ["sarx"] to represent the whole person.

"FLESH" ["sarx"] in the following two Bible texts refer to the whole person:

Matthew 19:4,5

"Have you not read... a man shall leave his father and mother and be joined to his wife, and the two shall become
KJV: one **flesh?"**
RSV: **one?"**

Romans 3:20

KJV: No **flesh**
RSV: No **human being**
will be justified in his sight by the works of the law...

Acts 27:37

In the ship were
KJV: 276 **souls.**
RSV: 276 **persons.**

The **Greek** word for **"SPIRIT"** ["pneuma"] is not only translated as **"LIFE"** but also as **"WIND."**

Likewise, the **Hebrew** word for **"SPIRIT"** ["ruach"] has been translated [in the KJV]

33 times as **"BREATH"** and
117 times as **"WIND."**

In **John 3:8** [following] the word **"WIND"** and the word **"SPIRIT"** were translated from **one** Greek word ["pneuma"]. **The same Greek word means both "wind" and "spirit."** This verse and **Revelation 13:15** demonstrate that the **"spirit"** which

goes back to God at death is the same **"breath of life"** that God breathed into Adam's nostrils.

John 3:8

The **WIND** [pneuma] blows where it wills, and you hear the sound of it, but you do not know whence it comes or wither it goes; so it is with every one who is born of the **SPIRIT** [pneuma].

Revelation 13:15

...it was allowed to give
KJV: **life** [pneuma]
RSV: **breath** [pneuma]
to the image of the beast.

For the **"spirit"** to **"return to God,"** is **not wind or breath** making its way through the starry heavens to Paradise. The **spirit, breath** or **wind** returns the same way as does the **dust.**

> **FACT:** **Man is a whole unit of which one part cannot exist by itself in a conscious state.**

PREVIEW

In our next outline we will consider the so-called "scientific proof" that spirits of the dead return to speak with people living on this earth.

Is God Really Like That? Outline No. 15

The Occult and Satanism

By studying Outlines 9, 10, and 11, we learned that **the dead are really dead** – that no dead person continues to live on in a <u>conscious</u> state in either heaven or "hell."

Why then do we hear so much about **people who claim they have communicated with the spirit of some deceased friend or relative?**

Any preacher, man, woman, or child who claims to have talked with the "spirits of the dead" has been **deceived by one of the <u>devil's</u> angels!** Your Bible makes it plain that the **"spirits of devils"** [evil angels] are doing their best to deceive you:

Ephesians 2:2
...the prince of the power of the air, **the spirit** that is now at work in the sons of disobedience.

Revelation 12:7-9
Now **war** arose **in heaven, Michael and his angels** fighting against the **dragon;** and the dragon and his angels fought, but they were **defeated** and there was no longer any place for them in heaven. And the great dragon was thrown down, that ancient **serpent,** who is called the **Devil** and **Satan,** the <u>deceiver</u> <u>of</u> <u>the</u> <u>whole</u> <u>world</u> – he was **thrown down to the earth,** and his angels were thrown down with him.

1 Timothy 4:1
Now the Spirit expressly says that in later times some will depart from the faith by giving heed to **deceitful spirits** and **doctrines of demons...**

2 Corinthians 4:3,4
And even if our gospel is veiled, it is veiled only to those who are perishing. In their case **the god of this world** has **blinded the minds** of the unbelievers, to keep them from seeing the light of the gospel...

John 12:31
...now shall **the ruler** [KJV = "prince"] **of this world** be cast out.

———————————————

When people talk about their communication with the "spirit" of their dead relative or friend, we often hear, **"It sounded exactly like him. I'd know his voice anywhere! And he told me things that only the two of us could possibly know!"**

Comedians do an excellent job imitating many different voices. **Why should we be surprised** at the ability of evil angels to do the same thing? And **who would be naïve enough to think we could keep secrets from angels?!**

Satan operates the largest **detective agency** in the world. He has all sorts of records available – on those living and on those who have died. He not only knows the facts, but he has millions of **audio-video cassettes** to use on the friends and relatives of the dead!

The Hebrews, during Old Testament times, were just as curious about the future as most of us are today. The problem for them was the temptation to consult a fortune teller! **We, today, have the same temptation!** Everyone wants to know the future. **But to attempt to find out about the future from fortune tellers was, and still is, forbidden:**

Isaiah 8:19

And when they say to you, "Consult the **mediums** and the wizards who chirp and mutter," should not a people consult their God?

Leviticus 19:31

"Do not turn to **mediums** or wizards; do not seek them out, to be defiled by them: I am the Lord your God...

Deuteronomy 18:9-12

There shall not be found among you any one who... practices divination, a soothsayer... or a sorcerer... or a **medium**... or a necromancer. For whoever does these things is an **abomination to the Lord.**

Galatians 5:19-21

Now the works of the flesh are plain... idolatry, **sorcery**... I warn you, as I warned you before, that those who do such things shall **not inherit the kingdom of God.**

Revelation 18:23

...**all** the **nations** were **deceived by thy sorcery.**

When we **knowingly** seek information from the devil, we lose the protection of holy angels. If one seeks the devil [fortune tellers] for information, **much of what the evil angels tell you will be the truth!** In this way the devil can lure you into thinking that he is **always** right!

One can read the predictions of psychics in tabloids, such as the National Enquirer, to see what the "experts" say will take place in the future; however, only a small percentage of their predictions come true! Also, can you imagine God informing His true prophets about the future lives of movie stars?!

Yes, Satan and his angels can make fairly accurate predictions, at times, because of the knowledge he has at his command. For example, Satan can have one of his secretaries figure up on the computer an airplane's flight time, weather conditions, and engine wear to come up with a fairly accurate date for it to crash. When he comes close, as he does many times, it is **not** a sign that his prophet is a true prophet. **The devil will only tell the truth when it is to his advantage to do so.**

Counterfeit prophets, in order to be believed – in order to create a following – must predict some things that are true. Present day psychics have predicted various catastrophes that will take place in **nature.** And if they predict 3 or 4 major events that really do take place, then one would naturally assume that their next prediction will also take place. Here is where great deceptions occur! **One of their false predictions deals with what will happen at the beginning of the millennium.** This will be studied in detail in a later outline.

According to **Jesus** and Bible writers, false Christs and false prophets will be a **major problem** in the days just before Jesus returns:

Matthew 24:24

For **false Christs** and **false prophets** will arise and show **great signs and wonders,** so as to **lead many astray;** if possible, even the very elect.

1 Timothy 4:1

Now the Spirit expressly says that in later times some will depart from the faith by giving heed to **deceitful spirits** and **doctrines of demons...**

Revelation 16:13,14

And I saw, issuing from the mouth of the dragon... **demonic spirits,** performing **signs,** who go abroad to the **kings of the whole world,** to assemble them for battle on the great day of God the Almighty.

Revelation 12:12

But woe to you, O earth and sea, for the **devil** has come down to you in great wrath, because he **knows that his time is short!**

Ephesians 6:12

For we are **not contending against flesh and blood,** but against the principalities, against the powers, **against the world rulers of this present darkness,** against the **spiritual hosts of wickedness** in the heavenly places.

1 John 4:1

Beloved, **do not believe every spirit,** but **test the spirits** to see whether they are of God; for many false prophets have gone out into the world.

Why is it that people are so gullible when **false prophets** come along? Could the reason be that the main line churches are not providing a satisfying brand of Christianity? **Could it be that God has not been presented as a "God of love," but rather a two-faced God who threatens you with eternal torture if you do not perfectly follow all of His laws?**

Both holy angels and evil angels have and can come in the form of men. **How can one tell the difference?**

Five tests people can and should make regarding professed prophets:

[1] – Are their **prophecies accurate?** Do most of their prophecies come true?

[2] – Do any of their teachings **contradict Holy Scripture?**

[3] – Do they **exalt Jesus?** If a prophet claims that Jesus was just a good man rather than God and Creator, then you can know for sure that prophet is a counterfeit.

[4] – Do they teach and keep <u>all</u> of the commandments of God?

[5] – **"By their fruits you shall know them."** Do they try to get their way by **force,** or do they follow the example of **Jesus** by promoting **love, peace,** and the **freedom of choice?**

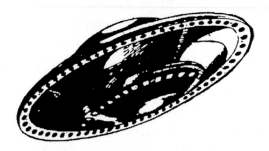

Neil Armstrong, when he was on his moon mission, sent messages back telling of two **UFO's** that followed them to the moon and landed with them. Of course these messages were censored so that the public did not hear them. The U.S. government is not going to admit that they are defenseless against "beings from outer space." **Buzz Aldrin** even **took color moving pictures** of them.

After studying the Bible for many years **I am absolutely convinced, without a shadow of a doubt, that the controversy between good and evil [between Jesus and Satan] is confined to this world** – that is, no other intelligent beings are directly involved. **There is no way that intelligent beings from other inhabited planets could be allowed to visit the battle ground of the most important controversy in the history of the universe!** Also, I believe that Satan and his angels were confined to this world after Jesus died and rose from the grave. At that time Satan was conquered – and the rest of the universe then realized that Jesus had "bought us back."

Anyone who has studied the reports of **UFO** sightings understands that they can materialize, and then become completely invisible instantaneously. **Radar picks them up** – then they disappear.

We can know for sure that all UFO occupants are from angels disguised in several different shapes, sizes, colors, and personalities. They sometimes **heal** and sometimes **kill.** Sometimes they give spiritual messages during which they quote the Bible. Sometimes they seduce sexually. **When UFO occupants appear openly, as they are beginning to do now, they will convince people who have not studied the Bible for themselves, that God's laws have been changed.**

The more we study the more we realize how many **millions [if not billions] will be deceived** by Satan, and all because they did not study Holy Scripture for themselves – or were not willing to change their thinking because of their traditions.

Satan is delighted when people think of him as a reddish imp with horns and a forked tail, carrying a pitch fork. Actually, he can come in the form of a handsome man of great intelligence with superhuman power. Satan and his angels can either change themselves into human forms, or they can accomplish their aims by working through people. **Their most effective methods are not by demon possession,** but through angelic voices, beautiful hair, handsome men, a delicate touch, hypnotic fragrances, and sensuous forms.

Many times **Satan** uses Christian principles to further his own cause. At times **he works the same types of miracles as holy angels work, in order to deceive** – mostly to deceive people into believing that people do not die at death, but keep on living in a different spiritual state.

Once in a while we still find someone who believes that seeing UFOs is nothing more than someone's imagination gone wild! Some still believe the government's lies about UFOs being nothing more than weather balloons! If that is the case, then people like President Jimmy Carter, Prince Charles, J.Edgar Hoover, and General Douglas MacArthur, who all claim they saw UFOs, were not the great men we thought they were! Also, hundreds of Air Force and civilian pilots should have their licenses revoked! And those who still believe our government when it claims that there was never a UFO crash near Roswell, New Mexico [in spite of all the eye witness accounts] are rather naïve. The wreckage was found by William Brazel and his children July 2, 1947. A local radio station in Albuquerque was warned not to continue the broadcasting of the eye witness accounts because of **"national security."** Now, tell me, what do "weather balloons" have to do with national security?!

Where is it that evil angels manufacture their UFOs?

Our own government does not have aircraft that can fly nearly as fast, nor maneuver nearly as well, as what has been seen by thousands. Most have heard reports of UFOs flying in and out of the water near the Bermuda Triangle. Is it possible that our earth has hollow sections in which individuals can reside?

Admiral Richard Byrd spoke of his experiences in and around the North and South Poles between 1947 and 1956. Our government stopped his radio accounts, and forbade him from even talking about his experiences. Admiral Byrd claimed to have seen iceless regions of green vegetation and animal life, from which fresh water flows, at the North Pole. He spoke of an opening inside the earth at the North Pole. Various explorers have discovered that the air warms as they get near both the North and South Poles. **As the winter weather gets colder, animals migrate north instead of south!** Dr. Raymond Bernard, in his book, The Hollow Earth, wrote that authors William Reed, Marshall Gardner, and Amadeo Giannini – as well as Admiral Byrd – came to the conclusion that the center of our earth has plenty of space between the North and South Poles in which thousands of highly intelligent beings dwell!

Does the Bible indicate that evil angels might dwell within our earth?

There are various Bible texts which **could** indicate such. As with many Bible texts, the wording could be taken in more than one way. **For example**, 200 years before Columbus, Giordano Bruno was burned at the stake for saying that our earth revolves around the sun! **After all, the church at that time had the Bible to back up their decision:** "Four angels standing at the four corners of the earth." "Deceive the nations which are in the four corners of the earth" [Rev 7:1; 20:8; Eze 7:2; Isa 11:12]. Did not Joshua command the sun to stand still? "Sun, stand thou still… the sun stood still" [Joshua 10:12,13; **review Outline No. 9-7**].

Therefore, the following Bible texts, even though they do not prove much, are worthy of our consideration:

Revelation 12:9

The great dragon was cast out, that old serpent called the devil, and Satan, which **deceiveth the whole world;** he was cast out **into the earth,** and his angels were cast out with him.

Revelation 5:2,3

"Who is worthy to open the scroll and break its seals?" And no one in heaven or **on** earth or **under the earth** was able to open the scroll or to look into it.

Job 1:7

The Lord said unto Satan, "Whence cometh thou?" Then Satan answered the Lord and said, from going to and fro **in the earth,** and from walking up and down **in it.**"

Revelation 5:13

Every creature which is in heaven, and on the earth, and **under the earth…** I heard saying, "Blessing and honor and glory and power be unto Him that sits upon the throne, and under the Lamb…

1 Samuel 28:7-13

The **witch [medium] of Endor** said to King Saul after he had sought out the advice of a medium, **"I see a god coming up out of the earth."**

Revelation 9:1,2

I saw a star fallen from heaven to earth, and he was given the key of the shaft of the **bottomless pit;** he opened the shaft of the bottomless pit, and from the shaft rose smoke like the smoke of a great furnace, and the sun and the air were darkened with the smoke from the shaft.

Genesis 1:2

The earth was without form, and **void...** The dictionary says "void" = "an empty space."

Are there Bible texts which indicate that Satan and his angels [demons] have anything to do with UFOs?

Revelation 16:13,14

And I saw, issuing from the mouth of the dragon... **demonic spirits,** performing **signs,** who go abroad to the **kings of the whole world,** to assemble them for battle on the great day of God the Almighty.

Ephesians 6:12

For we are not contending against flesh and blood, but against the principalities, against the powers, against the world rulers of this present darkness, against the **spiritual hosts of wickedness in the heavenly places.**

Ephesians 2:2

...the **prince of the power of the air,** the **spirit** that is **now at work** in the sons of disobedience.

Revelation 9:11

They have as king over them the **angel of the bottomless pit;** his name in Hebrew is Abaddon [destroyer], and in Greek he is called Apollyon [destroyer].

2 Thessalonians 2:9,10

The coming of the lawless one by the **activity of Satan** will be with all **power** and **pretended signs and wonders,** and with all **wicked deception** for those who are to perish, because they refused to love the truth and so be saved.

Ezekiel 10:9-13

And I looked, and behold, there were four wheels beside the cherubim, one beside each cherub; and the appearance of the wheels was like sparkling chrysolite. And as for their appearance, the four had the same likeness, as if **a wheel were within a wheel.** When they went, they **went in any of their four directions without turning as they went...** they were called in my hearing the **whirling wheels.**

[Perhaps UFOs are an imitation of what Ezekiel saw. Regardless, Ezekiel's vision was symbolic.]

Clairvoyant Lorraine Warren, who had a good reputation for getting good results when attempting to contact "spirits of the dead," said, after investigating a "haunted house," "Whatever is here is, in my estimation, most definitely of a negative nature. It has nothing to do with anyone who had once walked the earth in human form. It is right **from the bowels of the earth!"** [*The Amityville Horror* by Jay Anson]

There have been hundreds, if not thousands, of people who have been abducted and hypnotized by various types of UFO occupants; some described as "little green or gray men," 3 ½ feet tall, with oversized heads with no hair or ears, slits for eyes, that communicate via mental telepathy.

And there have been more than 20 of these UFO occupants that have been recovered – regardless of the lies that our government heads tell us.

Many times people are driving along a road – usually at night – when, after viewing a bright object in the sky, their car motors stop. Some are returned to their cars after two or three hours; however, they are not aware that two or three hours have elapsed. These abducted individuals experience various phy-sical and psychological problems, including the inability to sleep soundly without nightmares. What they experienced when being examined on the UFOs is not remembered except when they have someone hypnotize them!

For an example of the above experiences, I watched on A&E's TV *Unsolved Mysteries* about four men who went camping in northern Maine one evening. What bothered them at the time was a camp fire they had built which they figured would last two or three hours, was almost burned out after what seemed

to them about 20 minutes. All they remembered was seeing a UFO come close to them while they stood near the shore. The four men, who moved to different parts of the country [Jack & Jim Weiner, Chrlie Foltz, and Chuck Rak], remembered nothing about when they were inside the UFO until several years later when they all agreed to be hypnotized. **Each of the four men, several years later, under hypnosis, gave the very same detailed account of what they had unknowingly experienced!**

[An excellent 123 page book that gives a detailed account, including proof, concerning the UFO occupants and how they relate to world leaders, may be purchased for $8. including postage: *UFO's: Aliens or Demons?* by D.M. Pottenger, CHJ Pub, 1103 W, Main, Middleton, Idaho, **83644**.]

Why are UFO occupants allowed to abduct individuals – sometimes even killing them?

I do not know <u>all</u> the answers. Some, of course, are guilty of **knowingly rejecting Truth** when they read it in their own Bibles. Their deception is prophesied in:

2 Thessalonians 2:9,10

The coming of the lawless one by

the **activity of Satan** will be with all **power** and **pretended signs and wonders,** and with all **wicked deception** for those who are to perish, **because they refused to love the truth** and so be saved.

What I <u>do</u> know is how any genuine Christian can keep from being abducted!

<u>No. 1</u> Stay away from them. Do not seek them out – even if you are curious.

<u>No. 2</u> Whenever you see or hear a UFO, command, in the name of Jesus, for them to leave: **"<u>In the name of Jesus, I command you demons to get away from us and stay away</u>."** You should never play around with UFOs any more than you should play with a **Ouija Board.**

<u>No. 3</u> Avoid those who deal with spiritualism, mediums, fortune tellers, channeling, and those who teach reincarnation and other doctrines which contradict the Bible.

Unless one knows what Holy Scripture teaches, he or she is a good candidate for Satan's deceptions. When Satan openly impersonates Jesus just before the beginning of the millennium, he will quote many Bible texts, miraculously heal the sick, and even appear to raise people from the dead.

2 Corinthians 11:13,14

For such men are false apostles, deceitful workmen, disguising themselves as apostles of Christ. And no wonder, for even Satan disguises himself as an angel of light.

Yes, Satan will deceive <u>most</u> people when he impersonates Jesus. Because they have refused to learn the facts about Satan, and because they have rejected Truth when it was presented to them [2 Thess 2:9,10 Column a], they will actually <u>believe</u> they are ready for Jesus to return when they are not:

Matthew 7:21-23

"Not every one who says to me, Lord, Lord, shall enter the kingdom of heaven, but he who does the will of my Father who is in heaven. On that day many will say to me, 'Lord, Lord, did we not **prophesy** in your name, and **cast out demons** in your name, and do **many mighty works** in your name?' And then will I declare to them, 'I never knew you; depart from me, you evildoers.'

Daniel 12:1,2

At that time shall arrive Michael, the great prince who has charge of your people. And there shall be a time of trouble, such as never has been since there was a nation till that time; but at that time your people shall be delivered, every one whose name shall be found written in the book. And many of those who **sleep** in the dust of the earth shall awake, some to everlasting life, and some to shame and everlasting contempt.

Satan deceives in various ways:

[1] – For those who have no real purpose in life Satan has a **superb amusement program.** Many people would be bored to death if their radios, televisions, movie theaters, baseball, football, hockey, bowling, card games, and cocktail parties were **all** taken away! Yes, people <u>can</u> benefit from amusement. But when amusements comprise **most** of their **free time** they no longer have time for the most serious aspects of life – nor time to establish a continuous personal relationship with Jesus.

[2] – Heaven is full of **music.** From such a rich musical background Satan has learned to use music to his own advantage. <u>Some</u> of his music has a hypnotic effect upon the subconscious. **This greatly aids his youth movement.**

[3] – Modern psychologists know that a person's character and disposition are usually formed during the first six or seven years of his life. Satan knows that it is to his advantage if **little children** get **<u>most</u>** of their **education** in front of a **television** set, in **crowded**

nurseries, and/or in **fatherless homes.** He has succeeded in influencing political leaders to structure the economy so that **mothers must help fathers pay the rent,** taking them out of the home. **Satan and his army work exceedingly long and hard in trying to break up homes.**

[4] – **Physical health** has a positive or negative effect upon mental, emotional, and spiritual health. Many self-centered businessmen advertise products that they **<u>know</u>** are detrimental to health. **The average American diet is atrocious!** It is slowly but surely weakening America.

[5] – **Alcohol, tobacco, hard drugs, and over-the-counter drugs** easily trap our children and youth – as well as adults. **Emotional instability** causes people to try to escape. **Suicides are on the increase,** not only because of the **"rat race"** but because of the breakup of the home, unfaithfulness, lack of love and commitment, and **lack of an understanding of how God really thinks.**

[6] – Satan tries <u>not</u> to make life too complicated as long as we neglect prayer, Bible study, and meditation. Otherwise, more people would **"wake up"** and turn to heaven for help.

[7] – Satan has a **great recruiting plan. He accepts everyone regardless of background.** He does not care how long you have been a Christian, just as long as he gets you in the end.

[8] – Satan has been quite successful in substituting the theory of **evolution** in place of the Bible creation account [in public schools]. To the average public school student, it is **"common knowledge"** that it took **millions of years** to evolve upward from a mud hole, through the monkey stage, to our present stage. This, of course, **discredits our Creator.** I still marvel at how many Christians refuse to believe that God created us in six days as recorded in the book of Genesis – and still believe that God will raise us up from the dead and give us new bodies "in the twinkling of an eye" when Jesus returns! **How people can believe one and not the other is a big mystery!**

[9] – Satan has gotten the religious leaders of many denominations to adopt a **counterfeit law,** eliminating one, two, or three of the original ten.

[10] – **Religious persecution.** Satan's method is **force.** Jesus' method is **freedom of choice.**

[11] – Causing people to **fear** is one of Satan's most successful ideas. Satan's environment helps to create many real and imaginary **fears:**

> Fear of loss of love
> Fear of financial loss
> Fear of unemployment
> Fear of sickness
> Fear of accidents
> Fear of bodily harm
> Fear of harm to family
> Fear of death
> Fear of a burning hell
> Fear of God

<u>You</u> do <u>not</u> have to fear the devil!

Jesus gave the apostles and all Christians authority over the devil:

<u>Mark 6:7-13</u>

And he [Jesus] called to him the twelve... and gave them **authority over the unclean spirits...** And they cast out many demons...

<u>Luke 9:1</u>

And he called the twelve together and gave them power and **authority over all demons..**

<u>Luke 10:1,17</u>

After this the Lord appointed seventy others, and sent them on ahead of him, two by two, into every town and place where he himself was about to come. The seventy returned with joy, saying, "Lord, even the <u>demons</u> are subject to us <u>in</u> your <u>name.</u>

Beware of being fooled by **Casper the friendly ghost.** <u>All</u> ghosts have evil intent. Their goal is to deceive you, one way or another.

The importance of understanding the great deception coming upon this world <u>very</u> <u>shortly</u> cannot be over emphasized.

Satan <u>will</u> appear, and claim to be Jesus Himself. <u>Most</u> inhabitants of this world will be deceived! The Bible text, **"There is a way that <u>seems</u> right to a man, but its end is the way to death."** [Prov 14:12]

It is quite <u>possible</u> that Satan will try to imitate the second coming of Jesus in a three-mile long UFO! Those who have not studied and accepted the Bible will be deceived.

Those who accept the worldly evolution theory rather than the Bible explanation, will actually believe the UFO occupants who say that people were created with the help of more advanced civilizations from other planets in the universe.

Our national leaders are trying to learn <u>how</u> UFOs can travel thousands of miles per hour! They figure that <u>any</u> compromise is worth the ability to conquer and control the world. **The idea of a one world government is from the devil himself.**

Jesus insists upon freedom of choice; however, He will not allow the deception to go on forever. **He can and will veto Satan's plan to take over the world when He decides the time is right.**

One of the things that will stop world domination will be great destruction by **the natural forces of nature. The U.S., as well as the rest of the world, will suffer greatly** – from the east coast to the west coast. This is something that God will <u>allow</u> because of man's rebellion against His ways and against His laws.

The time for UFO occupants to boldly show themselves is very, very soon! Very soon the lies of our national and world leaders will be exposed!

In the fall of 1989, a huge wave of UFO sightings and encounters were reported in the city of Voronezh in the Soviet Union. Many teenagers, as well as forty adults, witnessed things difficult to believe. **Some of the UFO occupants were ten feet tall, having three eyes! They would appear and then quickly disappear.** One teenager disappeared when one of the UFO occupants pointed a tube at her. She reappeared only after the UFO had shot off into the heavens.

On Sept 14th, 1994, 62 school children [ages 6 to 12] saw a UFO land in their school yard during recess in broad daylight, in Ruwa, Zimbabwe. They described these strange beings as being black with long heads, eyes as big as rugby balls, thin arms and legs. **That was some recess!**

On **June 5, 2002,** aliens emerged from a UFO in Antalya, **Turkey,** a seaport on the Mediterranean. It had landed in a **school yard** during the day. The **60 students** described an alien 6 ft. tall, red rays from his eyes, and a very large head. The **Turkish newspapers,** Milliyet and Aksam, wrote about the event in their June 6, 2002, edition.

Is God Really Like That?
Outline No. 16

Lazarus and The Rich Man

Luke 16:19-31

There was a **rich man,** who was clothed in purple and fine linen, and who feasted sumptuously every day. At the gate lay a **poor man** named **Lazarus,** full of sores, who desired to be fed with what fell from the **rich man's table;** moreover, the **dogs** came and licked his sores. The **poor man died** and was **carried by the angels** to **Abraham's bosom.** The **rich man also died** and was **buried;** and in **Hades,** being in torment, he lifted up his **eyes,** and saw **Abraham** far off and **Lazarus in his bosom.** And he [rich man] called out, "Father Abraham, have mercy upon me, and send Lazarus to dip the end of his **finger** in water and cool my **tongue,** for **I am in anguish in this flame."** But Abraham said, **"Son,** remember that you in your lifetime received good things, and Lazarus in like manner evil things; but now **he is comforted** here, and **you are in anguish.** And besides all this, between us and you a **great chasm** [or gulf] has been fixed, in order that those who would pass from here to you may not be able, and none may cross from there to us." And he [the "rich man"] said, "Then I beg you, **father,** to send to my father's house, for I have **five brothers,** so that he may warn them, lest they also come into this place of torment." But Abraham said, "They have Moses and the prophets; let them hear them." And he said, "No, Father Abraham; but **if someone goes to them from the dead,** they will repent." He said to him, "If they do not hear Moses and the prophets, neither will they be convinced if some one should **rise from the dead."**

Judges 9:8-15, in the Old Testament, describes a conversation between an olive tree, cedar tree, fig tree, and grape vine! **Jesus,** also, used **parables** in the New Testament as His method of teaching:

Mark 4:11

And he said to them, "To you has been given the secret of the kingdom of God, but for those outside everything is in **parables."**

Matthew 13:34,35

All this **Jesus** said to the crowds in **parables;** indeed **he said nothing to them without a parable.** This was to fulfil what was spoken by the prophet: "I will open my mouth in **parables,** I will utter what has been hidden since the foundation of the world."

Jesus used the **parable** of the **Rich Man and Lazarus** [Luke 16:19-31] to show the place of the Jewish nation in the history of Christianity. This parable is often misunderstood; yet, with a little study, it **can** be understood.

Some believe this was a familiar parable of the times in which Jesus lived, like "<u>Snow White and the Seven Dwarfs</u>" is today. Daniel Whitby wrote that this parable is found in the <u>Gemara Babylonicum</u>.

This story must be <u>either</u> literal fact, or a parable; **one or the other.** Any attempt to blend the literal and figurative would be totally unacceptable. To take this account literally would result in some rather ridiculous results:

[1] – Those being tormented would be within speaking distance of the saved! Some "heaven" that would be!

[2] – The righteous would sit, watch, and listen to those being tormented.

[3] – In with the heavenly music would be heard the shrieks of the tortured.

[4] – While praising God we would be able to hear the cursing of those in the "fires" of "hell."

[5] – A mother, with all her natural motherly instincts, would be able to hear the cries of her son or daughter from the flames, and see the agonized facial expressions as he or she suffers from the burning heat!

OTHER REASONS WHY THIS IS THOUGHT TO BE A PARABLE:

[A] – It is the **last** of a **long series** of parables. The theme of this parable fits in with the theme of the preceding parables.

[B] – Many religious commentators and scholars consider this to be a parable: John Wesley, Daniel Whit-by, Lightfoot, Bloomfield, Gill, and hundreds of others. **However,** the fact that many scholars agree that this is a parable does not make it so. Other evidence is necessary.

[C] – Those who believe in the "immortality of the soul" believe in a conscious **"soul"** that goes to a place of torment. In <u>this</u> parable parts of the **body** are mentioned: **eyes, Abraham's bosom, finger,** and **tongue.** How can we say that <u>half</u> of the account is <u>actual</u> <u>fact</u> and <u>half</u> is a <u>parable</u>, and then build a doctrine on the whole – especially when the rest of the Bible says otherwise?

[D] – If this account was literal we would have to assume that <u>both</u> the <u>righteous</u> and the <u>unsaved</u> receive their rewards immediately at death. This would be in direct contradiction with what Jesus said and taught.

[E] – It is at the second coming of Jesus that angels gather the saved:

Matthew 24:30,31

...then will appear the sign of the Son of man in heaven, and then all the tribes of the earth will mourn, and they will see the Son of man coming on the clouds of heaven with power and great glory; and he will send out his **angels** with a loud trumpet call, and **they will gather his elect** from the four winds, from one end of heaven to the other.

[F] -- According to the apostle **Paul,** the living and the resurrected **saints** are **"caught up together"** when Jesus returns the second time:

1 Thessalonians 4:15-17

For this we declare to you by the word of the Lord, that we who are alive, who are left until the coming of the Lord, **shall not precede those who have fallen asleep.** For the Lord himself will descend from heaven with a cry of command, with the archangel's call, and with the sound of the trumpet of God. And the dead in Christ will rise first; then we who are alive, who are left, shall be **caught up together with them in the clouds to meet the Lord in the air;** and so we shall always be with the Lord.

[G] – According to the author of the book of Hebrews, **Abraham never went to heaven:**

Hebrews 11:8,13,39,40

By faith **Abraham** obeyed... These all **died** in faith, <u>not</u> having received what was promised... And all these, though well attested by their faith, did not receive what was promised, since God had foreseen something better for us, that apart from us they should not be made perfect.

[H] – The **"hell"** in this parable [Luke 16:23] is the **"hades"** hell. All Bible texts referring to a burning hell use the word **"gehenna." "Hades"** simply means **"grave." There is no fire in "Hades."** [Review Outline No. 13]

As you consider the details of this parable, continually ask yourself this question: "Does this sound like a real life situation that my **God of love** would actually set up?

Luke 16:19

There was a **RICH MAN** who was clothed in purple and fine linen, and who feasted sumptuously every day.

RICH MAN = JEWISH NATION

Why? Why is the **"Rich Man"** symbolic for the **Jewish nation?** The **Jewish nation was rich** inasmuch as they had received directly from God the promises of heaven, the law, the covenants, and the Redeemer Himself!

Romans 3:1,2

Then what advantage has the Jew?... Much in every way. To begin with, the Jews are entrusted with the Oracles of God.

Romans 9:4,5

They are **Israelites,** and to them belong the sonship, the glory, the **covenants,** the giving of the **law,** the worship, and the **promises;** to them belong the **patriarchs.** And of their race, according to the **flesh,** is Christ.

Luke 16:20,21

At the gate lay a **POOR MAN** named **Lazarus,** full of sores, who desired to be fed with what fell from the rich man's table; moreover the **DOGS** came and licked his sores.

POOR MAN = GENTILES

Why? Why is the **"poor man"** **Lazarus** a symbol of the Gentiles [anyone who was not Jewish]? The **Gentiles** were **poor** when it came to the special blessings of heaven. They had **no prophets** of their own, and they were deprived of the blessings of heaven because the Jewish nation refused to share with them as God had instructed.

The Jewish people considered the **Gentiles** to be **"dogs"** [Matthew 15:21-28]. **Lazarus** represents the **Gentiles who accept Jesus as their personal Savior.** All who accept **Jesus** as their personal Savior are said to be **"Abraham's seed"** and **"heirs according to the promise."**

Galatians 3:29

And if you are Christ's, then you are **Abraham's offspring, heirs** according to promise.

The Scribes and Pharisees taught that riches were a sign of God's special blessing. They figured that rich people had a much better chance of getting to heaven than poor people. Even the disciples believed this:

Matthew 19:23-25

And Jesus said to his disciples, "Truly, I say to you, **it will be hard for a rich man to enter the king-dom of heaven.** Again I tell you, it is easier for a camel to go through the eye of a needle than for a rich man to enter the kingdom of heav-en. When the **disciples** heard this they were greatly astonished, say-ing, **"Who then can be saved?"**

Luke 16:22

The **poor man died** and was carried by the **angels** to Abraham's bosom.

It is at the **second coming of Jesus** that the **angels** transport people [Matt 24:30,31 See page 16-2b.5].

According to **Jesus,** neither the saved nor the unsaved receive their rewards immediately at the time of death [See Mathew 25:31-34].

Jesus told us that we would receive our rewards when He returns and raises us from the dead [See Luke 14:14 and Revelation 22:12].

Lazarus was not carried to **heaven,** but to **"Abraham's bosom."** **Abraham never went to heaven** [Heb. 11:8,13,39,40 See **16-3a.G**]. Being in "Abraham's bosom" means being in agreement with Abraham

– being in favor of Abraham. We use the same expression today when we speak of a **"bosom friend"** or **"bosom buddy."**

At feasts in Bible times the guests reclined on couches. The one closest to the honored guest was said to be leaning on his bosom [John 13:23].

Luke 16:22,23

> The **rich man also died** and was **buried**; and in **Hades**, being in torment, he lifted up his **eyes**, and saw Abraham far off and **Lazarus in his bosom.**

HADES = THE GRAVE

In this parable the **rich man** was **"buried."** Where is a person put when he is buried? In the **grave**, of course.

The **"burning hell"** of the Bible = **"gehenna"** [See Outline No. 13]. In the above verse the **rich man went to "Hades" = the grave.** There is no **"fire"** in the grave [**Review Outline No. 13**].

Luke 16:24,25

> And he [the rich man] called out, "Father Abraham, have mercy upon me, and send Lazarus to dip the end of his **finger** in water and cool my **tongue**, for I am in anguish in this flame." But Abraham said, "**Son**, remember that you in your lifetime received good things, and Lazarus in like manner evil things; but **now he is comforted** here, and **you are in anguish.**

Here Abraham called the **"rich man," "Son."** The Jewish nation was the offspring of Abraham. The **"rich man"** – the **Jewish nation** – who was "rich" with the special revelations from heaven, was **"in anguish." The Jewish nation is still in anguish today.** No nation has been persecuted more than the Jewish nation down through the centuries. Today the Jewish nation fears for its very existence.

Ezekiel 23:28,29

> For thus says the Lord God: Behold, I will deliver you into the hands of those whom you hate, into the hands of those from whom you turned in disgust; and they shall deal with you in hatred, and take away all the fruit of your labor…

Lazarus – the Gentiles – are now **"comforted"** in that the truth of the Gospel has now gone to all the world. Now **everyone** has an equal opportunity to know Jesus, **including the Jews.** The Jew, like everyone else, can accept Jesus as his or her personal Savior – which will make them **"spiritual Jews"** in the same way that the converted Gentiles become **"spiritual Jews."**

Luke 16:26

> And besides all this, between us and you a great chasm [or gulf] has been fixed, in order that those who would pass from here to you may not be able, and none may cross from there to us."

Here the **"great chasm"** is too wide to jump over, but **narrow enough to allow a conversation across it!** A **"soul"** or **"ghost"** should, in theory, be able to just float across!!

The Jewish people had separated themselves from the Gentiles. <u>They</u> were the ones who had caused a **"great chasm"** or gulf. Thinking themselves closer to God than the Gentiles, they refused to allow non-Jews to come near.

Today a **"great chasm"** has been created by the **"<u>Gentiles</u>."** The United States is one of the few countries of the world which has not persecuted the Jewish people. Eighteen centuries of tears and prayers at the <u>Wailing Wall</u> have been to no avail.

Luke 16:27,28

And he [the "rich man"] said, "Then I beg you, father, to send him to my father's house, for I have five brothers, so that he may warn them, lest they also come into this place.

The "five brothers" <u>possibly</u> represent the entire world divided up into the five races:

Indian – red
Malayan – brown
Mongolian – yellow
Negro – black
Caucasian – white

Luke 16:29-31

But Abraham said, "They have Moses and the prophets; let them hear them." And he said, "No, Father Abraham; but if some one goes to them from the dead, they will repent." He said to him, "If they do not hear Moses and the prophets, neither will they be convinced if some one should rise from the dead."

The Jewish nation, as a whole, did not believe "Moses and the prophets." In other words they **rejected Jesus** even though His coming as the Messiah was foretold. **No, they** did <u>not</u> believe when Jesus rose from the grave – just like Jesus said they would not!

Most of the Jews did <u>not</u> believe that Jesus was the Messiah. They believed what their religious leaders told them. **God expects all of us <u>not</u> to rely upon the word of <u>our</u> religious leaders** – especially now that we can study the Bible for ourselves.

What the Jews looked for in a Messiah was one who would use **force** to conquer their enemies. The same is true today – most Christians look for God to come and **force** everyone to do things His way. **That will not happen.**

Is God Really Like That?
Outline No. 17

The End of Sin
and Sinners

Are the wages of sin death, or are the wages of sin eternal life in torment?

Romans 6:23

For the wages of sin is **death,** but the **free gift** of God is **eternal life** in Christ Jesus our Lord.

Ephesians 2:8,9

For by **grace** **you have been saved** through faith; and this is not your own doing, it is the **gift** of God – not because of works, lest any man should boast.

Why is it that some Christians want **grace** for themselves, but so-called **justice** for others?! To some Christians, **"justice"** = **eternal life in torment!!**

THINK: Heard over CNN, on June 9, 2003, was the news of a 7 year old boy who weighed only 34 lbs. Because he had disobeyed, his parents locked him in a closet for over a month. He was given no food whatsoever for a whole week! **Would you call that "justice"?**

Could you do that to one of your own children? If your answer is, **"No, of course not,"** then you have

no right to teach your children that God would ever do such a thing! By believing that God would even think of torturing His children throughout eternity because they were **"bad,"** you are saying that **you are more loving than God!!** No human being is more loving or just than God!

To create man without man's consent, and then torture him [either physically or mentally] forever for not following all of His laws, is **not** justice! Any Creator who would even think of doing such a thing could never be a **"God of love."** He could be mistaken for a devil!

It is interesting how people who think logically most of the time, and have the ability to read the Bible for themselves, will fail to think logically when some "well-educated," smooth-talking, good looking preacher tells them the "truth" of what will happen to them if they do not follow all of God's rules. They say, in effect, that **everyone has freedom of choice;** but if you decide not to "choose" His way, then your **"God of love"** will torture you throughout eternity! To teach our children such a "truth" is **child abuse** in the highest sense.

The Jewish leaders taught their followers that the Messiah was coming to destroy their enemies [the Romans]. People today are also wrongly taught that God is coming to torture His enemies with "fire" – forever and ever!

Our Creator has a perfect right to deprive anyone of eternal life who willfully disobeys His commands; **however,** he cannot torture the rebellious and still honestly call Himself a **"God of love,"** as the apostle John wrote in 1 John 4:8,16.

What does your Bible say will be the end of those who rebel?

Psalm 92:7

...the wicked... are doomed to **destruction for ever...**

Psalm 37:20

But the wicked **perish...** like smoke they **vanish** away.

Ezekiel 28:19

...you [Satan] have come to a dreadful end and **shall be no more for ever.**

Revelation 20:7,8,9,14,15

And when the thousand years are ended... fire came down from heaven and **consumed** them...

John 3:16,36

For God so loved the world that he gave his only Son, that whoever believes in him should **not perish** but have eternal life... He who believes in the Son has **eternal life;** he who does not obey the Son shall **not see life.**

Ezekiel 18:4,20

The **soul** that sins shall **die.**

Psalm 104:35

Let sinners be **consumed** from the earth, and let the wicked **be no more!**

Malachi 4:1-3

...all evildoers will be stubble; the day that comes shall burn them up... it will leave them neither root nor branch... And you shall tread down the wicked, for they will be ashes under the soles of your feet...

___

The preceding Bible text [Mal. 4:1-3] indicates that the saved and the unsaved **both end up on earth!** The unsaved will end up as **"ashes."** This puts **"hell"** [hades hell = the grave] right here on earth; not way down in the middle of the earth!

Keep in mind that even the ones who qualify for eternal life do not receive it, according to the apostle **Paul,** until the second coming of Jesus.   [I Cor. 15:51-53 & 14-2a.9]

There are **several types of fire** mentioned in your Bible. **The "fire" that will destroy the unsaved probably will be more than one type;** however, literal fire resulting from an imbalance of nature will be included – literal **fire** just as Noah's flood was caused by literal water - and possibly from the **"shaking"** of the **"powers of heaven"** as foretold by **Jesus** Himself -- **possibly a comet or planet flyby.**

Matthew 24:29-31

"Immediately after the tribulation of those days the **sun** will be darkened, and the **stars** will fall from heaven, and **the powers of the heavens will be shaken;** then will appear the sign of the Son of man in heaven, and then the tribes of the earth mourn, and they will <u>see</u> the Son of man coming on the clouds of heaven with power and great glory; and he will send out his **angels** with a <u>loud</u> trumpet call, and they will gather his elect from... one end of heaven to the other.

A Bible Example of the Final Destruction

2 Peter 2:6

...if by turning the cities of **Sodom** and **Gomorrah** to <u>ashes</u> he condemned them to **extinction** and made them **an example** to those who were to be **ungodly.**

Lamentations 4:6

....the punishment of **Sodom,** which was **overthrown in a <u>moment</u>...**

Luke 17:29,30

But on the day when **Lot** went out of **Sodom, fire** and **brimstone** rained from heaven and **destroyed them all – so it will be** when the Son of man is revealed.

Bible writers understood that the final end of those who do not qualify for eternal life, will be like the end of the Sodomites - as **"in a moment."**

Do you suppose that our **"God of love"** will recreate the unsaved into some type of **fireproof flesh** so that they can be tormented in **fire** without burning up?! At the present time, burning to death is one of the <u>quickest</u> ways to die. **Just one deep breath of the hot fumes** is enough to kill anyone! That is why so many people burn to death as a result of a cigarette catching bed sheets on fire. **If it was <u>not</u> a quick death, people would jump out of bed to get away from the fire!!**

Would God recreate the unsaved so that they could live without oxygen just so they could suffer more? **Do you really think that God would do such a thing to His children** because they disobeyed?

No, God is <u>not</u> <u>really</u> like that! God is love!

People who exercise their right to knowingly and willfully rebel against God, will die. **Everyone dies sooner or later.** God does <u>not</u> have to kill them! **No one can receive eternal life [immortality] unless it is given to him or her by the Creator!** Only God can create new life. **Even cloning will not extend life forever!** The devil can work miracles and extend life for a limited time; however, Satan cannot cause **anyone** [including himself] to live forever.

The **"wages of sin"** is **eternal death – <u>not</u> eternal life in torment!** After the <u>second</u> resurrection, spoken of in Revelation chapter 20, <u>all</u> who die will <u>stay</u> dead. The "second death" will be covered in our next outline.

FACT: By refusing
to give new life
to those who
knowingly rebel,
God will totally
eliminate all sin
and sinners from
the whole universe!

"Eternal Fire"

Matthew 25:41

Then he will say to those on his left hand, "Depart from me, you cursed, into the **eternal fire** prepared for the devil and his angels."

Matthew 25:46

And they will go away into **eternal punishment,** but the righteous into **eternal life.**

2 Thessalonians 1:9

They will suffer the **punishment** of **eternal destruction...**

Everyone understands what is meant by **"eternal destruction,"** but some are confused [because of tradition] about **"eternal punishment."** Think it through for yourself. What is the penalty for sin? Eternal **death.** The punishment = death – **not eternal life in torment!**

There is a **big difference** in punish**MENT** and in punish**ING.** Punish**ING** is a continuous action. Punish**MENT** is **not** continuous.

Bible texts refer to the punish**MENT.**

Ask yourself this question: "Would I enjoy heaven if I knew that one of my children was being tormented, either physically or mentally, in **"hell"**? What would it do to me, **today,** to find out that one of **my** children was trapped in a burning house? You, as a parent, and as a human being, love your children. **If "God is love,"** as the Bible writers claim He is, then for Him to arrange for His children to be in torment, would make life for Himself one continuous "hell"!

The Greek word for **eternal** or **everlasting** [aionois] is used in other parts of the New Testament in the same way. Hebrews 6:2 speaks of **"eternal judgment"** and Hebrews 9:12 speaks of **"eternal redemption."** Certainly these two Bible texts do not mean that the work of redemption will go on throughout eternity, and that the work of judgment is a never ending work.

"eternal redemption"
"eternal judgment"
"eternal punishment"

These all refer to the **result** rather than the process. It is the **punishMENT that equals eternal death; a death that really is eternal. The punishING is not eternal.**

"For ever and ever"

Revelation 20:10

And the devil who had deceived them was thrown into the **lake of fire** and brimstone where the **beast** and the **false prophet were,** and they will be tormented day and night **for ever and ever.**

Revelation 14:11

And the **smoke** of their torment goes up **for ever and ever;** and they have no rest, day or night, these worshipers of the beast and its image, and whoever receives the mark of its name.

Bible writers used the term **"for ever and ever"** differently than we use it today. **First,** remember that the book of **Revelation** is a **book of symbols.** The **"beast"** and the **"false prophet"** in the preceding verses, are **symbols** representing religious organizations. **No one can burn or torment a religious organization in a literal fire!**

Secondly, when we, as Bible students, understand how Bible writers used the term, **"for ever and ever,"** we can make good sense out of what Bible writers wrote concerning the final end of the unsaved.

Please note, in the following Bible texts, that Bible writers referred to **"for ever"** as the length of a person's life, or to even a shorter period of time:

Jonah 1:17 & 2:6

Jonah was in the belly of the **whale "for ever."** Matthew 12:40 says **"3 days & 3 nights"**

1 Samuel 1:22

The child **Samuel** was to abide in the tabernacle **"for ever."**

2 Kings 5:27

Leprosy was to cleave to Gehazi and his descendents **"for ever."**

Exodus 21:6

The **slave** was to serve his master
KJV: **"for ever"**
RSV: **"for life"**

The **Valley of Hinnom** [**"gehenna"** or **"hell"** in the KJV] was the **garbage dump** just outside one of the walls of the city of **Jerusalem.** **Carcasses** of animals and executed criminals were frequently thrown into this gully. What the fire did not burn, the maggots consumed. This **dump** was used as a **visual aid** of the complete destruction of those who would not receive eternal life.

Jeremiah 17:27

But if you do not listen to me, to keep the sabbath holy... I will kindle a **fire** in its gates, and it shall devour the palaces of **Jerusalem** and **shall not be quenched.**

A short time ago I, personally, visited Jerusalem, and **guess what?** This **"fire,"** spoken of in Jer. 17, was **not still burning** – even though it was **not to be quenched!**

"Smoke" which was to go up **"for ever"** is mentioned in other parts of <u>Revelation</u>:

Revelation 8:3,4

The **"smoke"** of the **incense** rose with the **prayers.**

Revelation 9:2,3

From the **"smoke"** of the bottomless pit came **"locusts."**

Revelation 9:17

"Smoke" came from the mouths of the **"horses."**

Revelation 15:8

The **"temple"** was filled with **"smoke"** from the **"glory of God."**

Revelation 18:9,10

The burning of **spiritual Babylon** will cause **"smoke."**

EXCELLENT EXAMPLE
of "smoke" that goes up "for ever and ever":

Isaiah 34:8-11,13,14

For the Lord has a day of vengeance... the streams of Edom shall be turned into **pitch,** and her soil into **brimstone;** her land shall become **burning pitch. Night and day** it shall **not be quenched;** its smoke shall go up <u>for</u> <u>ever</u>... none shall pass through it for ever and ever. **But the hawk** and the **porcupine** shall possess it, the **owl** and the **raven** shall dwell in it... **Thorns** shall grow over its strongholds... It shall be the haunt of **jackals** and the abode for **ostriches.** And **wild beasts** shall meet with **hyenas...**

The preceding description of the past destruction of Bozrah, an Edomite town about 20 miles southeast of the Dead Sea, shows us the **type of destruction** the unsaved will experience during the final end. <u>**After the fire has burned "day and night" "for ever,"**</u> we find the presence of <u>**living**</u> birds and beasts! **Thorns** were to grow**!**

What about "Purgatory"?

"Purgatory" is not mentioned in either the Old or New Testaments of the Bible. No one needs to pay for his or her sins through suffering. Jesus already paid for every sin at the cross. All one has to do is to accept His forgiveness. According to the apostle Paul, salvation is received by grace as a free gift:

Ephesians 2:8-10

For by **grace** you have been saved through faith; and this is not our own doing, it is the **gift** of God; **not because of works,** lest any man should boast. For we are his workmanship, created in Christ Jesus for good works, which God prepared beforehand, that we should walk in them.

The doctrine of **"purgatory"** is a **false doctrine** because it gives the idea that a person can either earn his right to heaven, or pay for his sins through either good works or through suffering. The good news is that **Jesus paid it. We accept this free gift by faith in the promises of Jesus.**

Satan is a well-educated, experienced, **UNHOLY SPIRIT.** He does not fight fairly. Anyone who does not study the Bible for himself, or who does not double-check what I, or any other theologian says, does not understand the danger in unnecessarily taking another's word on the subjects we have been studying in these outlines.

If I have been taught only tradition rather than Holy Scripture since I was three years old, it is understandable that I would have a difficult time believing what I read in the Bible. It will require changing my conscious and subconscious beliefs. Nevertheless, it is extremely important to understand that God really _is_ a "God of love" rather than One who acts like a devil. Remember, a God who truly _is_ a God of love, always acts as He really is: 100% true love. Remember that God loves _His_ children even _more_ than we love _our_ children!

Because of the influence of friends, parents, piers, pastors, and priests, my "heart" tells me something is drastically wrong about my thinking about how God thinks and acts.

Many times religious ideas are based upon only one or two Bible texts taken out of context. With a teachable attitude, your personal study, guided by God's Spirit, will result in the understanding that God really _is_ love – that He is not two-faced. He is the same yesterday, today, and for ever.
[Heb 13:8; Mal 3:6]

Is God Really Like That?
Outline No. 18

"Millennium"

The word, **"Millennium,"** is <u>not</u> found in the Bible. The word comes from two Latin words: **"mille"** meaning "a thousand," and **"annus"** meaning "a year." Now that we have lived past the year **2001**, we hear more and more talk about the "new millennium." The **"thousand years"** we study about here has resulted in many questions being asked by laity and clergy alike. In fact, **a misunderstanding of the events surrounding this "thousand years" will result in one of the biggest deceptions the devil has devised.**

Revelation 20:1-3

Then I saw an **angel** coming down from **heaven,** holding in his hand the key of the **bottomless pit** and a great **chain.** And he seized the **dragon,** that ancient **serpent,** who is the **Devil** and **Satan,** and **bound him** for a **thousand years,** and threw him into the pit, and shut it and sealed it over him, that he should deceive the **nations** no more, till the thousand years were ended. **After** that he must be **loosed** for a **little while.**

"Revelation Deciphered" is a **book** of the **22 chapters** of **Revelation** divided up **verse by verse** and **word by word. 293 symbols** are **deciphered,** using Scripture and logic to explain the meaning of each word as used in the prophetic book of Revelation. A **Dictionary** of the **293 symbols** serves as a quick reference to their meanings. Ask about **"Revelation Deciphered."**

"angel" = a messenger or message
"heaven" = the religious world
[See Revelation 14:6,7]
"bottomless pit" = a symbolic pit
Why? Because a <u>literal</u> pit has a bottom!
"chain" = a symbolic chain.
Why? Because the devil, being a spirit, could <u>not</u> be "bound" with a <u>metal</u> chain or with a <u>literal</u> rope!
"thousand years" = probably a literal **1,000 years.**
Why? Because, if we figured it in prophetic time as is done with <u>most</u> prophecies in the symbolic book of <u>Revelation</u> [one day = a year] it would come to 360,000 years. **Also, there may be some truth to the idea that the 7th thousand year period could be the "Sabbath millennium."** According to Usher's chronology, creation took place at **4004 BCE.** However, **no one knows for <u>sure</u> the exact date of creation.** According to Jewish chronology, we have over two hundred years to go before we come to the year six thousand. It is <u>possible</u> that <u>the</u> "millennium" <u>will</u> begin on the day the 7th thousand year begins.

Because the logical conclusion is that this "thousand years" is a <u>literal</u> thousand years, the **"bottomless pit"** in which Satan is **"chained"** could be our own earth.

First consider that <u>while</u> Satan is "chained" in this "bottomless pit," he will <u>not</u> be able to deceive the nations." Because <u>force</u> is <u>not</u> one of God's methods of dealing with sin and sinners, this must be talking about a **"chain of circumstances."**

As we study from the Bible what happens at the beginning, during, and at the end of the millennium, we will understand why this "chain" is a "chain of circumstances." In other words, something or some situation makes it impossible for Satan to tempt people!

<u>EVENTS</u> <u>AT</u> <u>THE</u> <u>BEGINNING</u> <u>OF</u> <u>THE</u> <u>MILLENNIUM</u>:

[1] **The second coming of Jesus**.

<u>Hebrews 9:27,28</u>

And just as it is appointed for men to die once, and after that the **judgment**, so Christ, having been offered once to bear the sins of many, **will appear a second time, not to deal with sin**, but to save those who are eagerly waiting for him.

<u>Matthew 24:27</u>

For as the lightning comes from the east and shines as far as the west, so will be the coming of the Son of man.

<u>Matthew 24:30,31</u>

Then will appear the sign of the Son of man in heaven... and they will <u>see</u> the Son of man coming on the clouds of heaven with power and great glory; and he will send out his **angels** with a <u>loud</u> trumpet call, and **they will gather the elect** from the four winds, from one end of heaven to the other.

<u>Revelation 6:14-16</u>

The sky vanished like a scroll that is rolled up, and every mountain and island was removed from its place. Then the kings of the earth and the great men... everyone, slave and free, hid in the caves and among the rocks of the mountains, calling to the mountains and rocks, "Fall on us and hide us from the face of him who is seated on the throne...

<u>1 Corinthians 15:22,23</u>

For as in Adam all die, so also in Christ **shall all be made alive**. But **each in his own order:** Christ the first fruits, then **at his coming those who belong to Christ**.

[2] **"<u>First</u>" resurrection, which raises the saved.**

<u>1 Thessalonians 4:16,17</u>

For the Lord himself will descend from heaven with a cry of command, with the archangel's call, and with the sound of the trumpet of God. And the **dead in Christ** will **rise <u>first</u>**; then we who are alive, who are left, shall be **caught up** together <u>with</u> them **in the clouds to meet the Lord in the air;** and so shall we always be with the Lord.

John 5:28,29

The hour is coming when all who are in the tombs will hear his voice and come forth, those who have done good, to the **resurrection of life**, and those who have done evil, to the **resurrection of judgment.**

Revelation 20:4-6

…They came to life, and reigned with Christ a thousand years. The rest of the dead did not come to life until the thousand years were ended.

---

[3] –The saved are taken "up" to be with Jesus.

The only Bible text that says that the saved go to heaven is in **Revelation 21:9-14** [following]. One must know the meanings of these symbols in order to understand what really happens:

"Bride" = The saved.

"Lamb" = Jesus.

"Twelve" -- Anything that has to do with the number "12" in the symbols of Revelation has to do with God's Church: 12 gates, 12 angels, 12 tribes,12 apostles, 12 stars, etc. [See Dictionary of Symbols in Revelation Deciphered]

Revelation 21:9-14

Then came one of the seven angels who had the seven bowls full of the seven last plagues, and spoke to me, saying, **"Come, I will show you the Bride, the wife of the Lamb."** And in the Spirit he carried me away to a great high mountain, and showed me the **holy city Jerusalem coming down out of heaven from God, having the glory of God…** with **twelve gates,** and at the gates **twelve angels**, and on the gates the names of the **twelve tribes** of the sons of Israel were inscribed… the wall of the city had **twelve foundations**, and on them the **twelve names of the twelve** apostles of the Lamb.

The idea that **Jesus** will suddenly appear somewhere in the Middle East and become a great spiritual leader in the midst of all the godless nations, does not agree with the predictions of Jesus who claimed He would return in a spectacular way so that everyone would see Him.

[4] The unsaved who are left here on earth will eventually die, and will stay dead until the second resurrection:

Jeremiah 4:23-27

I looked on the earth, and lo, it was waste and void; and to the heavens, and they had no light. I looked on the mountains, and lo, they were quaking, and all the hills moved to and fro. I looked, and lo, there was **no man**, and all the birds of the air had fled. I looked, and lo, the fruitful land had become a desert, and **all its cities** were laid in **ruins** before the Lord, before his fierce anger. For thus says the Lord, "The whole land shall be a desolation; **yet I will not make a full end.**

Jeremiah 25:33

And those **slain** by the Lord on that day shall extend **from one end of the earth to the other.** They shall not be lamented, or gathered, or buried; they shall be dung on the surface of the ground.

EVENTS DURING THE MILLENNIUM

[1] Judgment of the unsaved.

Revelation 20:4

Then I saw **thrones**, and seated on them were those to whom judgment was committed. Also I saw the **souls** [See Rev 14-1,2,3a] of those who had been beheaded for their testimony to Jesus and for the word of God, and who had not worshipped the beast or its image and had not received its mark on their foreheads or their hands. They **came to life**, and **reigned with Christ a thousand years.**

1 Corinthians 6:2,3

Do you not know that **the saints will judge the world?...** Do you not know that **we are to judge angels?**

Everyone has <u>already</u> been judged before Jesus comes back the <u>second</u> time; otherwise, no distinction could have been made between the saved and the unsaved; no way to divide the "sheep" from the "goats."

How long will/does it take Jesus to decide which people are safe to take to heaven? Some people tell me that ever since the year 1844 [the end of the 2300 year prophecy] that Jesus has been meeting with God the Father to go over the records of everyone who has ever lived, to see whether or not they qualify for eternal life. That is over 160 years! Does it really take that long to judge individuals?

When I get gasoline at an **Exxon** station, the instructions state: **"Remove card quickly."** Immediately I get an "ok" that my credit is good! Does Exxon have a better method than God in determining whether or not my record is clear!

Jesus reads our hearts. ["As he thinks in his heart, so is he" Prov 23:7 NKJV.] Jesus knows for sure whether we have a right relationship with Him. There is no guess work involved. Even people can know what others are thinking by their vibes, tone of voice, facial expressions, and body language. Spouses, at times, can read each other's minds. Jesus has no trouble determining our attitudes toward Him and His laws without having to go through any records! Our frame of mind when we die is what counts. There are people who have a right relationship with Jesus most of their lives, and who change at the very end of their lives. And there are what we call **"death bed conversions."** Only Jesus can read our innermost minds and know for sure whether we are for Him or against Him.

Some people claim that a person must be absolutely perfect in order to qualify for heaven. How stupid can one be to think that he or she is absolutely perfect! Furthermore, as someone has said, **"The closer we come to Jesus the more faulty we appear in our own eyes."** The reason given is that when we get a good look at Jesus, we do not look so good in comparison!

In Matthew chapter 5 Jesus makes it clear that He did not come to do away with the law [verse 17]. Then He proceeded to show how impossible it was for sinful men and women to be saved by keeping the letter of the law. He illustrates by saying that anyone who is **angry** with another breaks the law that says you shall not **kill**. And whoever looks at a woman lustfully **in his heart** [subconscious instincts] actually breaks the law of not committing **adultery**. And whoever marries someone who has been divorced commits adultery! **Jesus demonstrated how impossible it is to be absolutely perfect – how impossible it is to be perfect enough to <u>deserve</u> eternal life.** Whether we like it or not, our inherited negative tendencies are part of us, and always will be part of us until Jesus changes our hearts so that we naturally think no evil.

When Jesus was born of the virgin Mary, He was in no way sinful.

When is it that our hearts will be changed so that we never think evil? As we continue to yield ourselves to Jesus, asking for His help in our sanctification, changes will begin to take place to the extent that other people around us will notice a change in our attitudes, vocabulary, and dispositions:

<u>Galatians 5:22-25</u>

"The **fruit of the Spirit** is love, joy. peace, patience, kindness, goodness, faithfulness, gentleness, self-control...If we live by the Spirit, let us also walk by the Spirit,"

The longer we are genuine Christians, the more will be our spiritual growth. Yet the full and complete renewing of our minds will not take place until after Jesus returns:

<u>Hebrews 8:10</u>

"This is the covenant that I will make with the house of Israel **after those days,** says the Lord: **I will put my laws into their minds, and write them on their hearts...** And they shall not teach every one his fellow or every one his brother, saying 'Know the Lord,' <u>**for all shall know me,**</u> from the least of them to the greatest. For I will be merciful toward their iniquities, and I will remember their sins no more." [These verses are quoted from Jer 31:33,34; Eze 36:26 See Heb 10:16,17]

Every habit, either good of bad, causes an actual physical groove in our brains. When we form a new habit, the old grooves still remain. That is why we, every once in a while, slip back into some old habit. **When our minds are renewed**, "after those days," all the negative groves will be removed! All the negative thoughts and phobias will be "deleted" from our computer-like brains – just like we do with our computers! After that all of our tendencies will be as Jesus would have them – yet we will still have **freedom of choice**. From then on we will voluntarily choose the thoughts and actions that will please Jesus.

In the beginning Adam and Eve were created with programmed minds – minds that reflected the thinking of their Creator. Since then man has degenerated into what we have today – using only 20% of their brainpower. Adam and Eve used 100% of their brain power!

Men and women are judged by their attitudes toward what they know to be right. Because of a lack of knowledge, and because of early brainwashing in childhood, some adults know more than others. What is sin to some people is not necessarily sin to others!

Hebrews 10:26

For if we sin deliberately after receiving a knowledge of the truth, there no longer remains a sacrifice for sins.

To demonstrate the fact that everyone who is saved will not be absolutely perfect:

Revelation 22:11

"…do not seal up the prophecy of this book, for the time is near. Let the evildoer still do evil, and the filthy still be filthy, and the righteous still do right, and the holy still be holy."

Notice, above, that everyone is not "holy." And some of the lost are worse sinners than others. As I observe those around me I see many genuine Christians, yet I see very few, if any, what we would call "holy" people! For example, some fat people are genuine Christians. If they were "absolutely perfect" they would control their appetite! Is there really a difference in controlling appetite for food, or in controlling our desires for alcohol, drugs, tobacco, etc.?

The fact is that every law heaven has given to us to follow is for our own good! **Whenever we break the rules we suffer the penalty.** God does not give us cancer if we smoke, but the natural result could possibly be cancer. We are not forced to do anything. When a mother's infant is deformed because of her drug habits, it is not God who gives the baby crooked legs or a low IQ. God insists upon **freedom of choice.**

Heaven's plan was and is for people to learn by trial and error. Some learn quickly. Some never learn. Yet Jesus, our Creator, had the solution for sinners planned even before the creation of this world; before the creation of Adam and Eve:

Matthew 25:34

...inherit the kingdom **prepared for you from the foundation of the world.**

Ephesians 1:4

"Jesus... chose us in him before the foundation of the world..."

1 Peter 1:19,20

"...like a lamb without blemish or spot, He was destined before the foundation of the world..."

People are judged, not by occasional good deeds or occasional bad deeds, but by the general trend of their lives – by their **attitudes** toward Jesus and His laws.

Our state of mind at our death is what determines our eternal destiny. We know this to be true because of the following Bible texts:

Psalm 103:11,12

For as the heavens are high above the earth, so great is his steadfast love toward those who fear him; as far as the east is from the west, so far does he remove our transgressions from us.

Isaiah 43:25

I am He who blots out your transgressions for my own sake, and I will not remember your sins."

Micah 7:18,19

Who is a God like thee, pardoning iniquity... You will cast all our sins into the depths of the sea."

The above text, of course, refers to **confessed sins.**

1 John 1:9

If we confess our sins, he is faithful and just, and will forgive our sins and cleanse us from all unrighteousness. If we say we have not sinned, we make him a liar, and his word is not in us.

Romans 8:1

There is therefore now no condemnation for those who are in Christ Jesus.

When Jesus returns, there <u>will</u> be a people who, under no circumstances, will knowingly commit any sin. This group will be proof that God's ways are right – that those who have a close relationship with Jesus will receive all the help they need to withstand all the temptations of the enemy.

<u>Did Jesus take a chance</u> in coming to earth in the form of a man? Was there ever any question as to whether or not He would live a sinless life; that He would prove that He was right and Satan was wrong?

No, of course not. **Jesus**, our Creator, knows the end from the beginning:

Isaiah 46:9,10

"I am God, and there is none like me, declaring the end from the beginning, and from ancient times things not yet done."

Revelation 22:13

"I am the Alpha and the Omega, the first and the last, the beginning and the end."

Some think it is **not fair** that Jesus did not inherit weak tendencies as do all people who have been "born in sin." Jesus inherited no spiritual weakness from generations of DNA as we do. He did not inherit a temper as we see demonstrated in most human babies [even though He probably had to learn to walk]. **As humans, "our hearts are deceitful, and corrupt."** Not so with Jesus. **Adam and Eve could have lived sinless lives** – they had no inherited negative weakness, negative emotions, or negative tendencies as all people born today. **Some say that unless Jesus had all the negative traits as we do**, He would not be able to be sympathetic in what we go through. Would you say that Jesus had to have a drug or alcohol problem before He could sympathize with those who have such problems today? Of course not.

Actually Jesus was tempted more than we are. He was tempted to use His supernatural power for His own benefit, but He did not. One time,

when they tried to kill Him, He miraculously disappeared because "His time was not right" for His death and crucifixion.

Some believe that Jesus ascended to heaven to what they call the **"heavenly sanctuary."**

Hebrews 9:24

"For Christ has entered, not into a sanctuary made with hands, a copy of the true one, but **into heaven itself**, now to appear in the presence of God on our behalf."

There is nothing in heaven that is exactly like what was in the earthly sanctuary. No alter of sacrifice! No blood to sprinkle anywhere! The reference to **Jesus** being **our High Priest in heaven** is merely **symbolic**:

Hebrews 9:8-15

"…the way into the sanctuary is not yet opened as long as the outer tent is still standing (which is **symbolic** for the present age)… But when Christ appeared as a high priest… he entered once for all into the Holy Place taking **not the blood of goats and calves but his own blood** thus securing an eternal redemption… Therefore he is the mediator of a **new covenant…**"

No blood was shed in the heavenly sanctuary! The blood of Jesus, which covers all the sins of the saved, was shed on earth, not heaven.

Is Jesus now in heaven as our "High Priest" pleading for the Father to forgive our sins? Not according to Jesus Himself:

John 16:26,27

"…I do not say to you that I shall pray the Father for you; for the Father himself loves you…"

John 14:8,9,18

"Philip said to him, "Lord, show us the Father, and we shall be satisfied." Jesus said to him, "Have I been with you so long, and yet you do not know **me**, Philip? He who has seen me has seen the Father… **I will not leave you desolate;** I will come to you."

There is **<u>one</u> lawgiver** and **one judge.** When Jesus was here on earth He forgave people their sins – He did not have to check with heaven first! **Jesus does <u>not</u> have to get the Father's approval before He forgives sins of anyone!**

Our Creator, Jesus <u>could</u> have forgiven <u>His</u> children without dying on the cross! However, He had a reason for doing it like He did. **Jesus died on the cross to demonstrate the result of sin – and to demonstrate what He, God, was really like – in contrast to how He has been pictured in the Old Testament – as an angry, get even killer God, who has a violent temper.** Earthly parents do not have to die in order to forgive <u>their</u> children! **Jesus had an important reason for dying as He**

did, and He got His point across quite effectively to the angels, to humans, and to the inhabitants of the whole universe!

People who are eternally saved will have a delightful and important job to do – to travel to the ends of the universe to explain, first hand, the terrible results of rebellion against God and His laws. We will be able to say, **"I was there."**

Jesus, even though He took on the form of a man, was still 100% God. He is omnipresent. He can be everywhere at once! **Jesus raised Himself from the grave:**

John 10:17,18

"I lay down my life, that I may take it again. No one takes it from me, but I lay it down of my own accord. I have power to lay it down, and I have power to take it again."

Why was the book of Hebrews written? It was written to *bridge the gap* for the Jews from their many animal sacrifices [that God did <u>not</u> originally sanction – Review Outline No. 5] to total reliance upon the one sacrifice of Jesus.

Hebrews 10:4-6

For it is **impossible** for the blood of bulls and goats to take away sins. Consequently, when Christ came into the world, he said, "Sacrifices and offerings you [God] have not desired, but a body you have prepared for me; **in burnt offerings and sin offerings you [God] have taken no pleasure**.

Matthew 9:13

"Go and learn what this means, '**I desire mercy, not sacrifice.**' For I have come to call not the righteous but sinners.

The book of Revelation, which was written <u>after</u> the book of Hebrews, makes it clear that now all Christians are considered **"priests."** That is, each Christian can pray directly to the **lawgiver** and **judge** to ask for and receive forgiveness:

Revelation 1:5,6

"To him who loves us and has freed us from our sins by his blood, and made us a **kingdom of priests** to his God and Father…" [Also Rev 5:10]

This second judging is merely a review of the records by the saved.

Why would the saved be involved in reviewing the records of the unsaved? Unless there was an opportunity for the saved to review the records of the unsaved, the saved would wonder throughout eternity whether or not God had judged fairly their friends and/or relatives. **It <u>must</u> be made clear to the saved that God did <u>not</u> make any mistakes; that He judged correctly and fairly.**

Just suppose you were surprised that one of your grandmothers or grandfathers – or one of your sons or daughters was not included among the saved. Unless you were convinced in your own mind that God had judged correctly, you would soon begin to doubt God. On the other hand, **some people might be surprised that <u>YOU</u> made it to heaven!**

EVENTS AT THE END OF THE MILLENNIUM

[1] The unsaved will be raised to life toward the <u>end</u> of the millennium! They, again, surrender themselves to Satan, and will have no power to change without divine help.

[2] The symbolic "chain of circumstances" which bound Satan will be eliminated by the raising of the unsaved dead to life. Then Satan will deceive them again.

Revelation 20:5,7,8

The **rest of the dead did not come to life until the thousand years were ended…** And when the thousand years were ended, **Satan will be loosed** from his prison and will come out **to <u>deceive</u> the <u>nations</u>** which are at the four corners of the earth, that is, Gog and Magog, **to gather them for battle**; their number is like the sand of the sea.

The Bible does <u>not</u> say how long the unsaved will live on the earth while Satan is "deceiving" them again; however, it will be longer than we might think. **It will be long enough to prove a point.** In spite of all the evidence, the unsaved will continue to rebel against God and His ways. **The former Christians will suffer the most mental torment** as they realize how much they gave up for so little! Some will live longer than others. With all the modern technology, and all the modern methods of destruction and warfare, **Satan will convince the unsaved that they can conquer and eliminate the smaller, unarmed group of the saved!**

Surprise! Surprise! God will then reveal Himself and His superior power!

[3] All sinners will die sooner or later, including Satan and his angels. Satan will be the last to die.

The unsaved, when they see that their cause is useless, will die of various causes. **When they see how much they have given up for so little,** many will murder others whom they blame for giving them wrong advice and teaching them false doctrines about God and His ways [like the devilish doctrine of eternal torment] – people like preachers, parents, and secular rulers! Also, forces of nature will destroy as they did at the time of the flood; like what will happen during the upheaval of nature at Jesus' <u>second</u> coming. **The end result will be the elimination of all those who choose to rebel against God and His ways. Maybe Satan will self-destruct, as will some human beings:**

Ezekiel 28:11-19

…Thus says the Lord God: "You were the signet of **perfection**, full of wisdom and perfect in **beauty**. You were in **Eden**, the garden of God;… On the day that you were **created** they were prepared. With an anointed guardian cherub I placed you; you were on the holy mountain of God… **You were blameless** in your ways from the day you were **created**, till iniquity was found in you… so I cast you as a profane thing from the mountain of God, and the guardian cherub drove you out from the midst of the stones of fire. Your heart was proud because of your **beauty**… so **I brought forth fire from the midst of you; <u>it consumed you</u>, and I turned you to ashes** upon the earth in the sight of all who saw you… you have come to a **dreadful end** and **shall be no more for ever.**"

---

[4] – A new earth will be created.

Revelation 21:1-6

Then I saw a **new heaven** and a **new earth** and the first heaven and the first earth had passed away, and the sea was no more. And I saw the

holy city, new Jerusalem [Rev 21:9-14 = the saved] coming down out of heaven from God, prepared as a **bride** adorned for her husband; and I heard a great voice from the throne saying, "Behold, the dwelling of **God is with men.** He will dwell with them, they shall be his people, and God_himself shall be with them; he will wipe away every tear from their eyes, and **death shall be no more,** neither shall there be mourning nor crying nor pain any more, for the former things have passed away." And he who sat upon the throne said, **"Behold, I make all things new."** And he said to me, "It is done! I am the Alpha and the Omega, the beginning and the end. To the thirsty I will give water without price from the fountain of the water of life."

The misunderstanding of events surrounding the "thousand years" will result in one of the biggest deceptions the devil has ever devised!

Most religious people in the world, including most Christians [but not all Christians] look for Jesus to return and set up His earthly kingdom at the **BEGINNING** of the Millennium. As we have studied, the Bible does not teach this!

First will come a **counterfeit** of **antichrist.** The devil knows that everyone is looking for an antichrist. Then **following** the counterfeit will come the **real antichrist = Satan himself.** Satan, as the antichrist, will sound like we think Jesus would

sound. He will quote Scripture, work undeniable miracles, and even appear to raise the dead to life.

All those who expect Jesus to set up His kingdom here on earth at His **second** coming, will be deceived! They will be worshiping Satan, thinking that they are worshiping Jesus!

Most Christians do not realize that Zechariah 14 has been superceded by Revelation. They especially misapply Zechariah 14:16-21, which even speaks of the continuing of animal sacrifices! This prophecy was given on the condition that Israel would accept the Messiah when He came. They did not! Only by believing Revelation chapter 20 can we be kept from being deceived.

The elimination of all of the unsaved at the end of the millennium will not be accomplished as quickly as in Noah's flood. After the "New Jerusalem" descends from heaven, there will be a period of time before the unsaved die their eternal death.

Revelation 20:7-10

When the thousand years are ended, Satan will be loosed from his prison and will come out to **deceive the nations which are at the four corners of the earth...** they **surrounded** the camp of the saints and the beloved city, but fire came down from heaven and consumed them...

What kind of "fire" will destroy the unsaved?

Ezekiel 21:31,32

...I will blow upon you with the **fire of my wrath**; and **I will deliver you into the hand of evil men,** skilful to destroy. **You** shall be **fuel** for the **fire... you will be no more remembered...**

The unsaved will be destroyed from "cause to effect." Realizing that they have given up eternal life for so little, they will **murder each other by the millions.** Because of their great mental torment, some will die of **spontaneous human combustion.** Some will die from **literal fire** [Like people died in Noah's flood by the natural causes of the flood]. Eventually all who did not qualify for eternal **life will die the eternal death. No one can live again unless the Creator resurrects them and gives them new life.** This, according to Bible writers, will not happen.

FACT: **Eternal death will last the same length of time as eternal life. The dead stay dead!!**

18-14

Is God Really Like That?
Outline No. 19

Counterfeit lord

A few years ago someone tried to make me read an article which stated that there was a counterfeit lord god operating during Old Testament times. I figured the idea was so stupid that even I refused to read anything on the subject – until a year and a half later! At the present time I carefully and thoughtfully read anything which someone else wants me to read. I have repented for being so closed-minded. God guides my mind in different ways, one being the so-called "foolishness of preaching." Yes, God, at times, gets His message through via other people.

After much study and research, I have uncovered much Bible proof that Satan promoted his deception from the very beginning of this world's history. Jesus Himself proclaimed Satan was a liar from the beginning:

John 8:44

You are of your father the **devil,** and your will is to do your father's desires. He was a murderer from the beginning, and has nothing to do with truth, because **there is no truth in him.** When **he lies,** he speaks according to his own nature, for **he is a liar** and **the father of lies.**

2 Corinthians 11:13-15

For such men are false apostles, deceitful workmen, disguising themselves as apostles of Christ. And no wonder, for even **Satan himself disguises himself as an angel of light.**

There is no question whatsoever that Satan operates as a counterfeit "angel of light" <u>now</u>, during New Testament times. But **is it logical to think that Satan [Lucifer] did <u>not</u> do the same in <u>Old</u> Testament times?** After Adam's fall do you suppose Satan decided to take a universal vacation? **Jesus** made it clear that Satan was a liar from the **beginning!**

Ever since Lucifer [Satan] rebelled in heaven, there has been a great controversy between Jesus and Satan – a "war" that will continue until evil is finally eliminated:

Revelation 12:7-9

Now **war** arose in heaven, **Michael [Jesus] and his angels** fighting **against the dragon;** and the **dragon and his angels** fought... And the great **dragon** was thrown down, that ancient **serpent,** who is called the **Devil** and **Satan,** the **<u>deceiver</u> <u>of</u> <u>the</u> <u>whole</u> <u>world</u>** – he was thrown down to the earth, and his angels were thrown down with him.

Jude 1:6

And the **angels** that did not keep their own position but **<u>left</u>** their proper dwelling place...

Several Bible texts refer to Satan as a "god" or "ruler" of this world. Ever since Adam's fall, Satan and his angel followers have been working hard and long to deceive every human being possible:

2 Corinthians 4:4

…the **god of this world** has blinded the minds of the <u>un</u>believers, to keep them from seeing the light of the gospel…

John 12:31

[Jesus speaking] "Now is the judgment of this world, now shall **the ruler of this world** be cast out…"

Ephesians 2:1,2

…following **the prince of the power of the air,** <u>the</u> <u>spirit</u> **that is <u>now</u> <u>at</u> <u>work</u> in the sons of disobedience.**

1 John 4:1

Beloved, do not believe every spirit, but **<u>test the</u> <u>spirits</u>** to see whether they are of God.

1 Corinthians 8:5, 6

For although there may be **so-called gods** in heaven and on earth – as indeed there are **many "gods"** and **many "lords"** – yet for us there is one God…

Colossians 2:18

Let no one disqualify you, insisting on… **worship of angels,** taking his stand on visions…

Deuteronomy 32:16-18

They stirred him to jealousy with **strange gods… They <u>sacrificed</u> <u>to</u> <u>demons</u>** which were **no gods,** to **gods** they had never known, to **new gods** that had come in of late, whom your fathers never dreaded. You were unmindful of the **Rock** that begot you…

FACT: Satan deceived many people during Old Testament times, making them think that <u>he</u> was the <u>true</u> Lord.

<u>When</u> is it that Satan and his evil angels have the <u>RIGHT</u> to deceive God's followers? Because the same principle applies today, we need to know the following <u>FACT</u>:

FACT: Satan has the <u>right</u> to <u>deceive</u> when people willfully <u>rebel</u> against God or His laws.

Even people like Abraham, Moses, and Elijah [who later was translated into heaven] were, <u>at</u> <u>times</u>, allowed to be deceived.

The apostle Paul makes it clear that the Israelites, at times, worshiped the <u>counterfeit</u> lord:

Galatians 4:8-11

Formerly, when you did not know God, you were **in bondage to beings** that by nature are no gods; but now that you have come to know God, or rather to be known by God, **how can you turn back again to the** beggarly elemental **spirits, whose slaves you want to be once more?** You observe days, and months, and seasons, and years! I am afraid I have labored over you in vain.

Deuteronomy 32:17,18

They **sacrificed to demons...** you forgot the God who gave you birth.

The true Lord [Jesus] did not openly accuse Satan of being the "liar" and "murderer" that he really is, until Jesus came to this earth in the form of a man. **If God had openly condemned Lucifer from the beginning, a fair and unbiased trial would have been impossible!**

The same is true today when someone commits a crime. If a lawyer fears that his client cannot receive a fair trial because of newspaper and radio coverage, he will rightfully insist that the trial be held in a neutral location. **In order to receive a fair trial, Lucifer [Satan] had to be allowed to "hang himself."**

For the eventual good of the universe, God allowed evil to run its course so that forever afterwards every created being would know for sure, in his own heart, that rebellion should no longer be allowed. **Everyone will then be convinced in his or her own mind** that God and His ways are the only ways to receive genuine and lasting happiness.

Because God, **before the cross**, could not openly point a condemning finger at Satan, **people on earth had the disadvantage of not knowing whether or not they were being deceived by a counterfeit lord.** People, because of their rebellion and/or lack of faith, were forced to try to figure out the difference between the true Lord and the counterfeit lord. Nevertheless, people then, as well as people today, have nothing to fear **IF** they do not knowingly and willfully rebel against God or His laws.

Those who believe God's promises, study His Holy Word for themselves, and continue to establish a right relationship with Him, should have no fear of being deceived by Satan.

At times, Old Testament Bible writers were not sure **who** was directing them. **Notice the difference** in the following two Bible texts. **Speaking of the same event,** one text says it was **the Lord** who influenced King David to number Israel; the other text says it was **Satan!** The only way the following Bible texts would **not** contradict each other is if **"the Lord"** referred to the **counterfeit lord!** Here the writer of 2 Samuel referred to **Satan** as **"the Lord."**

2 Samuel 24:1,2

Again the anger of **the Lord** was kindled against Israel and he incited **David** against them, saying, "Go, **number Israel** and Judah." So the king said to **Joab**... "Go through all the tribes of Israel from **Dan to Beersheba...**"

I Chronicles 21:1,2

Satan stood up against Israel, and incited **David** to **number Israel.** So David said to **Joab**... "Go, number Israel from **Beersheba to Dan...**"

King David yielded to Satanic influences and **deliberately** did what he believed was contrary to God's desire; therefore, Satan had a license to **deceive** David into thinking that the genuine Lord God was directly responsible for the loss of 70,000 lives. King David admitted that he had "sinned greatly," "done very foolishly," and had "done very wickedly" [2 Sam 24:10,17; 1 Chron 21:8].

What kind of a **"God of love"** would force King David into making a choice that would result in the death of 70,000 people? [See 2 Sam 2 & 1 Chron 21] And would a **"God of love"** kill 70,000 people for one of David's sins? As David himself said, "It is **I** who **have sinned** and **done very wickedly. But these sheep, what have they done?"** [1 Chron 21:17]

What supernatural being "tried to kill Moses"?

Understanding that there is a counterfeit lord helps us to accept questionable statements for what they really are:

Exodus 4:21-26

And **the Lord** said to **Moses,** "When you go back to Egypt, see that you do before Pharoah all the miracles which I have put in your power... At a lodging place on the way [to Egypt] **the Lord** [counterfeit] **met him** [Moses] **and sought to kill him.** Then **Zipporah** [Moses' wife] took a flint and cut off her son's foreskin, and touched Moses' feet with it, and said, "Surely you are a bridegroom of blood to me! So he [the "lord"] let him [Moses] alone. Then it was that she said, "You are a bridegroom of blood," because of the **circumcision.**

In what form did the counterfeit lord appear to Moses? No one knows for sure, but possibly it was in the form of a man, as heavenly beings had appeared before and after Moses' time.

Anyone who believes that the <u>true</u> Lord God unsuccessfully tried to kill Moses, does not understand God's power! To create, all it took was a **"word"** from Him!

Psalm 33:6,9

By the **word** of the Lord the heavens were made... For he **spoke,** and it came to be...

If all it took were **"words"** to create, then all it would have taken to kill Moses were words! **The idea that the true Lord God tried to kill Moses and failed, does not make sense.** The counterfeit lord would have had no problem killing Moses **if** Holy angels had not <u>also</u> been present. **Satan's actions are limited.** He is allowed to go just so far, and no farther – according to the circumstances. As for **circumcision,** it was <u>never</u> part of God's <u>perfect</u> <u>will</u>. **Moses** was <u>not</u> the first person to practice circumcision. **Jesus said so.**

THINK!

Was it the true Lord God, or was it the counterfeit lord Satan who indicated that it was sinful for a woman to have her menstrual period, so that she must go to the priest and offer a <u>sin</u> offering?!

Leviticus 15:19,29,30

When a woman has a discharge of blood which is her regular discharge from her body, she shall be in her impurity for seven days… And on the eighth day she shall take **two turtle doves or two young pigeons,** and bring them to the priest, to the door of the tent of meeting. And the priest shall offer one **for a <u>sin</u> offering** and the other for a burnt offering; and the priest shall **make atonement for her unclean discharge.**

Only the counterfeit lord Satan would put down women and attempt to degrade them by making such a law. More of how the devil himself caused women to become second class citizens is covered in Outline No. 24.

THINK!

Would a "God of love" inspire a law that forced a man to choose between a life of slavery or his wife and children? No, of course not!

Exodus 21:1-6

When you **buy a Hebrew slave,** he shall **serve six years**, and in the 7th he shall go free, for nothing… If his master gives him a **wife** and she bears him **sons** and **daughters, the wife and her children shall be her master's** and he shall go out alone. **But if the slave plainly says, "I love my master, my wife, and my children;** I shall not go out free," then **his master shall bring him to the door or the doorpost; and his master shall bore his ear through with an awl; and he shall serve him for life.**

Jesus made it plain that <u>all</u> of the Old Testament laws were <u>not</u> from the true Lord God [Review Outline No. 1-1].

Two Different Kinds of Spirits!

1 Samuel 16:14

Now the **Spirit of the Lord departed** from **Saul,** and **an evil spirit from the Lord tormented him.**

The preceding Bible text says that the **"Spirit of the Lord"** departed from Saul; therefore, the **"evil spirit"** had to be the <u>counterfeit</u> lord Satan. Always keep in mind that people in OT times believed that there was only **one Lord** and that everything, either **good or bad,** came from that one Lord.

What caused Uzzah's death?

2 Samuel 6:6-9

Uzzah put out his hand to the ark of God and took hold of it, for **the oxen stumbled.** And the **anger** of the Lord was kindled against **Uzzah;** and **God smote him...** and **he died...**And **David was angry** because the Lord had broken forth upon **Uzzah...** So **David was afraid** of the Lord that day.

From a child <u>Uzzah</u> was taught that if he ever touched the sacred ark, for any reason, he would die. There are **two possibilities:**

[a] – He died because of his subconscious [heart] belief that he would die.

[b] – Satan killed him.

David believed in **one God** from which everything came, good or bad. **David actually believed that God had killed Uzzah,** and he did not think that was fair because he knew Uzzah was only trying to keep the ark from falling over.

Our God of love does <u>not</u> really get angry like humans do so that He loses control and kills someone! The <u>result</u> of the whole event was to cause David to become afraid! **"There is no fear in love"** [1 John 4:18].

Does the following sound like a God of love, or does it sound like the devil?

Numbers 31:1-41

...to execute the Lord's **vengeance... kill** every male among the **little ones,** and **kill** every woman who has known man by lying with him. But all the **young girls** who have not known man by lying with him, **keep alive for yourselves...**

PREVIEW

This subject of the counterfeit lord Satan is so important that an additional five more outlines of Bible proof will follow.

Is God Really Like That?
Outline No. 20

Counterfeit lord
Part 2

Who tormented Job?

Bible students who have not carefully studied the book of Job for themselves, often come to the wrong conclusion that it was the true Lord God who tormented Job.

Job, chapters one and two, tell the story of how Satan went to a heavenly council where **"all the sons of God"** met from different occupied planets. **God asked Satan where he was from – what planet he represented.** His answer was "from the earth." <u>Adam should have been there</u> to represent the earth; however, Adam sold out to Satan when he chose to follow the counterfeit lord rather than the true Lord God.

There is no Bible text which specifically says that there are other inhabited worlds; nevertheless, the following text [Job 1;6,7] seems to indicate that there <u>are</u> other inhabited worlds. The <u>"sons of God,"</u> it seems, were the leaders of various worlds – even though man is a unique creation made in the likeness of God.

Job 1:6,7

"Now there was a day when the <u>sons of God</u> came to present themselves before the **Lord,** and **Satan** also came among them. **The Lord said to Satan, 'From where have you come?'** Satan answered the Lord, 'From going to and fro on the **earth,** and from walking up and down on it."

Satan claimed that **Job** followed the true Lord God because God gave him <u>extra</u> protection. **This is encouraging:**

Job 1:8-12

And the Lord said to Satan, "Have you considered my servant Job, that there is none like him on the earth, a blameless and upright man, who fears God and turns away from evil?" Then Satan answered the Lord, **"Does Job fear God for nothing? HAVE YOU NOT PUT A <u>HEDGE</u> ABOUT HIM and his house and all that he has, on every side? You have blessed the work of his hands, and his possessions have increased in the land.** But put forth <u>your</u> hand now, and touch all that he has, and he will curse you to your face." And **the Lord said to Satan, "Behold, all that he has is in y<u>our</u> power;** only upon himself do not put forth your hand." So Satan went forth from the presence of the Lord.

It is encouraging to know that the true Lord God puts a "hedge" of protection around those who love and obey Him!

Satan told God, "Put forth <u>YOUR</u> hand now, and touch all that he has…" But then God told Satan, "All that he has is in <u>YOUR</u> power."

Therefore, what happened to Job was <u>Satan's</u> doings; not God's! The "fire of God" which "fell from heaven" and destroyed the sheep and the servants, was from the <u>counterfeit</u> lord Satan – as it was many other times in the Bible. And the tornado or hurricane that blew down the house that killed Job's sons and daughters was also from the counterfeit lord Satan!

Remember that everyone in those days believed in just <u>one</u> God. That meant that <u>everything</u> that happened, even in nature, was something that "God did."

So, when Job's three "friends" met Job, they believed that Job had some secret sin that caused God to torment him! And **Job** himself, knowing that he was doing everything he knew to be right, **wondered <u>why</u>** God was doing this to him! **In <u>Job 9:6</u> he speaks about God "who shakes the earth out of its place." In Outlines No. 9, 10, and 11 you learned the <u>natural</u> cause of the earth being shaken out of its place!** Speaking about himself, Job said:

Job 12:4

I am a **laughingstock** to my friends; I, who called upon God and he answered me, a just and blameless man, am a **laughingstock**.

It is not usually understood that the "Lord" who answered Job's questions was <u>not</u> the <u>true</u> Lord God. One clue that it was <u>not</u> the true Lord God was the way he answered Job. He did not give any <u>logical</u> answers as to <u>why</u> Job was being tormented. All that this counterfeit lord said was, "Look, I am the all-powerful God who created everything; who are you to question me!" This is **<u>not</u>** the way God **"reasons"** with sinners:

Isaiah 1:18

"Come now, let us **reason** together, **says the Lord**: though your sins are like scarlet, they shall be as white as snow…

A <u>second</u> <u>clue</u> is that the "Lord's" voice came out of the "whirlwind" rather than coming as a **"still small voice."**

Job 38:1-3

…the Lord answered Job out of the whirlwind: "Who is this that darkens counsel by words without knowledge? Gird up your loins like a man, I will question you…."

1 Kings 19:11-13

…the Lord was not in the wind… earthquake… fire… and after that a still small voice… Elijah heard it…

Who was responsible for the "fire from heaven" that killed 100 men?

2 Kings 1:9-12

"...But **Elijah** answered the captain of **fifty,** 'If I am a man of God, let fire come down from heaven and consume you and your **fifty.**' Then **fire came down from heaven, and consumed him and his fifty...** Again the king sent to him another captain of **fifty** men with his **fifty...** Then the **fire of God came down from heaven and consumed him and his fifty."**

Luke 9:52-55

They entered into a village of the Samaritains, to prepare for Him. But they did not receive Him... And when His disciples **James** and **John** saw this, they said, **"Lord do you want us to command fire to come down from heaven and consume them, just as Elijah did?** But He [Jesus] turned and **rebuked them,** and said, **"You do not know what manner of spirit you are of.**

Job 1:12,16

And the **Lord said to Satan,** "Behold, all that he [Job] has is in y**our power...** The **fire of God fell from heaven,** and burned up the **sheep** and the **servants...**

In Luke 9:52-55 [above] **Jesus said, in effect, "By asking Me to bring fire down from heaven like Elijah, you are talking like the devil!"**

Remember the rule: Compare everything written in the OT with what Jesus did and said in the NT.

Satan, when God allowed, was able to cause fire to come down from heaven to burn up people, sheep, or animal sacrifices – fire which people in OT times thought was from the <u>true</u> Lord God! It was <u>not</u>. In John 8:44 Jesus called Satan a murderer. [At times the "fire from heaven" was caused by nature being out of control.]

<u>FACT</u>: It is important to remember that the book of Job gives proof that the "fire from heaven" came from Satan.

Also, it is important to understand that God allowed Satan to deceive Job into thinking that he [Job] was talking to the genuine Lord God, when, in reality, Job was talking with the counterfeit lord Satan.

Serpent = Symbol of Sin and Satan

Revelation 12:9

And the great **dragon** was thrown down, that ancient **serpent,** who is called the **Devil** and **Satan,** the **deceiver** of the whole world – he was thrown down to the earth, and his angels were thrown down with him.

Unless we understand and accept the fact that the counterfeit lord Satan is allowed to deceive when people find fault with God or His laws, the following story could give us the wrong impression:

Numbers 21:4-9

From Mount Hor they set out by the way to the Red Sea... and the people became impatient on the way. And the **people spoke against God** and against Moses. **"Why have you brought us out of Egypt to die in the wilderness?** For there is no food and water, and we loathe this **worthless food."** Then **the Lord sent fiery serpents** among the people, and they bit the people, so that **many** people of Israel **died.** And the people came to Moses, and said, **"We have sinned,** for we have spoken against the Lord and against you; **pray to the Lord, that he take away the serpents from us."** So Moses prayed for the people. And **the Lord said to Moses, "Make a fiery serpent** and **set it on a pole;** and every one who is bitten,

when he sees it, shall live." So **Moses made a bronze serpent,** and set it on a pole; and if a serpent bit any man, he would **look at the bronze serpent and live.**

Once again the pattern is clear:

[A] – The people spoke against God, giving the counterfeit lord Satan license to deceive and indirectly kill people.

[B] – The true Lord God, because of Israel's rebellion, allowed poisonous snakes to come among the people. Some of the people died.

[C] – **The people said to Moses, "We are sorry; please pray that the Lord will take away the snakes."** However, the people were not really sorry that they had spoken against God. They felt that God had let them down; therefore, they were not truly repentant.

[D] – **The counterfeit lord answered Moses' prayer** and **told Moses to put a symbol of himself [Satan] on a pole!** Only the counterfeit lord would command them to do something that was against one of the ten commandments!! **The second commandment** forbade them from making **any graven image** [Ex. 20:4-6; Deut 5:8-10]! The counterfeit lord <u>Satan</u> had Moses and the people look at a symbol of <u>himself</u> in order to be healed!

[E] – **Satan was smart enough <u>not</u> to have the people <u>bow down</u> to the serpent on the pole.** That would have been too obvious a disregard for the commandments.

[F] – People are <u>not</u> saved by looking to Satan, symbolized by a serpent. People are saved by looking to Jesus, symbolized by the cross.

[G] – In the New Testament, as a counter move to Satan's Old Testament deception, the apostle Paul declared that <u>Jesus</u> <u>was</u> <u>made</u> <u>sin</u> <u>for</u> <u>us</u>:

<u>2 Corinthians 5:21</u>

For our sake he [God] made him [Jesus] to be sin who knew no sin, so that in him [Jesus] we might become the righteousness of God.

The same type of counter move was made in connection with the killing of animals as sacrifices for sin. **All of** the major Old Testament prophets wrote that animal sacrifices were <u>not</u> commanded by God [**Review Outline No. 5**]. **God said, in effect, "O.K., if you insist upon doing it the heathen way, the lamb will represent Jesus."** Yet even this did not accomplish its

purpose, because the Jewish nation rejected Jesus, **"the Lamb,"** when He came.

One of the good kings of Judah destroyed the evil serpent symbol of Satan:

<u>2 Kings 18:1-4</u>

"**Hezekiah...** did what was right in the eyes of the Lord... And he **broke in pieces the bronze serpent that Moses had made,** for until those days the people of Israel had burned incense to it"

Some non-Christian religions still use the serpent as a sign of something good or holy – like in **India** where they worship the **cobra.** They also worship the **bull,** which began with the worship of **Baal** [See Outlines No. 9 & 10]. In <u>**Matthew 10:16**</u> **Jesus** told His disciples to be **"wise as serpents, and harmless as doves." Jesus,** in effect, made a <u>contrast</u> between serpents and doves. **Jesus did <u>not</u> say, "be as harmless as serpents"!** The serpent got its bad reputation beginning in the <u>Garden of Eden</u>. In the book of <u>Ezekiel</u> Lucifer [Satan] is symbolized by the "king of Tyre":

<u>Ezekiel 28:11-19</u>

"You were the signet of perfection, full of wisdom and perfect in beauty. **<u>YOU WERE IN EDEN,</u> the garden of God...** you were on the holy mountain of God... You were blameless in your ways from the day **you were created...** Your heart was proud because of your beauty... you have come to a dreadful end and shall be no more for ever."

Revelation 12:9

And the great **dragon** was thrown down, that ancient **serpent**, who is called the **Devil** and **Satan**, the **deceiver** of the whole world – he was thrown down to the earth. And his angels were thrown down with him.

John 8:44

You are of your father the **devil...** He was a murderer from the beginning, and has nothing to do with the truth, because there is no truth in him. When **he lies,** he speaks according to his own nature, for **he is a liar and the father of lies.**

THINK!

Do the following commands equal child abuse, or are they laws of a genuine Lord God of love?

Deuteronomy 21:18-21

If a man has a **stubborn and rebellious son, who will not obey** the voice of his father or... mother... **all the men of the city shall** stone him to death... **and all Israel shall hear, and** fear.

Exodus 21:15,17

Whoever **strikes** his father or his mother shall be put to **death...** Whoever **curses** his father or his mother shall be put to **death.**

Did the true Lord, who now insists upon freedom of choice, ever outlaw religious freedom?

Deuteronomy 13:6-10

If your **brother... son... daughter... or your friend...** entices you secretly, saying, "Let us go and serve other gods... **you shall kill him...**"

Numbers 15:32-36

They found a man **gathering sticks** on the **sabbath...** And the Lord said to Moses, "This man shall be **put to death.**"

THINK!

Why take it out on the animals and birds?

Genesis 6:5-8

The Lord saw that the wickedness of men was great in the earth, and it grieved him to his heart. **So the Lord said, "I will blot out man whom I have created** from the face of the ground, **man** and **beast** and... **birds...** for **I am sorry that I have made them."** But Noah found favor in the eyes of the Lord.

THINK IT THROUGH:

If God really <u>did</u> "so love the world that He gave His only Son" [John 3:16], why would He ever say, "I am sorry that I have made them"? If God really <u>can</u> see the end from the beginning, and if, as the Bible says, the **plan of salvation** was thought up **"from the foundation of the world,"** why would God react so violently to man's wickedness, as if it had caught Him by surprise?

Isaiah 46:9,10

...for **I am God,** and there is none like me, **declaring the end from the beginning** and from ancient times things not yet done.

Revelation 22:13

"I am the **Alpha** and the **Omega,** the **first** and the **last,** the **beginning** and the **end.**"

Matthew 25:34

...inherit the kingdom prepared for you from the foundation of the world.

FACT: No one can genuinely love God who believes that He did, does, and will do the things many Christians teach and preach.

Is God Really Like That?
Outline No. 21

Counterfeit lord
Part 3

More proof of a counterfeit lord Satan!

Please note very carefully the following Bible text in Exodus 19:20-25. Think about what this Bible text is saying – that at times there were **two** who were operating as God!! Obviously, only one can be the true Lord. The other is the counterfeit lord.

Exodus 19:20-25
And the **Lord came down** upon Mount Sinai, to the **TOP** of the mountain; and the **Lord** called **Moses** to the **TOP** of the mountain, and **Moses went UP**. And the Lord said to Moses, **"Go DOWN and warn the people,** lest they break through to the **Lord** to gaze and many of them perish. And also let the priests who come near to the **Lord** consecrate themselves, lest the **Lord** break out upon them… do not let the priests and the people break through to come up to the **Lord, lest HE break out against them."** So **Moses went down** to the people and told them.

It is important to note that God did **not** say, **"I** will break out against them." No, the true Lord referred to another –

a counterfeit lord. In **Exodus 19:20-25** [21-1a.5] God called Moses **UP** to the **TOP** of the mountain to warn him about the counterfeit lord Satan at the **BOTTOM** of the mountain.

The **original Bible manuscripts** included **no punctuation** – **no** commas, question marks, quotation marks, periods, or **CAPITALS**. These were added hundreds of years later, and were the **opinions of the translators**; therefore, **whether or not "lord" was to be capitalized was the option of the translator.**

Also, any paraphrased translation [such as "The Living Bible"] **that changes the original third person to the first person, is not an accurate translation of the original Hebrew manuscript.**

Exodus 19:1-19 [following] covers more detail of that conversation:

[A] Israel camped at the foot of the mountain only three months after they left Egypt!!

Exodus 19:1,2
On the third new moon after the people of Israel had gone forth out of the land of Egypt, on that day they came into the wilderness of Sinai… and there Israel encamped before the mountain.

[B] Moses went up to hear what God had to say. God told Moses to tell the people that if they would obey Him, He would make them a holy nation; a kingdom of priests.

Exodus 19:3-6

And **Moses went UP to God,** and the Lord called to him out of the mountain, saying, "Thus you shall say to the house of Jacob, and tell the people of Israel: You have seen what I did to the Egyptians, and how I bore you on eagles' wings and brought you to myself. Now therefore, if you will obey my voice and keep my covenant, you shall be my own possession among all peoples; for the earth is mine, and you shall be to me a kingdom of priests and a holy nation"...

[C] Moses went down to the people and told them what God had promised. The people of Israel responded by saying, "All that the Lord has spoken we will do."

Exodus 19:7,8

So Moses came and called the elders of the people, and set before them all these words which the Lord had commanded him. And all the people answered together and said, "All that the Lord has spoken we will do."

[D] God told Moses that He would speak to the people through a thick cloud.

Exodus 19:9

And the Lord said to Moses, "Lo, I am coming to you in a thick cloud, that the people may hear when I speak with you, and may also believe you for ever"...

[E] God told Moses that "on the third day the Lord will come down upon Mount Sinai in the sight of the people... to set bounds" so that the people would not touch the mountain and die as a result. [Please note that the true Lord God told Moses that the counterfeit lord would come down upon Mount Sinai IN THE SIGHT OF ALL THE PEOPLE. This must have been the counterfeit lord because 1 John 1:18 tells us that "no one has ever seen God." God is a Spirit.]

Exodus 19:10-15

And the Lord said to Moses, "Go to the people and consecrate them today and tomorrow, and let them wash their garments, and be ready by the third day; for on the third day **the Lord will come down upon Mount Sinai in the sight of the people.** And you shall set bounds... whoever touches the mountain shall be put to death... he shall be stoned or shot; whether beast or man, he shall not live..." Be ready by the third day...

[F] On the third day there was thunder, lightning, a thick cloud, and a very loud blast. As a result the people trembled."

Exodus 19:16-19

On the morning of the third day there were thunders and lightnings, and a thick cloud upon the mountain, and a very loud trumpet blast, so that all the people trembled… the whole mountain quaked greatly. And as the sound of the trumpet grew louder and louder, Moses spoke, and God answered him in thunder….”

Because of the "fireworks" at Mount Sinai, the people of Israel became so afraid of God that they later requested of Moses that he alone communicate with God. They were too afraid of God to go near Him:

Exodus 20:18,19

Now when all the people perceived the thundering and the lightning and the sound of the trumpet and the mountain smoking, the people were afraid and trembled; and they stood afar off, and said to Moses, "You speak to us, and we will hear; but **let not God speak to us lest we die.**"

Fear is not caused by God.
Fear is evil.
Fear comes through people:

1 John 4:18

There is **no fear in love,** but perfect love casts out fear.

Isaiah 29:13

…their fear of me is a commandment of men learned by rote… [rote = thoughtless repetition].

Satan was well acquainted with **nature** and knew that something would happen on the **"third day"** that would cause Israel to be afraid -- that would cause the predicted **"long blast"** of the **"trumpet"** -- that would cause a severe earthquake [Ex 19:18,19]. By making the people of Israel believe that he was the real lord God, Satan was successful in making Israel fear God.

Ezekiel 28:11-19

"You were the signet of perfection, full of wisdom and perfect in beauty. You were **in Eden, the garden of God… YOU WERE ON THE HOLY MOUNTAIN OF GOD…**

This verse, above, is speaking about Satan. In a future outline you will receive Bible proof that Satan was in the Garden of Eden with Eve. **There is a strong possibility that this "holy mountain of God" refers to the mountain where Moses received the Ten Commandments from God.** If so, it would account for the fact that the people of Israel became afraid.

A Logical Question:

"Why would Satan have license to deceive Israel so soon after they left Egypt?" Because of their bad attitude toward Moses and toward God:

Exodus 16:2,3

And the **whole congregation** of the people of Israel **murmured** against Moses and Aaron in the wilderness, and said to them, **"Would that we had died by the hand of the Lord in the land of Egypt,**when we sat by the fleshpots and ate bread to the full; for you have brought us out into this wilderness to kill this whole assembly with hunger."

Exodus 17:3,4

…the people murmured against Moses, and said, "Why did you bring us up out of Egypt, to kill us and our children and our cattle with thirst? So Moses cried to the Lord, "What shall I do with this people? They are almost ready to stone me."

Acts 7:41-43

And they made a calf in those days, and **offered a sacrifice to idols…** But **God turned and gave them over to worship the host of heaven**, as it is written in the book of the prophets: "Did you offer to me slain **beasts** and **sacrifices**, forty years in the wilderness, O house of **Israel**? And **you took up the tent of Moloch,** and the **star of the god Rephan**, the **figures which you made to worship…**

Psalm 78:58-64

For they provoked him to anger with their **high places**; they moved him to jealousy with their **graven images**. When God heard, he was full of wrath, and **he utterly rejected Israel. He forsook his dwelling at Shiloh, the tent where he dwelt among men,** and delivered his power to captivity, and glory to the hand of the foe. He gave the people over to the sword, and vented his wrath on his heritage. **Fire devoured their young men…** Their priests fell by the sword.

David, in the above Psalm, clearly states that God [Elohim] **"forsook his dwelling"** in the earthly sanctuary! **WHO DO YOU SUPPOSE TOOK HIS PLACE?!** The following Bible texts from Numbers chapter 11, show that, because of Israel's rebellion, the **counterfeit lord** was allowed to masquerade as an angel of light! Israel and Moses thought they were communicating with a temperamental and unforgiving Lord God. **They were not!** They were dealing with the **counterfeit lord Satan** who did his best to make the true Lord God look bad.

> **FACT:** At times, the **true** Lord left the sanctuary ["tent"] and was replaced by the counterfeit lord!

Numbers 11:1,2

And the **people complained** in the hearing of the Lord about their misfortunes; and then the Lord heard it, his anger was kindled, and the **fire of the Lord burned among them,** and consumed some outlying parts of the camp. Then the people cried to Moses; and Moses prayed to the Lord, and the fire abated.

According to **Psalm 78:58-64** **"fire devoured their young men"** **AFTER** the Lord God had vacated the sanctuary; therefore, we must conclude that the **fire** was **literal, and that it was controlled by the counterfeit lord Satan.** Also note that the counterfeit lord will answer prayers in order to continue his deception. **Both** the **people** of Israel **and** Moses found fault with God:

Numbers 11:4-25

...the people of Israel also **wept** again, and said, **"O that we had meat to eat!** We remember the **fish** we ate in Egypt **for nothing,** the cucumbers, the melons, the leeks, the onions, and the garlic; but now our strength is dried up, and there is nothing at all but this **manna** to look at..." **Moses said** to the Lord, "Why have you dealt ill with your servant?

And why have I not found favor in your sight, that **you did lay the burden of all this people upon me?... If you will deal thus with me, kill me at once...** And the Lord said to Moses, **"Gather me seventy men of the elders of Israel... and bring them to the tent of meeting...** And I will come down and talk with you there; and I will take some of the spirit which is upon you and put it upon them; and they shall bear the burden of the people with you, that you may not bear it alone**... the Lord will give you meat, and you shall eat... until it comes out of your nostrils... because you have rejected the Lord...** So Moses... gathered seventy men of the elders of Israel,

and placed them **around the tent.** Then the Lord came down in the cloud and spoke to him, and took some of the spirit that was upon him and put it upon the seventy elders; and when the spirit had rested upon them, **they prophesied.** **But they did so no more.**

Numbers 11:31-33

And there went forth a **wind** from the Lord, and it brought **quails** from the sea, and let them fall beside the camp... about **two cubits [3 feet]** above the face of the earth. And the people rose all that day, and all night, and all the next day, and gathered the quails. He who gathered least gathered ten omers **[60 bushels];** and they spread them out for themselves all around the camp. While the meat was between their teeth, before it was consummed, the anger of the Lord was kindled against the people, and the Lord smote the people with a very great plague.

Because both Israel and Moses found fault, and blamed God for their problems, the counterfeit lord was allowed to indirectly kill many of them. **No one was forced to eat anything.**

Those who have studied the results of eating large quantities of meat immediately following a very simple diet know the **natural results**! People in modern times have died after doing such a foolish thing – and not because God struck them dead!

As usual, this Bible writer wrote as if God had done something which He merely allowed. And the counterfeit lord Satan did his best to make it look like it was an act of a vengeful God! **Moses** even told the <u>counterfeit lord Satan</u> [thinking that he was talking to the true Lord God] to **"kill me at once"** if you are going to treat me like that!

It was at the sanctuary **["tent of meeting"]** that the counterfeit lord Satan spoke to Moses and the 70 elders. The true Lord God had left the sanctuary because of the rebellion of Israel. Choosing 70 elders to help Moses <u>seemed</u> like a good idea; yet it turned out to be a major problem later on, just as the counterfeit lord knew it would be. **Moses** was to rely upon the **true Lord God** for the extra wisdom and strength he needed. It was the <u>counterfeit</u> lord that told the people, **"you shall eat meat until it comes out of your nostrils."** Our true God of love does <u>not</u> deal with people in that way!

The fact that "they prophesied" [only the one time] does not mean they were controlled by the true Lord God. Jesus Himself warned about counterfeits who would prophesy in His name:

Matthew 7:21

"Not every one who says to me, 'Lord, Lord,' shall enter the kingdom of heaven, but he who does the will of my Father who is in heaven. On that day many will say to me, **'Lord, Lord, did we** **not prophesy in your name, and cast out demons in your name,** and do many mighty works in your name?' And then will I declare to them, 'I never knew you; depart from me, you evildoers."

Is God Really Like That?
Outline No. 22

Counterfeit lord
Part 4

Did Jesus and the apostle John tell the truth?

1 John 4:12

No man has ever seen God.

John 5:17

And the Father who sent me has himself borne witness to me. His voice you have never heard, his form you have never seen.

John 6:46

Not that **any one** has seen the **Father** except him who is from God; he has seen the Father.

John 1:17,18

The law indeed was given through Moses; grace and truth came through Jesus Christ. **No one has ever seen God.** It is **God the only Son,** who is close to the Father's heart, who has made him known.

Exodus 24:9-11

Then **Moses** and **Aaron, Nadab, and Abihu,** and **seventy of the elders** of Israel went up, and **THEY SAW THE GOD OF ISRAEL;** and there was under his feet as it were a pavement of sapphire stone, like the very heaven for clearness. And he did not lay his hand on the chief men of the people of Israel; **THEY BEHELD GOD;** and ate and drank.

Did the apostle John and Jesus tell the truth that **"no man had ever seen God"**? If they did tell the truth [and I believe they did], then the **"God"** that Moses and the 70 elders saw and ate with was the **counterfeit lord Satan!**

Because Israel and Moses rebelled and found fault, the counterfeit lord had the license to **deceive** them!

Remember that the true Lord God had deserted the sanctuary, and that the counterfeit lord Satan had taken over in His place, and, that Moses and the 70 elders did not know the difference! [See Psalm 78:58-64; 21-3b.1].

Did God Command the Murder of Little Babies?

The Bible text which disturbs more Christians than any other, is where **"the Lord"** commanded **King Saul** to murder the **Amalekites** – including every man, woman, infant, and animal! This was done **for revenge,** not for what these Amalekites had done, but what their **parents** had done years before!

1 Samuel 15:1-11

And **Samuel** said to **Saul,** "The Lord sent me to anoint you king over the people of Israel; now therefore hearken to the words of the Lord. Thus says the Lord of hosts, **"I will punish what Amalek did to Israel** in opposing them on the way, when they came out of Egypt." Now **go and smite Amalek, and utterly destroy** all that they have; do not spare them, but **kill** both **man** and **woman, infant** and **suckling,** and sheep, camel and ass.

Christians who understand that a **counterfeit lord** operated during Old Testament times, are not concerned about a **"Lord God"** who **appeared** to have devilish traits! The **genuine Lord God** is love, and He always acts the part of a **"God of love." Always!** [1 John 4:8,16].

1 Samuel 8:7-9

And the **Lord said** to Samuel, **"hearken to the voice of the people** in all that they say to you; for they have not rejected you, but **they have rejected me from being king over them.** According to all the deeds which they have done to me, **from the day I brought them out of Egypt even to this day;** forsaking me and **serving other gods,** so they are also doing to you. Now then, hearken to their voice; only **you shall solemnly warn them,** and show them the ways of the king who shall reign over them."

Because the people of Israel **demanded** a king to rule over them – even though they knew that God did not want them to be ruled by a king – and because of the total rebellion of King Saul, the counterfeit lord Satan had a free hand in deceiving Israel in every way possible.

The command to kill every man, woman, infant, and animal shows that this command did not come from the true Lord God!

FACT: Revenge is not a Godly trait! God does not break His own law which forbids murder!

John 14:7-10

If you had known me, you would have known my Father also; henceforth you know him and have seen him." Philip said to him, "Lord, show us the Father, and we shall be satisfied." **Jesus said** to him, **"Have I been with you so long, and yet you do not know me,** Philip? **He who has seen me has seen the Father...** Believe me that I am in the Father and the Father in me."

Jesus, our perfect example of what the genuine Lord God is like, always taught and practiced the **opposite of revenge.** He repeatedly taught that people should always **return good for evil:**

Matthew 5:38-49

You have heard that it was said, **"An eye for an eye and a tooth for a tooth."** But I say to you, do not resist one who is evil. But if any one strikes you on the right cheek, turn to him the other also... **You have heard that it was said, "You shall love your neighbor and hate your enemy." But I say to you, Love your enemies and pray for those who persecute you, so that you may be sons of your Father who is in heaven;** for he makes his sun rise on the evil and on the good, and sends rain on the just and on the unjust... You, therefore, must be **perfect [Luke 6:36 says "merciful"],** as your heavenly Father is perfect.

The idea that **"God will get you"** if you do wrong is believed by millions of Christians around the world. **"And I hope he does"** is usually insinuated by the tone of voice! Does this philosophy agree with God's thinking? No, it does not.

If the natures of **God** and **Satan** are really that much alike, why should we be so quick to bad-mouth the devil?

Perhaps the devil is not so bad after all!! If God and Satan really *do* think and act alike, why is One so much better than the other?

Please do not jump to negative conclusions about God as have many of our youth. My years of research have made it possible for me to prove by the Bible that:

1 John 4:8,16

"God is love... God is love."

> ## FACT: If God acted like most Christians claim He does, He would not be a God of love; He would be like the devil!

Circumstantial evidence has led most people to the wrong conclusions about God. **Incriminating evidence** planted by the enemy has, in most cases, swayed the jury toward a **"guilty"** verdict when it comes to judging God!

Does God Make Mistakes?

Does God have to learn by trial and error?

Hebrews 8:6,7

Christ has obtained a ministry which is as much **more excellent than the old** as **the covenant he mediates is better,** since it is enacted on **better promises.** For **if that first covenant had been faultless, there would have been no occasion for a second.**

Hebrews 8:6,7, above, **makes it crystal clear that the "first covenant" was faulty!** God did not make a mistake with an "old covenant." Why? Because He was not the one who made it in the first place!!

God does not make mistakes! The deception was allowed because the people of Israel offered animal sacrifices not authorized by God through which it was **"impossible"** to **"take away sins."** God took **"no pleasure"** in these sacrificial offerings [Hebrews 10:4-6, column b].

Hebrews 8:6,7 [above] does not say that God was the author of the first covenant – the one that was **not** faultless; only that **His covenant was better!**

How do we know that it was the counterfeit lord Satan who made the faulty covenant with Israel? Exodus 24:3-11: The covenant was made with the lord with whom Moses and the 70 elders ate and drank. For Bible texts that say no person has ever seen God. **review Outline No. 22-1a.**

Everlasting Covenant
by The true Lord God
Began Before Creation
Lasts Forever

1 Peter 1:19,20

"…a lamb without blemish or spot. He was destined **before the foundation of the world** but was made manifest at the end of the times for your sake."

Revelation 13:8

"…every one whose name has not been written **before the foundation of the world** in the book of life of the Lamb that was slain."

Ephesians 1:4

"…he chose us in him **before the foundation of the world.**"

Old Covenant
by The counterfeit lord Satan's
Began in the Wilderness
Ended At the Cross

Exodus 24:3-11

Moses came and told the people all the words of the Lord and all the ordinances; and all the people answered with one voice, and said, **"All the words which the Lord has spoken we will do."** [5] And he sent young men of the people of Israel, who **offered burnt offerings and sacrificed peace offerings of oxen to the Lord…** And Moses took the **blood** and threw it upon the people, and said, "Behold **the blood of the covenant** which the Lord has made with you in accordance with all these words." Then Moses and Aaron, Nadab, and Abihu, and seventy of the elders of Israel went up, and **they saw the God of Israel...** they beheld God, and ate and drank.

Hebrews 10:4-6

For it is **impossible that the blood of bulls and goats should take away sins.** Consequently, when Christ came into the world, he said, **"Sacrifices and offerings you have <u>not</u> desired,** but a body you have prepared for me; **in burnt offerings and sin offerings you have taken no pleasure."**

Colossians 2:14 – KJV

Blotting out the handwriting of <u>ordinances</u> that **was against us,** and took it out of the way, nailing it to his cross.

New Covenant
The <u>true</u> Lord God's
Began With Adam & Eve
Lasts Forever

Matthew 25:34

Then the King will say to those at his right hand, "Come, O blessed of my Father, inherit the kingdom prepared for you **from the foundation of the world."**

1 Peter 1:19, 20

Quoted in 22-4b

Why Satan was allowed to cause the genuine "God of love" to be feared is a mystery; however, he <u>was</u> allowed to do so.

Hebrews 12:18-24

You have <u>not</u> come to something that can be touched, a blazing fire, and darkness, and gloom, and a tempest, and the sound of a trumpet, and a voice whose words made the hearers beg that not another word be spoken to them. (For they could not endure the order that was given, "If even an animal touches the mountain, it shall be stoned to death." Indeed, so terrifying was the sight that Moses said, "I tremble with fear.") But you have come to Mount Zion and to the city of the living God, the heavenly Jerusalem, and to innumerable angels in festal gathering, and to the assembly of the firstborn who are enrolled in heaven, and to God the judge of all, and... to Jesus, the mediator of a new covenant.

<u>New Testament</u> writers knew more about the true character of God than did Old Testament writers. **Jesus** made this plain by the way He disregarded and/or condemned certain ceremonial laws [See Outline No.1].

Romans 16:25,26

...the preaching of Jesus Christ, according to the revelation of **the mystery which was kept secret for long ages, but is now disclosed** and through the prophetic writings is made known to all nations...

Ephesians 3:4,5

When you read this you can perceive my insight into the **mystery** of Christ, which was **<u>not</u> made known** to the sons of men **in other generations as it has now been revealed to his holy apostles...**

Colossians 1:25,26

...I became a minister... to make the word of God fully known, the **mystery hidden for ages and generations,** but now been revealed to the saints.

Notice in the following Bible texts how the New Testament writer corrected the Old Testament writer.

Numbers 21:5,6

And the people spoke against God and against Moses, "Why have you brought us up out of Egypt to die in the wilderness? For there is no food and no water, and we loathe this worthless food." Then **the Lord** sent fiery serpents among the people, and they bit the people, so that many people of Israel died.

1 Corinthians 10:9,10

We must not put the Lord to the test, as some of them did and were **destroyed by serpents**; nor grumble, as some of them did and were **destroyed by the Destroyer.**

Num. 21:5,6 indicated that it was __God__ who killed people.

1 Cor. 10:9,10 makes it clear that He did __not__:

FACT: God does __not__ lose control of His emotions as do people!

at the end of two months, she returned to **her father, who did with her according to his vow** which he had made. She had never known a man. And it became a custom in Israel that the daughters of Israel went year by year to lament the daughter of Jephthah...

Is God Really Like That?
Outline No. 23

Counterfeit lord
Part 5

Did the true Lord God inspire a human sacrifice?!

Judges 11:29-40

Then the **Spirit of the LORD** came upon Jephthah... ³⁰And **Jephthah made a vow** to the LORD, and said, "If thou wilt give the Ammonites into my hand, then whoever comes forth from the doors of my house to meet me, when I return victorious from the Ammonites, shall be the LORD'S, and **I will offer him up for a burnt offering.**" So Jephthah crossed over to the Ammonites to fight against them; and **the LORD gave them into his hand...** ³⁴Then Jephthah came to his home at Mizpah; and behold, **his daughter came out to meet him** with timbrels and with dances; she was **his only child;** beside her he had neither son nor daughter. And when he saw her, he rent his clothes, and said, "Alas, **my daughter! you have brought me very low, and you have become the cause of great trouble to me;** for I have opened my mouth to the LORD, and **I cannot take back my vow.**"... ³⁹And

at the end of two months, she returned to **her father, who did with her according to his vow** which he had made. She had never known a man. And it became a custom in Israel that the daughters of Israel went year by year to lament the daughter of Jephthah...

Above we have a Bible story that is hard to believe! It illustrates perfectly how the <u>counterfeit</u> <u>lord</u> <u>Satan</u> continued to deceive those who were not truly dedicated to the true Lord God. The <u>true</u> Lord God would <u>never</u>, <u>never</u>, <u>never</u> inspire anyone to offer up a human sacrifice!!

The "Spirit of the Lord" that inspired Jephthah to offer his daughter as a human sacrifice definitely was <u>not</u> the <u>true</u> Lord God! The story **shows how far Israel had fallen away from the true Lord** – being deceived into thinking they were communicating with the true Lord when, in reality, they were being deceived by the counterfeit lord Satan. **Yes, Jephthah actually "did with her according to his vow" [Judges 11:39].**

The **"Spirit of the Lord"** that came upon Jephthah" was actually the <u>counterfeit</u> lord Satan. **The <u>true</u> Lord God never helped someone in battle so that he could offer a human sacrifice in His honor!** During Old

Testament times a **"vow"** was different than a promise. A promise could be broken; a vow could not. **JESUS: "Let what you say be simply 'Yes' or 'No'; anything more than this comes from evil"** [Matt. 5:37].

The sorry fact is that **human sacrifices were not uncommon** in those days. Israel, at that time, was totally under the control of the <u>counterfeit</u> <u>lord</u> <u>Satan</u>. This is why the apostle Paul wrote against **worshiping angels!** [See Colossians 2:18] Satan is a fallen angel. Probably the only reason this story found its way into the Bible is because she was his only child. If Jephthah had had more than one child, this story would never have made the front page!

The Bible makes it plain that Jephthah **did** offer his own daughter as a human sacrifice, thinking that he was pleasing the true Lord God by doing so! In fact, he was so spiritually blind that he could not come to blame <u>himself</u> for his foolish vow, and he didn't dare blame God! So he blamed his daughter – as if it was <u>her</u> fault!

FACT: **The true Lord God <u>never</u> tells anyone to do something contrary to what He has already commanded.**

Even Abraham was deceived, by the <u>counterfeit</u> lord, into offering Isaac as a human sacrifice!

Just suppose that a supernatural being woke **YOU** up in the middle of the night, told you that he was the true Lord God, and told you to kill your son or daughter!! **Would you do it? Why not?** Because God has instructed you, by way of the Bible, <u>not</u> to kill! Besides that, you have learned that violence and force are not God's methods.

If there was one thing that God repeatedly warned Israel against, it was the offering of their children as human sacrifices! **Molech** was a Canaanite god of fire who **demanded the sacrifice of children.**

Leviticus 18:21

You shall not give any of your children to devote them by fire to **Molech,** and so **profane the name of your God;** I am the Lord.

Leviticus 20:1-3

The Lord said to Moses, "Say to the people of Israel, **Any man...** who gives any of his children to **Molech** shall be put to death... I myself will set my face against that man, and will cut him off from among his people, because he has given one of his children to **Molech**, defiling my sanctuary and **profaning my name."**

Acts 7:41-43

And they made a calf in those days, and offered a sacrifice to the idol... But **God** turned and **gave them over to worship the host of heaven,** as it is written in the book of the prophets: "Did you offer to me slain beasts and sacrifices, forty years in the wilderness, O house of Israel? And you took up the tent of **Molech,** and the star of the **god Rephan,** and figures which you made to worship..."

The counterfeit lord Satan took advantage of Abraham's occasional lack of faith, yet Satan was not allowed to defeat him.

Genesis chapters 15 thru 22 gives us an account of Abraham's ups and downs. At times Abraham showed great faith. At other times Abraham showed a complete lack of faith. It was **during the times when Abraham lacked faith in the promises of the true Lord God that Satan was allowed to deceive him:**

Genesis 15:1-6

...the Lord came to **Abram** in a **vision,** "Fear not, Abram, I am your shield; your reward shall be very great." But Abram said, "O Lord God, what will you give me, for **I continue childless...** And he the Lord, **[possibly in the form of a man]** brought him outside and said, "Look toward the heaven, and number the stars... so shall your descendants be." And he believed the Lord; and he reckoned it to him as righteousness.

Some time **after** the above promise was made and accepted by Abraham, Abraham began to wonder exactly **how** God's promise would be fulfilled. **Sarah,** having all the physical signs of being **past the childbearing age** – and wanting to be a good wife, suggested that Abraham have a child by her maid, **Hagar.** At first Sarah experienced the natural human jealousy when Hagar bore Abraham a son; then the jealousy turned into a Satanic jealousy:

Genesis 16:1-16

Now Sarai [later changed to Sarah], Abram's wife, bore him no children. She had an **Egyptian maid** whose name was **Hagar;** and Sarai said to Abram [later changed to Abraham], "Behold now, the Lord has prevented me from bearing children; go in to my maid; it may be **that I shall obtain children by her."** And Abram hearkened to the voice of Sarai... And he went into Hagar, and she conceived; and when she had conceived, she looked with contempt on her mistress. And Sarai said to Abraham, **"May the wrong done to me be on you!** I gave my maid to your entrance, and when she saw that she had conceived, she looked on me with contempt. **May the Lord judge** between you and me!" But Abram said to Sarai, "Behold, your maid is in your power; do to her as you please." Then **Sarai dealt harshly with her,** and she fled from her. The **angel of the Lord** found her by a spring of water in the wilderness... The angel of the

Lord said to her, **"Return to your mistress, and submit to her... I will greatly multiply your descendants that they cannot be numbered for multitude...** you shall bear a son; you shall call his name **Ishmael...** He shall be a wild ass of a man, his hand against every man and every man's hand against him... And Hagar bore Abram a son; and Abram called the name of his son, whom Hagar bore, **Ishmael.** Abram was **86 years old** when Hagar bore Ishmael to Abram.

Isaac, born to Abraham and Sarah 14 years later when Abraham was 100 years old [Genesis 21:5], was God's **perfect will. Ishmael,** born to Abraham and Hagar, was God's **permissive will** [Review Outlines No. 4 and 5]. Having children by a wife's maid was customary in Abraham's day, yet it was **not** God's **perfect will.**

Even though Hagar helped to arouse Sarah's jealousy and anger by her "contempt," **Sarah acted like the devil** when she was harsh enough with Hagar to cause her to flee. **Sarah believed that Ishmael and Hagar would die in the wilderness. Abraham was at fault** for not stopping Sarah from doing it.

There is a question as to **who** promised Hagar a multitude of descendants. It **is possible** that the counterfeit lord Satan could have predicted the obvious hostile results down through the ages. **The conflict between the Arabs and Jews today is the predicted result of Abraham's and Sarah's wrong choices.**

Abraham agreed with his wife, Sarah that the only way God's promise was to be fulfilled was for Abraham to have a son by Sarah's maid, Hagar. **This gave the counterfeit lord Satan the license to deceive.**

Did Abraham's and Sarah's attitude toward God's promise get better as time went on?

Genesis 17:15-19 tells how **"Abraham fell on his face and laughed"** when God's promise was again given that Sarah would bear a son. In Genesis chapters 18 and 19, one or more of Abraham's visitors is referred to as:

> [a] a man
> [b] an angel
> [c] the Lord

Today both holy angels and evil angels appear in the form of men.

Evil angels will, at times, perform miracles that will help people – as a method of deception. Only by comparing their __words__ by what the Bible teaches, can we tell the difference between the holy angels and evil angels.

Hebrews 13:2

Do not neglect to show hospitality to strangers, for thereby **some have entertained angels** unawares.

__Gen 18:1,2,9-15__ tells how **Sarah laughed** when, again, she and Abraham were given God's promise that she would bear a son.

__Genesis 21:8-21__ tells how __both__ Abraham and Sarah **acted like the devil** when dealing with **Ishmael. Sarah was willing to kill Abraham's number one son! Abraham** caved in to Sarah's demand that he **"cast out this slave woman with her son."** This demand was motivated by jealousy and self-centeredness. **Abraham** gave Hagar and her son some bread, a skin of water, and sent them away into the wilderness. **Abraham was being led by the __counterfeit__ lord Satan when he yielded to his wife's Satanic demand. Abraham __should__ have come up with a better solution.** A generous share of the inheritance could have been given to Ishmael when he was older and better able to make it on his own.

Certainly it was the counterfeit lord Satan who told Abraham, "do whatever Sarah says."

How do we __know__ that it was the __counterfeit__ lord Satan who told Abraham to offer his son, Isaac, as a human sacrifice? __Because__:

[1] The true Lord God __never__ commands anyone to do something contrary to what He has commanded in the past.

[2] __Abraham's__ __lack__ __of__ __faith__ in God's promises is obvious.

[3] Abraham was actually willing to kill Sarah's only son!

Genesis 22:1-17

"__God__ __did__ __tempt Abraham__"[KJV]

James 1:13

Let no one say when he is tempted, "I am tempted by God"; for **God** cannot be tempted with evil and he himself **tempts no one.**

Satan saved one of his most far-reaching deceptions for when Abraham was older and weaker – about age 120 [although Abraham did live to be 175]. Approximately 20 years had passed since Abraham had driven Ishmael and Hagar into the wilderness. Bible records of this 20 years are silent. Following this 20-year period Abraham received instruction from **"God"** to sacrifice his son, Isaac, as an animal sacrifice! **After __failing__ this test, there is no record __in__ __the__ __Bible__ of the true Lord ever speaking to Abraham again!**

Abraham was fully aware of God's laws against human sacrifices! Because the true Lord God had not yet clearly and openly exposed the counterfeit lord Satan, **the counterfeit lord** was allowed to **"tempt"** Abraham. The only way the true Lord tempted or "tested" [RSV] Abraham was to allow the counterfeit lord Satan to confuse and deceive him.

"Take... your only son, Isaac."

Isaac was not his only son. He also had Ishmael.

"Offer him there as a burnt offering."

The true Lord God never tells anyone to do something contrary to what He has commanded. Our **"God of love"** would never command anyone to kill his son by driving a knife through his heart, for **any** reason, let alone for a "test."

"God will provide himself a lamb."

Abraham lied to Isaac. Abraham actually believed that Isaac would be the offering. Perhaps Abraham figured that Isaac would run away if he had time to think about it! As a boy, possibly around 17 years old, what would you have done?

"The angel of the Lord called to him."

It is interesting to note that **"God"** told Abraham to kill his son, and that an **"angel of the Lord"** stopped him from doing so! **God sent an angel to stop Abraham from carrying out the command of the counterfeit lord Satan.**

"Now I know that you fear God."

This kept the counterfeit lord Satan from being exposed before his time. God already knew Abraham's heart. "God searches the hearts of men" [Rom 8:27; 1 Sam 16:7]. God was able to read **Job's mind,** knowing that he would not yield to Satan [Job chapters 1 and 2]. **The only way Abraham could have passed the test was to refuse to sacrifice his son!** Abraham should have said, "I cannot do it; it is contrary to Your law! **God gave laws before He gave the 10 commandments on Mt. Sinai in Exodus chapter 20.**

Exodus 17:28

The Lord said to Moses, "How long do you refuse to keep my commandments and my laws?"

"Behind him was a ram."

A ram was provided for the burnt offering because such was part of God's **permissive will** [See Outline No. 5]. Abraham believed that offering animal sacrifices was God's desire, and God chose not to tell him otherwise.

Hebrews 11:8-10

By faith Abraham obeyed when he was called to go out to a place which he was to receive as an inheritance; and he went out, not knowing where he was to go. By faith he sojourned in the land of promise, as in a foreign land, living in tents…

Note in the above verses that even though Abraham is credited with great faith when he moved to a foreign land, **it does not credit him with great faith when he tried to sacrifice Isaac as a human sacrifice!**

Abraham failed the test when he believed the true Lord God would command him to do something that He had forbidden him to do in the past. **God never contradicts Himself by telling us to do something contrary to one of His laws.**

No Scripture says so, yet I believe Satan was taken completely by surprise when Jesus died on the cross. **Satan expected the true Lord God to step in and stop the human sacrifice of Jesus just as He had done with Isaac.** Satan never planned on a death, resurrection, and his own eternal defeat.

Satan was defeated at the cross. Satan expected God to rescue Jesus from the cross, after which Jesus would set up an earthly kingdom as predicted in Zechariah chapter 14 – which would have been fulfilled **if** the Jewish nation had accepted Jesus as the Messiah He claimed to be.

Is God Really Like That?
Outline No. 24

Counterfeit lord
Part 6

The study and evaluation of **different vocabularies and writing styles by different authors** of the Bible, has helped us to understand that there were three or four main authors of the historical Old Testament books which were, at a later date, integrated or merged together into the one Old Testament we have today.

For example, any Bible student can recognize two different accounts of both the flood story and the creation story – something like how the four Gospels were written. All four Gospel authors were inspired by God to write the account of what happened during the time of Jesus – what Jesus said and did. Nevertheless, there are minor differences in the narrative. This does not mean that one Gospel was inspired more than another because of the minor differences that do exist.

Because of our long held traditions, the idea that there are two different Genesis stories is difficult to believe. **It is only natural to have serious doubts** concerning new ideas on subjects we have always accepted as

Truth. **Before you accept or reject these new ideas**, realize that certain facts are not the same as we have always believed:

[a] – Genesis 1 & 2 were <u>not</u> written by the same Bible writer.

[b] – God is referred to by different names in Genesis 1 & 2.

[c] – The order of events are different in Genesis 1 & 2.

[d] – In Gen. 1 God made man and woman at the same time.

[e] – In Gen. 1 God told them they could eat of <u>ANY</u> tree.

[f] – In Gen. 2 God is quoted as saying that, if man would eat the fruit of the tree of knowledge, he would die the very same day. This prediction did not come true.

There is no doubt whatsoever that the **unfair put down of women,** and the infamous **double standard,** began before Adam and Eve left the Garden of Eden. The **true Lord** God allowed, but was **not the cause of** the terrible treatment that women have suffered throughout the ages.

There is no question that we have two different accounts of the creation story. <u>Genesis 1:1 thru</u>

2:3 is the <u>first</u> account. **Genesis 2:4b thru 2:25** is a <u>second</u> account. Because these two accounts of the creation story are quite different, **it is important that we analyze the contents of these two accounts carefully to see if we can detect the presence of the counterfeit lord Satan in either of the two.** After all, **<u>Ezekiel 28:11-19, Revelation 12:9, & John 8:44</u> make** it crystal clear that **<u>Satan</u>** and his angel followers left heaven, ended up **<u>in the Garden of Eden,</u>** and that Satan was **a "<u>liar and murderer from the beginning.</u>"**

Even though it was the counterfeit lord who told Adam that it was wrong to eat of the tree, Adam <u>believed</u> it was the true Lord God. It was counted as sin because Adam <u>believed</u> the command was from the <u>true</u> Lord God [See James 4:17].

How are Chapters 1 & 2 different?

Genesis 1:1 thru 2:4

"In the beginning God **[Elohim]** created the heavens and the earth."

Day <u>one</u>: God **[Elohim]** made light and darkness; day and night.

Day <u>two</u>: God made the firmament [sky] and divided the waters above from the waters below.

Day <u>three</u>: God made the dry land and the seas; plants yielding seed, and fruit trees.

Day <u>four</u>: God made the sun, moon, and stars.

Day <u>five</u>: God made the fish, sea monsters, and everything that lives in the water, and **<u>birds</u>**.

Day <u>six</u>: God made **<u>man</u>, <u>woman</u>,** beasts, cattle, and what-ever creeps on the ground:

Genesis 1:26-31

Then God **[Elohim]** said, "Let us make man in our image, after our likeness... So God created man in his own image, in the image of God he created **<u>him</u>; <u>male</u>** and **<u>female</u>** he created **<u>them</u>...** **(29)** And God said, "Behold, I have given you every plant yielding seed which is **upon the face of all the earth, and <u>every</u> <u>tree</u>** with seed in its fruit; **you shall have them for food.**" And God blessed them, and God said to them, **"Be fruitful and multiply, and fill the earth..."** And God saw **EVERYTHING** that he had made, and behold, it was **<u>VERY</u> <u>GOOD</u>.** And there was evening and there was morning. A **sixth day.**

Now notice the difference in chapter 2

Genesis 2:4-6

In the day that the Lord God made the earth and the heavens, when **no plant** of the field was yet in the earth... for the Lord God had not caused it to rain... there was **no man** to till the ground; but a **mist went up from the earth and watered the whole face of the ground.**

Genesis 2:7

Then the Lord God [Yahweh] formed man of dust from the ground, and breathed into his nostrils the breath of life; and man became a living being.

Genesis 2:8,9

And the Lord God **[Yahweh] planted a garden in Eden,** and **there he put man** whom he had formed. And out of the ground the Lord God made to grow **every tree** that is pleasant to the sight and good for food, the **tree of life** also in the midst of the garden, and the **tree of knowledge of good and evil.**

Genesis 2:15-17

The Lord God **[Yahweh]** took the **man** and **put him in the garden of Eden** to till it and keep it. And the Lord God commanded the man, saying, "You may freely eat of every tree of the garden; but of the tree of the knowledge of good and evil you shall not eat, for **in the day that you eat of it you shall die.**"

Genesis 2:18

Then the Lord God **[Yahweh] said, "It is not good that the man should be alone;** I will make him a helper fit for him." So out of the ground the Lord God formed every **beast** of the field and every **bird** of the air, and brought them to the man to see what he would call them...

Genesis 2:21,22

So the Lord God **[Yahweh]** caused a **deep sleep** to fall upon the **man,** and **while he slept took one of his ribs** and closed up its place with flesh; and the **rib** which the Lord God had taken from the man he **made into a woman** and brought her to the man.

Genesis 1:1 to 2:3 describes a **different order** than found in **Genesis 2:4-22.** Because these chapters disagree, both of them cannot be 100% right!

Genesis 1:1 to 2:4

[1] – **Day 3** God created plants and fruit trees.

[2] – **Day 5** God [Elohim] created birds.

[3] -- **Day 6** God [Elohim] created beasts. God created both male and female. God gave them every plant and every tree to eat.

Genesis 2:4-22

[1] – A mist watered the ground.

[2] – **Man** was made from the dust.

[3] – God [Yahweh] planted a garden in Eden.

[4] – God [Yahweh] put the <u>man</u> in the garden.

[5] – God told them they could eat of every tree <u>except</u> the tree of knowledge of good and evil.

[6] – The "Lord God" told <u>Adam</u> he would die the <u>same</u> <u>day</u> if he ate the forbidden fruit.

[7] – God created the beasts and <u>birds</u>.

[8] – God made Eve out of one of Adam's ribs.

[9] – God presented the woman to Adam.

Review of the Differences:

[A] – In <u>Genesis 1</u> God [Elohim or El] created the fruit trees on the 3rd day, and created man and woman on the 6th day. <u>Gen. 2</u>: Yahweh made the garden of Eden, and fruit trees, <u>after</u> God created man.

[B] – In <u>Gen. 1</u> God created the <u>birds</u> on the 5th day. In <u>Gen. 2</u>, on the 6th day.

[C] – In <u>Gen. 1</u> God created <u>both</u> man and woman on the 6th day. In <u>Gen</u> <u>2</u> God created only man before He planted the Garden of Eden.

[D] – In <u>Gen. 1</u> God gave Adam and Eve permission to eat of <u>every</u> tree, including the fruit trees. In <u>Gen</u>. <u>2</u> <u>Adam</u> was forbidden to eat of the tree of knowledge.

[E] – In <u>Gen. 1</u> God created <u>both</u> man & woman at the <u>same</u> time. In <u>Gen</u>. <u>2</u> God created Eve as an after thought; from a rib of Adam.

[F] – <u>Gen. 2</u> quotes the "Lord God" as saying that <u>Adam</u> would die if he <u>ate</u> the forbidden fruit: "In the <u>day</u> that you <u>eat</u> of it you shall die." But in <u>Gen. 3</u> we read a different story:

Genesis 3:1-7

Now the **serpent** was more subtle [cunning, crafty, skillful] than any other wild creature that the Lord God had made. He said to the woman, **"Did God say, 'You shall not eat of any tree of the garden'?"** And the woman said to the serpent, "We may eat of the fruit of the trees of the garden; but God said, 'You shall not eat of the fruit of the tree which is in the midst of the garden, neither shall you <u>touch</u> it, **lest you die.'"** But the serpent said to the woman, **"<u>You</u> <u>will</u> <u>not</u> <u>die</u>...** So when the **woman saw that the tree was good for food,** and that it was to be **desired to make one wise,** she took of its fruit and ate; and she also gave some to her husband, and he ate.

Because it is obvious that two different Bible writers gave two different accounts of the story of creation, **each one using a different name for God,** it will not break any rules for us to consider the possibility that we are dealing with some of the deception of the counterfeit lord.

First of all, we know that the true Lord God does not threaten His children in this manner. Would YOU say to YOUR children, "You have a choice. You can either obey me or not, but if you disobey me, I will kill you!" "No." Do you think that you are more loving, more reasonable, or more like a "God of love" than our heavenly Father?

Secondly, we know that God does not lie! The threat of Genesis 2:17 was a lie! Neither Adam nor Eve died the day they ate the fruit!

Genesis 2:16

And the Lord God commanded the **man,** saying, "You may freely eat of every tree of the garden; but of the tree of the knowledge of good and evil you shall not eat, for **in the day that you eat of it you shall die."**

The use of the Hebrew *mot tamut* repeats the word **"die"** so that there is no mistaking the message of the author. **Adam and Eve did not die that "day." If the true Lord God had really said it, Adam and Eve**

would have died the same day! Do you really think that our 'God of love' told his children, "You have complete freedom of choice, but if you disobey Me, even once, I will strike you dead"!!**

Thirdly, how did the counterfeit lord know what the Lord had told them? Because it was he himself, the counterfeit lord Satan, who was allowed to deceive Eve. And, if it had been the true Lord God who threatened them in the first place, Satan would have known that God does not lie! Satan knew they would not die that day because he was the "god" who threatened Adam in the first place! There was nothing wrong with the fruit! The true Lord God tempts no one to disobey Him [James 2:13].

Also, it is **probable** that the counterfeit lord Satan was the one who pronounced all the **curses** upon Eve, Adam, and even upon himself! **This was the beginning of the terrible role to which women have been subjected since the beginning!** The Genesis 2 version that Eve was made out of one of Adam's ribs makes it seem like woman is inferior to man. Men and women are **equal;** but playing **different roles** in life. **Millions today, especially the youth, are "turned off" to God because they have been misinformed about what He is really like.**

Alan M. Dershowitz, Professor of law at Harvard University, in his interesting book, The Genesis of Justice, indicates that God Himself had to learn by trial and error!

Attorney Dershowitz has a brilliant, logical mind that comes to the correct conclusions PROVIDED the Bible writers wrote only what God actually did do! Dershowitz, being educated in orthodox Hebrew parochial schools, knows what the Hebrew text says. He actually believes that God inspired every word Bible writers wrote. Christians who actually believe that God personally dictated every word of the Bible, can see logic in Dershowitz's following conclusions:

> **"The nature of God's punishments raises profound questions – for Christians, Jews, and Muslims alike – about His concept of justice.** He punishes Eve by inflicting the pain of childbirth on *all* women and by making *all* women submissive to men. He punishes Adam by requiring *all* men to toil for their bread... **punishment should be limited to the specific person or persons who violated the law, not to innocent descendants...** punishment should be proportional to the harm caused. **God,** of course, constantly violates these rules throughout the Bible – **He kills without warning, punishes innocent children for the sins of their parents, and imposes disproportionate punishments...** Moreover, **the nature of the punishment God inflicted on all women raises the most profound issues of fairness.** God directly commanded Adam, not Eve, to refrain from eating of the Tree of Knowledge. Yet it was **Eve, and all future Eves,** who were **punished most severely,** not only in absolute terms, but also relative to Adam and future Adams: 'Toward your husband will be your lust, yet he will rule over you.' Here we have the origin of the infamous **double standard** regarding sex... it is neither logical nor moral that husbands should rule over wives... Until the twentieth century, women were legally subordinate to men in nearly all countries." [The Genesis of Justice, pp 32-36]

Adam sinned because he believed the lie of Genesis 2 rather than what God told him and Eve as recorded in Genesis 1 – the lie being that it was wrong to eat of the Tree of Knowledge.

God told Adam they could eat of ANY tree.

But doesn't the Bible say that "ALL SCRIPTURE" is inspired by God?

It depends on which translation you read. In most translations it reads as follows:

> **2 Timothy 3:16 [RSV]**
> "All scripture *is* inspired by God and ..." [Margin: "Or, every scripture inspired by God is..."]

In the original Greek, "**is**" is not included. The "**is**" was **added** by the Bible translators. In other words, Bible translators thought the word should be added to make the text say what **they** thought it should say. **Some translations have it as it was in the original Greek:**

2 Tim. 3:16

Revised Version
"Every scripture
inspired of God
is profitable for teaching,
for reproof..."

American Standard Version

"Every scripture
inspired of God
is also profitable..."

New English Bible

"Every inspired scripture
has its use for teaching
the truth and refuting
error..."

Because we are considering the possibility of the counterfeit lord Satan having his influence in the book of Genesis, **and because we assumed that fire came down from heaven** to burn up the animal sacrifices, we ask, **"Did the genuine Lord God tell Cain and Abel to offer animals on the altar, or was it the counterfeit lord?"**

In Outline No. 5 we studied the many Bible texts which made it clear that it was **not** the genuine Lord God who told them to sacrifice animals!

Isaiah 66:3,4

"He who slaughters an ox is like him who kills a man; he who **sacrifices a lamb,** like him who breaks a dog's neck... These have chosen their own ways, and their soul delights in **their abomination... they did what was evil in my eyes, and chose that in which I did not delight."**

It is interesting to note that **Cain did not lose his life** because he killed Abel. He was allowed to travel to a place where he actually built up a city!

No doubt it was the counterfeit lord Satan who brought fire down from heaven [See Job 1:16] to burn up Abel's animal sacrifice – a sacrifice which did not originate as one of the true Lord God's commands. Cain was not only angry enough to kill Abel [possibly as an accident], but he was also very confused. **Actually Cain's offering was more in harmony with what was right than was Abel's.** [See Outline No. 5]

Review

The lie of Satan that God kills started in Eden when Satan said, in effect, "God says you will die in the very same day you eat the fruit."

Is God Really Like That?
Outline No. 25

15 Bible Proofs that a counterfeit "god" deceived people in Old Testament times

Reason No. 1
Simple logic:

2 Cor. 11:13,14

For such men are false apostles, deceitful workers, disguising themselves as apostles of Christ. And no wonder, for **even Satan disguises himself as an angel of light**.

2 Corinthians 4:3,4

In their case **the god of this world** has **blinded the minds** of the unbelievers, to keep them from seeing the light of the gospel...

We know for sure that Satan and his angel followers work in these New Testament times to deceive people. Why, then, would they not have attempted to deceive mankind in Old Testament times?! **They did, with much success.**

Reason No. 2
Satan was a liar and a murderer from the beginning:

John 8:44

Jesus speaking
You are of your father the devil …He was a murderer from the beginning… he is a liar and the father of lies.

Revelation 12:7-9

Now war arose in heaven, Michael and his angels fighting against the **dragon…** And the great dragon was thrown down, that ancient **serpent,** who is called the **Devil** and **Satan,** the **deceiver** **of** **the** **whole** **world** – he was **thrown down to the earth,** and his angels were thrown down with him.

Reason No. 3
Satan was in the Garden of Eden:

Ezekiel 28:13-15

You were in Eden, the garden of God… You were blameless in your ways from the day you were created, till iniquity was found in you.

To review what deceptions Satan used in the Garden of Eden, see Outline No. 24. Remember that God did **not** have to learn by trial and error.

> **Remember the rule:**
> **Always compare**
> **everything written**
> **in the O.T.**
> **with what Jesus**
> **did and said**
> **in the New Testament.**

Reason No. 4
The terms "lord" and "Satan" are used interchangeably:

2 Samuel 24:1,2

Again the anger of **the Lord** was kindled against Israel and he incited **David** against them, saying, "Go, **number Israel** and Judah." So the king said to **Joab**... "Go through all the tribes of Israel from **Dan to Beersheba**..."

I Chronicles 21:1,2

Satan stood up against Israel, and incited **David** to **number Israel**. So David said to **Joab**... "Go, number Israel from **Beersheba to Dan**..."

---

2 Samuel 24:1,2 states that it was **"the Lord"** who incited King David to number Israel. 1 Chronicles 21:1,2 says that it was **"Satan"** who incited King David to number Israel. **Both Bible texts refer to Satan.** God would not incite King David to do what David felt was against His commands.

Reason No. 5
Some Old Testament laws were not from God.

Exodus 21:23-25

If any harm follows, then you shall give life for life, eye for eye, tooth for tooth, hand for hand, foot for foot, burn for burn...

Leviticus 24:19,20

Anyone who maims another shall suffer the same injury in return; fracture for fracture...

Yet, in the New Testament Jesus said:

Matthew 5:38, 43-45, 48

"You have heard that it was said, 'An eye for an eye and a tooth for a tooth.' But I say to you... if any one strikes you on the right cheek, turn to him the other also... "You have heard that it was said, 'You shall love your neighbor and hate your enemy.' But I say to you, Love your enemies and pray for those who persecute you, so that you may be children of your Father in heaven; for he makes his sun rise on the evil and on the good, and sends rain on the righteous and on the unrighteous. Be perfect, as your heavenly Father is perfect."

Note, above, how diplomatic Jesus was when He referred to this Old Testament "eye for an eye" get even law: "You have heard that it was said… but I SAY to you, "Love your enemies." WHY? "So that you may be children of your Father in heaven." When Jesus said, "But I SAY," He was claiming to have greater authority than the source of this particular Old Testament "eye for an eye" law! These words of Jesus in Matthew 5:38-48 [Above] show that some of the O.T. laws did not originate with God. The 'eye for an eye" law came either directly or indirectly from the counterfeit lord, Satan.

Counterfeit OT law:
A sin for a woman to have her menstrual period:

Leviticus 15:19,29,30

When a woman has a discharge of blood which is her regular discharge from her body, she shall be in her impurity for seven days… And on the eighth day she shall take two turtledoves or two young pigeons, and bring them to the priest, to the door of the tent of meeting. And the priest shall offer one for a sin offering and the other for a burnt offering; and the priest shall make atonement for her unclean discharge.

THINK!

Was it the true Lord God, or was it the counterfeit lord Satan, who indicated that it was sinful for a woman to have her menstrual period, so that she must go to the priest and offer a sin offering?!

Only the counterfeit lord Satan would put down women, and attempt to degrade them, by making such a law. More of how the devil himself caused women to become second class citizens is covered in Outline No. 24.

Counterfeit OT law:

Exodus 21:1-6

When you buy a Hebrew slave, he shall serve six years, and in the 7th he shall go free, for nothing… If his master gives him a wife and she bears him sons and daughters, the wife and her children shall be her master's and he shall go out alone. But if the slave plainly says, "I love my master, my wife, and my children; I shall not go out free," then his master shall bring him to the door or the doorpost; and his master shall bore his ear through with an awl; and he shall serve him for life.

THINK!

Would a "God of love" inspire a law that forced a man to choose between a life of slavery or his wife and children? No, of course not! Jesus made it plain that some of the Old Testament laws were not from the true Lord God.   [Review Reason No. 5]

Reason No. 6
At times, Israel worshiped the counterfeit lord:

Deuteronomy 32:17,18

They sacrificed to demons...
you forgot the God who gave you birth.

Galatians 4:8-11

Formerly, when you did not know God, you were in bondage to beings that by nature are no gods; but now that you have come to know God, or rather to be known by God, how can you turn back again to the beggarly elemental spirits, whose slaves you want to be once more? You observe days, and months, and seasons, and years! I am afraid I have labored over you in vain.

Reason No. 7
The true Lord never sanctioned a human sacrifice:

Judges 11:29-40

Then the **Spirit of the LORD** came upon Jephthah... [30]And **Jephthah made a vow** to the LORD, and said, "If thou wilt give the Ammonites into my hand, then whoever comes forth from the doors of my house to meet me, when I return victorious from the Ammonites, shall be the LORD'S, and **I will offer him up for a burnt offering."**

The true Lord God would never, never, never inspire anyone to offer up a human sacrifice!! The "Spirit of the Lord" that came upon Jephthah" was actually the counterfeit lord Satan. **The true Lord God never helped someone in battle so that he could offer a human sacrifice in His honor!** [Review Outline 23-1]

Reason No. 8
It was the counterfeit lord who took advantage of Abraham's lack of faith to make him believe God wanted him to sacrifice Isaac.

It was not the true Lord God who tempted/tested Abraham [Gen 22:1-17]:

James 1:13

Let no one say when he is tempted, "I am tempted by God"; for **God** cannot be tempted with evil and he himself **tempts no one.**

It was the counterfeit lord who deceived Abraham into thinking that the true Lord wanted him to sacrifice Isaac.

The true Lord God never tells anyone to do something contrary to what He has commanded. [Review Outline No. 23-2]

Reason No. 9
The true Lord God did not try to kill Moses and fail:

Exodus 4:21-26

At a lodging place on the way [to Egypt] **the Lord** [counterfeit] **met him** [Moses] **and sought to kill him.**

The <u>true</u> Lord God would only have to speak in order to get rid of Moses:

Psalm 33:6,9

By the **word** of the Lord the heavens were made... For he **spoke,** and it came to be...

Reason No. 10
The book of Job proves Satan operated in the earth during Old Testament times:

Job 1:6,7

"Now there was a day when the <u>sons</u> <u>of</u> <u>God</u> came to present themselves before the Lord, and Satan also came among them. The Lord said to Satan, 'From where have you come?' Satan answered the Lord, 'From going to and fro on the earth, and from walking up and down on it."

Adam should have been the one attending this meeting in heaven as the representative of the earth. The true Lord God challenged Satan: "Have you considered my servant Job?"

Reason No. 11
The fire that fell from heaven came from Satan, not God:

Job 1:12,16

And the Lord said to Satan, "Behold, all that he [Job] has is in y<u>our</u> power... The fire of God fell from heaven, and burned up the sheep and the servants...

2 Kings 1:9-12

"...But **Elijah** answered the captain of **fifty, '**If I am a man of God, let fire come down from heaven and consume you and your **fifty.'** Then **fire came down from heaven, and consumed him and his fifty...** Again the king sent to him another captain of **fifty** men with his **fifty...** Then the **fire of God came down from heaven and consumed him and his fifty."**

Luke 9:52-55 NKJV

They entered into a village of the Samaritains, to prepare for Him. But they did not receive Him... And when His disciples James and John saw this, they said, **"Lord do you want us to command fire to come down from heaven and consume them, just as Elijah did?** But **He** [Jesus] turned and **rebuked them,** and said, **"You do not know what manner of spirit you are of.**

In the preceding Bible text, Jesus said, in effect, "By asking Me to bring fire down from heaven like Elijah, you are talking like the devil!"

Reason No. 12
The Old Covenant came from the counterfeit lord:

Hebrews 8:6,7

Christ has obtained a ministry which is as much **more excellent than the old** as **the covenant he mediates is better,** since it is enacted on **better promises.** For **if that first covenant had been faultless, there would have been no occasion for a second.**

Hebrews 8:6,7 makes it crystal clear that the "first covenant" was faulty! God does not make mistakes! The deception was allowed because the people of Israel offered animal sacrifices not authorized by God, through which it was **"impossible"** to **"take away sins"** [Hebrews 10:4-6; 22-4b.1] **This old covenant was made with the lord with whom Moses and the 70 elders ate and drank.**

Reason No. 13
Moses and the 70 elders ate and drank with the counterfeit lord Satan:

Exodus 24:9-11

Then **Moses** and **Aaron**, **Nadab**, and **Abihu**, and **seventy of the elders** of Israel went up, and **THEY SAW THE GOD OF ISRAEL**;

and there was under his feet as it were a pavement of sapphire stone, like the very heaven for clearness. And he did not lay his hand on the chief men of the people of Israel; **THEY BEHELD GOD**; and ate and drank.

In the New Testament the apostle John wrote that no one had ever seen God:

1 John 4:12

No man has ever seen God.

John 5:17

And the **Father** who sent me has himself borne witness to me. **His voice you have never heard, his form you have never seen.**

John 6:46

Not that **any one** has seen the **Father** except him who is from God; he has seen the Father.

John 1:17,18

The law indeed was given through Moses; grace and truth came through Jesus Christ. **No one has ever seen God.**

Reason No. 14
The true Lord God referred to the counterfeit lord as lord:

Exodus 19:20-25

And the Lord came down upon Mount Sinai, to the TOP of the mountain; and the Lord called Moses to the TOP of the mountain, and Moses went UP. And the Lord said to Moses, "Go DOWN and warn the people, lest they break through to the Lord to gaze and many of them perish. And also let the priests who come near to the Lord consecrate themselves, lest the Lord break out upon them... do not let the priests and the people break through to come up to the Lord, lest HE break out against them."

In the preceding Bible text God called Moses **UP** to the **TOP** of the mountain to warn him about the counterfeit lord Satan at the **BOTTOM** of the mountain.

The original Bible manuscripts included no punctuation or capitals; therefore, whether or not "lord" was to be capitalized was the option of the translator. Also, any paraphrased translation [such as "The Living Bible"] that changes the original third person to the first person, is not an accurate translation of the original Hebrew manuscript.

Reason No. 15
At times the true Lord God was replaced in the sanctuary [tent] by the counterfeit lord:

Psalm 78:58-64

For they provoked him to anger with their **high places;** they moved him to jealousy with their **graven images.** When God heard, he was full of wrath, and **he utterly rejected Israel... He forsook his dwelling at Shiloh, the tent where he dwelt among men,** and **delivered his power**

to captivity and **glory** to the hand of the foe.... **Fire devoured their young men...** Their priests fell by the sword.

Whenever Israel rebelled against God or His laws, the counterfeit lord had the right to deceive and destroy – like the fire that devoured their young men.

If we, today, knowingly and willingly rebel against God's laws, Satan is given permission to deceive us, in the same way he was allowed to deceive people in Bible times.

HOW THE BIBLE WAS WRITTEN

Why did God allow Bible writers to write as if He had actually done things which He had merely allowed? Why were not all of the facts revealed to each Bible writer from the beginning?

Please keep in mind that <u>God</u> <u>is</u> <u>on</u> <u>trial</u>! **Remember that** the great controversy is between Michael **[Jesus]** and Satan **[Lucifer]**. **[Review Outline No. 2]**

Revelation 12:7-9

Now **war** arose in heaven, **Michael and his angels** fighting against the **dragon;** and **the dragon and his angels fought,** but they were defeated and there was no longer any place for them in heaven. And the great **dragon** was thrown down, that ancient **serpent,** who is called the **Devil** and **Satan,** the deceiver of the whole world – he was thrown down to the earth, and his angels were thrown down with him.

The great controversy is between Jesus and Satan. Both have their angel followers – millions of them! And who is it that is coming from heaven to raise the dead? **None other than Jesus:**

Daniel 12:1,2

At that time shall arise **Michael,** the great prince who **has charge of your people.** And there shall be a time of trouble, such as never has been… but at that time your people will be delivered, everyone whose name shall be found written in the book. And many of **those who sleep in the dust of the earth shall awake,** some to everlasting life, and some to shame and everlasting contempt.

Lucifer [Satan] accused **Michael** [Jesus] of being unfair. **Satan was defeated at the cross.** Yet Satan still tries to convince the millions of angels, people, and the inhabitants of unfallen worlds, that he is being treated unjustly.

Revelation 12:10-12

And I heard a loud voice in heaven, saying, "Now the salvation and the power and the kingdom of our God and the authority of his Christ have come, for **the accuser of our brethren** has been thrown down, who **accuses them day and night before our God.** And they have **conquered him by the blood of the Lamb** and by the word of their testimony, for they loved not their lives unto death. Rejoice then, **O** <u>heaven</u> **and** <u>you</u> <u>that</u> <u>dwell</u> <u>therein</u>! But woe to you, O earth and sea, for **the devil** has come down to you in great wrath because he **knows that his time is short!**

In order for the inhabitants of the whole universe to be convinced that God's ways are right – that doing and thinking His way is the only way to permanent happiness, the **rules of spiritual warfare must be the same** for both the forces of evil and the forces of good; otherwise the inhabitants of the universe would consider it not a fair fight. What is right and fair for the forces of good has to be right and fair for the forces of evil. What one side is allowed to do, so is the other.

For example, **both holy angels and evil angels can and do appear as men**. **Both God and the devil have and do appear in the form of men**. **In** Genesis 18 both angels <u>and</u> the Lord appeared in the form of men:

Genesis 18:1,2,22

And the **Lord** appeared to him by the oaks of Mamre, as he sat at the door of his tent in the heat of the day. He lifted up his eyes and looked, and behold, **three <u>men</u>** stood in front of him... **The <u>Lord</u> said...** So the <u>men</u> turned from there, and went toward Sodom; but **Abraham still stood before the <u>Lord</u>**.

Hebrews 13:2

Do not neglect to show hospitality to strangers, for thereby some have **entertained angels unawares.**

Psalm 34:7

The **angel of the Lord** encamps around those who fear him, and **delivers** them.

Because holy angels have the right to appear as men, so do evil angels. Evil angels can and do act in the same way as holy angels – in order to deceive those who do not study the Bible for themselves.

Matthew 7:21-23

Not every one who says to me, "Lord, Lord," shall enter the kingdom of heaven, but he who does the will of my Father who is in heaven. On that day many will say to me, "Lord, Lord, did we not **prophesy** in your name, and **cast out demons** in your name, and do **many mighty works** in your name? And then will I declare to them, "I never knew you; depart from me, you evil doers."

John 16:2,3

"The hour is coming when **whoever kills you will think he is offering service to God.** And they will do this because they have not known the Father nor me."

2 Corinthians 11:13-15

For such men are false apostles, deceitful workmen, disguising themselves as apostles of Christ. And no wonder, for **even Satan himself disguises himself as an angel of light.** So it is not strange if his servants also disguise themselves as servants of righteousness.

John 8:44 [Jesus]

You are of your father **the devil...** He was a **murderer** from the beginning, and **has nothing to do with the truth,** because there is **no truth in him.** When he **lies,** he speaks according to his own nature, for **ho is a liar and the father of lies.**

The **method which God has chosen** to vindicate Himself and His ways, is to **allow Satan to hang himself. Satan is not allowed to force anyone to sin; therefore, God can not use force – unless it is force to prevent evil men and evil angels from hurting those who have yielded themselves to Him.** In the end, the lies of Satan will be revealed. **Jesus,** when He came to earth, **demonstrated what God is like!** The best way to know what God is really like [how He thinks and how He acts] is to **study the life and teachings of Jesus. Jesus is our visual aid!**

Heaven will not force you or anyone else to believe. Those who study the Bible for themselves, asking Jesus to reveal the Truth to them as individuals, will be able to see through the deceptions of Satan. When they observe **miracles** – when they **listen to various preachers** – because they know, by way of Holy Scripture, what is right and what is counterfeit, **they will instinctively know the source of miracles, and the source of what they hear preached.**

The story of **Santa Claus** is a **myth.** Some children are disappointed and some are shocked when they learn that Santa Claus does not really bring them toys which he has made at the North Pole! **So it is with Christian children** when they learn that certain traditions they have been taught are nothing more than **myths!** – like the idea that God gives us freedom of choice, but if we do not choose His way he will kill us, then give us new life, and torment us in "hell fire" forever!!

Because both the forces of evil and the forces of good must abide by the same rules of spiritual warfare, God does not force truth upon anyone, and neither is the devil allowed to force his deceptions upon anyone.

For this reason God did not force Bible writers into believing that all good and all evil did **not** come from Him. **God allowed people to detect Satan's lies on their own.**

> **FACT: It was not until Jesus came to this earth to live in the form of a man, that He openly exposed Satan.**

The New Testament Gospels were written by four different men. Each Gospel writer described the events of the life and teachings of Jesus; however, the details vary to a certain extent. **Because the details of the stories are not always the same, does not mean that these Gospel writers were not inspired by God.** Each of the Gospel writers remembered things that especially impressed him. **For example,** only **Dr. Luke** wrote of Jesus restoring the ear that Peter had cut off. It impressed him the most because he was a doctor! God inspired them to write an account of His life and His teachings, and they did so as they, as individuals, saw and remembered them.

> **FACT: Because all details of the Gospels are not exactly the same, does not mean that the Gospel writers were not inspired.**

In the <u>Old</u> Testament the **first five books** of the Bible [Pentateuch] were **written the same way as the Gospels.** Each writer wrote as he remembered the facts. But even if the facts are not exactly the same, still the writers were inspired by God in the same way as were the Gospel writers. Remember that Bible writers were the **penmen;** <u>not</u> the **pen.** God did <u>not</u> dictate every word as they wrote. The important question is, "Did the personal beliefs of the Bible writers, and the times in which they lived, affect the way they wrote?"

No Bible scholar today believes that Moses wrote every word of the first five books of the Bible. <u>Genesis 36</u> lists kings who lived long after Moses had died. Some texts describe Moses

in the third person. In one chapter Moses went into a Tabernacle before he had built one. And humble Moses certainly would not have written:

> <u>**Deuteronomy 34:10**</u>
> And there has not arisen a prophet since, in Israel, like Moses, whom the Lord knew face to face.

As we continue this study, we will discover more than enough evidence that at least **parts** of the first five books of the Bible were <u>**rewritten**</u> **by at least four different people at different times.**

At the beginning of the nation of ancient Israel **there was just** one priesthood. **All** Levites **were priests. They recorded the history and traditions as they were passed down from generation to generation. However, there came a time when** ancient Israel divided into two separate nations **with** two different and divided priesthoods. **The nation of** Israel [the ten tribes] **was the** northern kingdom, **and** Judah **[including the tribe of Benjamin] became the** southern kingdom.

The northern kingdom, Israel, **had priests that were descendants of** Moses. **The southern kingdom,** Judah, **had priests that were descendants of** Aaron. **Israel and Judah operated as separate, independent nations for** 200 years **before the Assyrians destroyed**

and scattered Israel = "the lost ten tribes of Israel." After Israel was destroyed, Judah existed for another 100 years.

King Solomon **was responsible for the breakup of the nation of Israel into northern and southern kingdoms; therefore, it was** because of him **that the** two competing priesthoods **were created.**

These two kingdoms became both political and religious enemies. Each nation told and retold the stories from Creation, Noah's flood, their stay and escape from Egypt, the giving of the law at Sinai, and the history of their kings, to their present day. **Eventually they** <u>wrote</u> **down all of these historical facts; but they did so in the light of how** <u>they</u> **perceived them, depending on whether they lived in the north, or in the south.**

On the following page is **an example** of how the stories of the Gospel writers sometimes varied. What is interesting, and even amusing, is how even saintly **John** showed how annoyed he was over Peter's constant boasting. **There is no way the apostle John could have forgotten how Peter walked on the water!**

<u>Also,</u> **the story of** <u>Noah's</u> <u>flood</u> **is reproduced so one can see how the accounts of two different Bible writers were combined to make one story. Each story makes sense by itself.**

The Flood
Genesis 6:5 to 8:22

J = Regular Type P = Bold Type

[6:5] And <u>Yahweh</u> saw that the evil of humans was great in the earth, and all the inclination of the thoughts of their heart was only evil all the day.

[6] And <u>Yahweh</u> regretted that he had made humans in the earth, and he was grieved to his heart.

[7] And <u>Yahweh</u> said, "I shall wipe out the humans which I have created from the face of the earth, from human to beast to creeping thing to birds of the heavens, for I regret that I have made them."

[8] But Noah found favor in <u>Yahweh's</u> eyes.

[9] These are the generations of Noah: Noah was a righteous man, perfect in his generations. Noah walked with <u>God</u> [Elohim]. [10] And Noah sired three sons: Shem, Ham, and Japheth.

[11] And the earth was corrupted before <u>God</u> [Elohim], and the earth was filled with violence.

[12] And <u>God</u> [Elohim] saw the earth, that it was corrupted, for all flesh had corrupted its way on the earth.

[13] And <u>God</u> [Elohim] said to Noah, "The end of all flesh has come before me, for the earth is filled with violence because of them, and here I am going to destroy them with the earth.

[14] Make yourself an ark of Gopher wood, make rooms in the ark, and pitch it outside and inside with pitch.

[15] And this is how you shall make it: Three hundred cubits the length of the ark, fifty cubits its width, and thirty cubits its height.

[16] You shall make a window for the ark, and you shall finish it to a cubit from the top, and you shall make an entrance to the ark in its side. You shall make lower, second, and third stories for it.

[17] And here I am bringing the flood, water over the earth, to destroy all flesh in which is the breath of life from under the heavens. Everything which is on the land will die.

[18] And I shall establish my covenant with you. And you shall come to the ark, you and your sons and your wife and your sons' wives with you.

19] And of all the living, of all flesh, you shall bring <u>two</u> to the ark to keep alive with you, they shall be <u>male</u> and <u>female</u>.

[20] Of the birds according to their kind, and of the beasts according to their kind, and of all the creeping things of the earth according to their kind, <u>two</u> <u>of</u> <u>each</u> will come to you to keep alive.

[21] And you, take for yourself of all food which will be eaten and gather it to you, and it will be for you and for them for food.

[22] And Noah did according to all that <u>God</u> [Elohim] commanded him – so he did.

[<u>Genesis 7:1</u>] And <u>Yahweh</u> said to Noah, "Come, you and all your household, to the ark, for I have seen you as righteous before me in this generation.

[2] Of all the <u>clean</u> <u>beasts</u>, take yourself <u>seven</u> <u>pairs</u>, male and female; and of the beasts which are <u>not</u> <u>clean</u>, <u>two</u>, male and female.

[3] Also of the <u>birds</u> of the heavens <u>seven</u> <u>pairs</u>, male and female, to keep alive seed on the face of the earth.

[4] For in seven more days I shall rain on the earth forty days and forty nights, and I shall wipe out all the substance that I have made from upon the face of the earth."

[5] And Noah did according to all that Yahweh had commanded him.

[6] And Noah was six hundred years old, and the flood was on the earth.

[7] And Noah and his sons and his wife and his sons' wives with him came to the ark from before the waters of the flood.

[8] Of the clean beasts and of the beasts which were not clean, and of the birds and of all those which creep upon the earth,

[9] Two of each came to Noah to the ark, male and female, as God [Elohim] had commanded Noah.

[10] And seven days later the waters of the flood were on the earth.

[11] In the six hundredth year of Noah's life, in the second month, in the seventeenth day of the month, on this day all

the foundations of the great deep were broken up, and the windows of the heavens were opened.

[12] And there was rain on the earth, forty days and forty nights.

[13] In this very day, Noah and Shem, Ham, and Japheth, the sons of Noah, and Noah's wife and his sons' wives with them came to the ark.

[14] They and all the living things according to their kind, and all the beasts according to their kind, and all the creeping things that creep on the earth according to their kind, and all the birds according to their kind, and every winged bird.

[15] And they came to Noah to the ark, two of each, of all flesh in which there is the breath of life.

[16] And those which came were male and female, some of all flesh came, as God [Elohim] had commanded him. And Yahweh closed it for him.

[17] And the flood was on the earth for forty days and forty nights, and the waters multiplied and raised the ark, and it was lifted from the earth.

[18] And the waters grew strong and multiplied greatly on the earth, and the ark went on the surface of **the waters.**

[19] And the waters grew very strong on the earth, and they covered all the high mountains that are under all the heavens.

[20] Fifteen cubits above, the waters grew stronger, and they covered the mountains.

[21] And all flesh, those that creep on the earth, the birds, the beasts, and the wild animals, and all the swarming things that swarm on the earth, and all the humans expired.

[22] Everything that had the breathing spirit of life in its nostrils, everything that was on the dry ground died.

[23] And he wiped out all the substance that was on the face of the earth, from human to beast, to creeping thing, and to birds of the heavens, and they were wiped out from the earth, and only Noah and those who were with him in the ark were left.

[24] And the waters grew strong on the earth a <u>hundred</u> <u>and</u> <u>fifty</u> <u>days</u>.

[Genesis 8:1] And <u>God</u> [Elohim] remembered Noah and all the living, and all the beasts that were with him in the ark, and <u>God</u> passed a wind over the earth, and the waters were decreased.

[2] And the fountains of the deep and the windows of the heavens were shut, and the rain was restrained from the heavens.

[3] And the waters receded from the earth continually, **and the waters were abated at the end of a <u>hundred</u> <u>fifty</u> <u>days</u>.**

[4] And the ark rested, in the seventh month, in the seventeenth day of the month, on the mountains of Ararat.

[5] And the waters continued receding until the tenth month; in the tenth month, on the first of the month, the tops of the mountains appeared.

[6] And it was the end of forty days, and Noah opened the window of the ark which he had made.

[7] And he sent out a <u>raven</u>, and it went back and forth until the waters dried up from the earth.

[8] And he sent out a <u>dove</u> from him to see whether the waters had eased from the face of the earth.

[9] And the <u>dove</u> did not find a resting place for its foot, and it returned to him to the ark, for waters were on the face of the earth, and he put out his hand and took it and brought it to him to the ark.

[10] And he waited seven more days, and he again sent out a <u>dove</u> from the ark.

[11] And the <u>dove</u> came to him at evening time, and here was an olive leaf torn off in its mouth, and Noah knew that the waters had eased from the earth.

[12] And he waited seven more days, and he sent out a <u>dove</u>, and it did not return to him ever again.

[13] And it was in the six hundred and first year [of Noah's life], in the first month, on the first of the month, the waters dried from the earth. And Noah turned back the covering of the ark and looked, and here the face of the earth had dried.

[14] And in the second month, on the twenty-seventh day of the month, the earth dried up.

[15] And <u>God</u> [Elohim] spoke to Noah saying,

[16] "Go out from the ark, you and your wife and your sons' wives with you.

[17] All the living things that are with you, of all flesh, of the birds, and of the beasts, and of all the creeping things that creep on the earth, that go out with you, shall swarm in the earth and be fruitful and multiply in the earth."

[18] And Noah and his sons and his wife and his sons' wives went out.

[19] All the living things, all the creeping things and all the birds, all that creep on the earth, by their families, they went out of the ark.

[20] And Noah built an altar to <u>Yahweh</u>, and he took some of each of the clean beasts and of each of the clean birds, and he offered sacrifices on the altar.

[21] And <u>Yahweh</u> smelled the pleasant smell, and <u>Yahweh</u> said to his heart, "I shall not again curse the ground on man's account, for the inclination of the human heart is evil from their youth, and I shall not again strike all the living as I have done.

[22] All the rest of the days of the earth, seed and harvest, and cold and heat, and summer and winter, and day and night shall not cease."

Is God Really Like That?
Outline No. 27

HOW THE BIBLE WAS WRITTEN
Part 2

Review of Outline No. 26

In the New Testament the Gospels were written by four different men. Each Gospel writer was inspired to write an account of the life and teachings of Jesus; however, the details of the stories vary to a certain extent. Because the details of the stories in the Gospels are not exactly the same, does not mean that the Gospel writers were not inspired by God. You were given an example in the story of Jesus walking on the water.

In this outline you will learn how the books from Genesis to 2 Kings were written and re-written, and when. You will learn why the writers of the first five books did not always agree.

Before Solomon became king, **King David** made **Jerusalem** both the religious and political capital. He brought the **ark of the covenant** to Jerusalem. It was later placed in Solomon's Temple after Solomon's Temple was built.

King David appointed two chief priests in Jerusalem. David's priest from the northern part of his kingdom was **Abiachar**, a descendant of **Moses** [the only priest who had escaped King Saul's massacre of the priests of **Shiloh**]. David's priest from the south was **Zadok**, a descendant of **Aaron**.

David also established a permanent army, not dependant on volunteers, from the 12 different tribes. This system was continued under **King Solomon.**

After King David's death, King Solomon did several things that made the northern part of his kingdom very angry:

[1] **King Solomon drove chief priest Abiachar** [the descendant of **Moses** from **Shiloh**] out of Jerusalem [1 Kings 2;26], leaving only the chief priest **Zadok**, the descendant of **Aaron**, in Jerusalem.

[2] King Solomon spent most of the **tax** money on military defenses in Judah.

[3] He established **12 districts** among the **10 northern** tribes, and appointed the head of each district.

[4] He forced each man who lived in the northern 10 tribes to **work free one month out of each year.** Men of **Judah** were **not** required to do free labor.

[5] King Solomon **gave a Phoenician king**, who was one of his many fathers-in-law, a northern tract of land which included **20 cities**, in exchange for the cedars of Lebanon from which he built **Solomon's Temple** in Jerusalem.

[6] **Solomon built altars** upon which people sacrificed **animals** or sometimes even **human babies**, in order **to please his heathen wives**. Of course, these unwise practices resulted in thousands of bitter enemies among the northern ten tribes.

> **FACT:** King Solomon
> was responsible
> for the 10 tribes
> of Israel rebelling
> against Judah.
> He was an extremely
> <u>un</u>wise king!

When **King Solomon died,** the people in the north asked his son, **Rehoboam**, if he intended to follow in his father's footsteps. When he said, **"Yes,"** they declared their independence. Their first act was to stone to death Solomon's leader who had forced them to work a whole month free labor each year!

Their new king, **Jeroboam**, in order to keep his citizens from going to Jerusalem several times a year on **religious holidays** [taking thousands of animals with them for sacrifices] established **new religious centers** in the north along with **new holidays, new symbols** [two golden <u>calves</u> instead of the two golden cherubs in Solomon's Temple], and **new priests**. Now the **Levites**, descendants of **Moses**, could be employed as priests in the north.

> **FACT:** Israel and Judah,
> as separate kingdoms,
> lived side by side
> for 200 years.

The priests who descended from **Moses** believed that <u>they</u> were the true priests! And the priests who descended from **Aaron** believed that <u>they</u> were the true priests! It is **easy** to see **why** the writings of the **Jerusalem priests** and the **Shiloh priests** did not always agree!

After Solomon became king and outlawed the priests from the north [who were descendants of Moses], two versions of Israel's history were written by **"J"** [from Judah in the south], and by **"E"** [from Israel in the north].

The author of Who Wrote the Bible? referred to the Bible writers who wrote and edited the first few books of the Bible as **J, E, P, & D.** To avoid unnecessary confusion, we will do the same in this outline. **J** refered to God as **Yahweh. E** refered to God as **Elohim.** Writer **D** wrote **Deuteronomy.** **P** = the writings of **priests.**

[An excellent book on this subject is, **Who Wrote the Bible? by Richard Elliott Friedman**, Summit Books, 1230 Avenue of the Americas, New York, NY 10020 www.simonsays. com, or at your local book store] **[Excellent videos on Who Wrote the Bible?** shown on A&E TV, New Video Group, Suite 201, 250 Park Ave. South, New York, NY 10003]

The **J** stories, that tried to make the **Aaron** priests look better than the northern priests [who were descendants of **Moses**], would hardly be welcomed in Israel. And the **E** stories, that tried to make the **Moses** priests look better than the **Aaron** priests of Jerusalem, would not be welcomed by those who lived in Judah, or by those who fled from Israel to Judah when the Assyrians destroyed the northern kingdom. [Religious leaders fleeing from the Assyrians took their religious documents with them to Judah.] **Both versions were well known; therefore, one could not get away with excluding the other. The solution was to combine the two documents.** Someone took the two different works, cut them up, and pieced them together into one document. This is **why we have two flood stories and two Genesis stories.** [See 25-6,7]

P, a priest from Judah, took both the histories of **J** and **E**, spliced their stories together putting them in the order he preferred, and added many laws which favored the priests who descended from Aaron. Because he was a priest from Jerusalem in the southern nation of Judah, he tried to make the Aaron priests look good, and the priests who descended from Moses look bad. In **JE** any Levite could be a priest. **But when P combined the two versions, he wrote that only descendants of Aaron could be priests.**

For example, consider the story of Moses striking the rock at Meribah to get water for the people and animals. The **E** story in **Exodus** made hitting the rock an **act of obedience.** But when we read the **P** story in **Numbers,** hitting the rock became an **act of disobedience!**

Exodus 17:2-7

The Lord said...you shall **strike the rock,** and water shall come out of it, that the people may drink.

Numbers 20:2-13

The Lord said to Moses, "Take this rod, and assemble the congregation, you and Aaron your brother, and **tell the rock** before their eyes to yield its water..." And Moses lifted up his hand and **struck the rock** with his rod **twice...** And the Lord said to Moses and Aaron, "Because you did not believe in me, to sanctify me in the eyes of the people of Israel, therefore you shall not bring this assembly into the land which I have given them."

P did his best to make Moses look bad and Aaron look good! **P** did not tell the golden calf story because Aaron was the bad guy who made the golden calf for the people to worship! Joshua was on Mt. Sinai at the time waiting for Moses. Joshua used to stand guard in the Tabernacle, but **P** could not tell that story because, according to **P**, only a priest can enter the Tabernacle. **P's** rules said that anyone entering the Tabernacle who was not a priest, would be killed.

P produced a work that was to take the place of **JE**. **JE** wrote of God as being kind, merciful, and forgiving.

P wrote about a lawgiver who expected perfect obedience.

According to **JE**, miracles in Egypt were the result of using **Moses' staff**. **P** wrote they were the result of using **Aaron's staff**.

J wrote in the first half of the story in Numbers 25:1-15, that the Israelite men were attracted to **Moabite** women. But in the second half of the same story, **P** wrote they were **Midianite** women. **Moses's wife was a Midianite! Phinehas, Aaron's grandson, became the hero and was promised that the priesthood would be in his family's future.**

In the **JE** version only **Caleb** returned with a positive report. However, in **P's** account there are two faithful spies: **Caleb and Joshua!**

P wrote before Solomon's Temple was destroyed. **How do we know?** The laws all through **P** say that sacrifices must take place at the entrance of the Tabernacle, and nowhere else. And this law was to be "forever." **A priest would not write a law that said sacrifices could only be offered at a place that no longer existed. P** wrote after the fall of the northern kingdom when **E** had already gone south and had been combined with **J**.

How can a scholar tell the difference in who wrote what? They can tell by the writer's vocabulary, grammar, emphasis, the stories they include or exclude, and the name they use for God [either Yahweh or Elohim]. The story of Noah's flood, printed in Outline 26-5b thru 7b, shows that the **J** writer referred to God as **Yahweh**, and that the **P** writer referred to Him as **Elohim** [translated **"God"** in most translations].

Chronology

1011 to 971 BCE -- **King David** ruled Israel.

970 to 931 BCE -- **King Solomon** ruled Israel. He put up pagan altars [1 Kings 11:1-8]

931 BCE – Israel split into two nations.

931 to 913 BCE – **Rehoboam** ruled Israel in the north. He put up pagan altars to keep his citizens from going to Jerusalem to worship.

E, in the north, produced a history beginning with Moses that favored priests that descended from Moses. **E** wrote between **922** and **722 BCE**.

J, in the south, produced a history beginning with Moses that favored priests who descended from Aaron. **J** wrote between **848** and **722 BCE**.

735 to 715 BCE – **Ahab & Jezebel** ruled Israel in the north. They promoted **Baal** worship.

729 to 686 BCE – **Hezekiah** ruled Judah in the south. **Hezekiah** destroyed the pagan altars.

722 BCE – Assyrian army destroyed Israel.

P wrote an alternative to **JE** that offended **P's** ancestor, Aaron.

639 to 608 BCE – **Josiah** ruled Israel in the north. **Josiah** "discovered" the Torah that Jeremiah wrote. **Josiah** destroyed pagan altars.

D No. 1 - **Probably written by Jeremiah.**

622 BCE – **Priest Hilkiah** told **King Josiah** he had discovered an old manuscript, which **motivated Josiah to tear down the heathen altars put up by King Solomon and King Rehoboam.** Actually the "discovery" was written shortly before it was "discovered," by a priest from Shiloh of the northern kingdom, that included a systematic history of the Jews from Deuteronomy through Joshua, Judges, 1 & 2 Samuel, and 1 & 2 Kings. Evidence that points to **Jeremiah** as the **"D"** author is outlined in Who Wrote the Bible? by Richard Elliott Friedman. The **Talmud** identifies the writer of the books of Kings as **Jeremiah**. The **D** writer listed many rules and regulations concerning priests and sacrifices. **D ruled that sacrifices should be made only at one central place: Jerusalem.** However, **Jeremiah** declared that the **Levites** could be official priests anywhere. **D** took one history of the kings of Israel, and one history of the kings of Judah, cut them up and pieced them together into one document. **Jeremiah** knew the priestly laws, but he did not like them:

Jeremiah 8:8

"How can you say, 'We are wise, and the law of the Lord is with us'? But, behold, the false pen of the scribes has made it into a lie.

587 BCE – King Nebuchadnezzar of Babylon captured and burned Jerusalem. Jews were exiled to Babylon. Many fled to Egypt. David's 400 year old royal family no longer ruled, even when that prophecy said that it would last "forever" [2 Samuel 7:13-16]. After Zedekiah rebelled, King Nebuchadnezzar, executed **Zedekiah's** sons in front of him; then blinded him. **Most of the Jews fled to Egypt, where they had started as slaves. In 587 Nebuchadnezzar destroyed Solomon's Temple,** but only **after the ark** of the covenant containing the ten commandments was hidden.

The **Tabernacle**, because it was actually inside of Solomon's Temple, was destroyed in the fire that destroyed the Temple. The Temple was 60 cubits [about 90 ft.] long and 20 cubits [30 ft] wide. This was large enough to house the Tabernacle which was only 30 x 10 cubits = 45 x 15 ft.

By the way, the **golden cherubs** that were inside the Tabernacle and the Temple were each 10 cubits tall, had a human head, the body of a four-legged animal, and the wings of a bird.

D No. 2 written after 587 BCE

D No. 1 was written **before 587 BCE**.
D No. 2 was written **after 587 BCE**, and was made to revise **D No. 1**.
It described the end of Judah and

David's kingdom. **Jeremiah** began his ministry as a prophet during **King Josiah's** reign. **Josiah** destroyed the heathen altars Solomon set up. **Jeremiah was a priest of Shiloh** in the **northern kingdom of Israel – a descendant of Moses.**

The **first edition** had to be written before **King Josiah** died in 609 BCE. The **second edition** had to have been written after the Babylonian destruction of Jerusalem and exile in 587 BCE. = a difference of only 22 years. It was written by the same person – probably **Jeremiah**.

516 BCE – Second Temple dedicated.

Final Revision by Ezra

After the destruction of Jerusalem in 587 BCE, someone else thought it necessary to produce another Torah for the unity and future of the Jewish people. The highly qualified individual, who was at the right place at the right time, was **Ezra**. He was a priest, scribe, and lawgiver. **Ezra and Moses are the only two men known as lawgivers. Ezra** had the backing of the secular rulers, and was given the power to enforce the laws. According to Jewish tradition, the original scroll of the Torah and other books of the Bible were burned up in the fire that destroyed Solomon's Temple in 587, but Ezra was able to restore them.

Ezra produced a work that reconciled the opposing forces. Even though Ezra's descendants were of **Aaron, he could not insist that the only place one could offer a sacrifice was at the Temple,** because the Temple had been **destroyed! Ezra** retained as much of the original texts as possible without major contradictions. Ezra combined the two different pictures of God. Ezra had to include all the famous stories that we are familiar with, because they were all well known by the time he wrote. **Ezra added Numbers chapter 15**.

Ezra wrote in the days of the second Temple [dedicated in 516 BC], in which there was no ark of the covenant nor cherubs. The Most Holy Place was probably just an empty room. **Ezra** began each major section of his work with **P** stories or **P** laws. He used these priestly documents as his framework. He cut up the **Book of Generations** which contained the genealogies from Adam onward, and divided it up between the stories in Genesis. **Ezra never** referred to God as **Yahweh**, only as El or Elohim [the chief pagan god was El].
El, like **Yahweh**, was not identified with any force of nature.
El was associated with bulls, known as **Bull El**.

God revealed His name, Yahweh, for the first time, to Moses, at the burning bush:

Exodus 3:13-15

And Moses said to Elohim, Behold, when I come to the children of Israel, and say to them, The **Elohim** of your fathers has sent me to you, and they shall say to me, What is your name? What shall I say to them?... say to them, **Yahweh**, the Elohim of your fathers...

Is God Really Like That?
Outline No. 28

Armageddon

All Christians, at one time or another, talk about Armageddon. Their concept of Armageddon is usually what they have been **taught by religious leaders,** and what they have seen portrayed in **movies** and **television. Movie makers** have made millions, capitalizing on the interest and ignorance of the general public.

When serious trouble rears its ugly head in one or more parts of the world, some people tell us, "Armageddon is right upon us; the world is about to end!"

Most people believe about Armageddon what they have been told by others – especially religious leaders. After all, **"my preacher certainly is a man of God who studies the Bible, is led by God's Spirit, and prays for the revelation of Truth"** – as if other preachers who disagree with him do not!

There <u>was</u> a time when people had an <u>excuse</u> for not studying the Bible for themselves, but that time has passed.

Armageddon is mentioned only in the Book of Revelation. Everyone has heard of the **"7 last plagues,"** but few know that **Armageddon is one of the plagues!**

Armageddon begins in the 6th plague, and ends in the 7th plague.

Revelation is a book of **symbols;** therefore, it is important to understand the meanings of the symbols before we can know the truth about Armageddon. **First** we will read the Bible texts; then we will diagnose the symbols:

Revelation 16:12
The **sixth** angel poured his bowl on the great **RIVER EUPHRATES,** and its **WATER** was **dried up,** to prepare the way for the **KINGS FROM THE EAST**

<u>ARMAGEDDON</u> – The word itself means, "mountain of Megiddo" or "mount of the congregation."

<u>MOUNTAIN</u> is symbolic for government:

Zechariah 8:3
Jerusalem shall be called the faithful city, and the **mountain** of the Lord of hosts, the holy **mountain.**

Hebrews 12:22
...you have come to **Mount Zion** and to the city of the living God, **the heavenly Jerusalem...**

Isaiah 66:20
...my holy **mountain...** Jerusalem...

Revelation 17:3,9,10

...the 7 heads and 7 **hills [KJV: mountains]** on which the woman is seated...

NOTE: Ask about "Revelation Deciphered" by Paul G. Sweitzer, which covers all **22 chapters** of the book of Revelation, **verse by verse**, and includes a **Dictionary of 293 Symbols.**

RIVER EUPHRATES – **All water** in the book of Revelation = **people** – regardless of whether the water is a river, sea, fountain of water, or lake:

Revelation 17:15

The **waters** that you saw, where the harlot is seated, are **peoples** and **multitudes** and **nations** and **tongues.**

The literal river Euphrates used to flow under the walls of the literal city of Babylon. Cyrus, commander of the Medo-Persian armies, dammed up the Euphrates to prevent water from flowing under the city walls. In this manner Cyrus **dried up** the section of **the Euphrates river** which flowed under the city walls, allowing him and his army to enter the city and conquer ancient Babylon.

KINGS FROM THE EAST = **God and His followers.** There is no Scripture which specifically states the identity of the **"kings from the east;"** nevertheless, certain Bible texts indicate that God and His followers come, **symbolically, from the east:**

Isaiah 41:2

Who stirred up **one from the east** whom **victory** meets at every step? He gives up nations before him, so that he **tramples kings** underfoot...

Revelation 7:2

Then I saw another angel ascend
[RSV] from the rising of the **sun**
[KJV] from the **east** with the **seal of the living God...**

Revelation 5:10

...and has made them
[RSV] a kingdom
[KJV] kings and priests to our God, and they shall reign on earth...

Ezekiel 43:2

...the glory of **the God of Israel came from the east;** and the **sound** of his coming was **like the sound of many waters** and the **earth shone with his glory.**

Rev 16:12 – Deciphered

The sixth phase of the withdrawal of holy angels results in the exposure of Satan's ["dragon's] **counterfeit religious organization** ["beast"] along with her apostate followers ["false prophet"]. This prepares the way for the followers of Jesus ["kings from the east"] [to be acknowledged as followers of Truth].

Because Bible readers have skipped over the **obvious symbolism** in these verses, most have misunderstood "Armageddon." One should not interpret **half** of a text as **literal** and

half as **symbolic,** and come to any logical conclusions – especially in the symbolic book of Revelation. **Continue reading** and you will see clearly that this account is obviously symbolic**:**

Revelation 16:13-16

And I saw, issuing from the **mouth** of the **DRAGON** and from the **mouth** of the **BEAST** and the **mouth** of the **FALSE PROPHET, three foul spirits** like **FROGS;** for they are **demonic spirits,** performing **signs,** who go abroad to the **KINGS** of the **whole world,** to assemble them for **battle** on the great day of God Almighty… And they assembled them at the place which is called in Hebrew **Armageddon.**

FACT: Demonic spirits, "like frogs," do not really come out of the mouths of "dragons" and "beasts."

Armageddon is a **spiritual battle** between the **"beast"** and the **"Lamb."** Does this mean one gulp and no Lamb? **No, the Lamb will win:**

Revelation 17:13,14

These ["kings" – leaders] are of one mind and give over their power and authority to the **beast; and will make war on the Lamb,** and the **Lamb will conquer** them, for he is Lord of lords and King of kings, and **those with him are called and chosen and faithful.**

DRAGON =

[a] – Satan
[b] – A power through which Satan works.
[c] -- Paganism

Revelation 20:1-3

…the **dragon,** that ancient **serpent,** who is the **Devil** and **Satan.**

Revelation 12:3-17

…a great red **dragon**… 7 heads… 10 horns… **dragon… serpent… Devil** and **Satan,** deceiver of the whole world…

BEAST =

[a] – A political power
[b] – A religiopolitical power
[c] – Satan – dragon

Revelation 13:1-18

…**beast** rose out of the sea…

Revelation 11:7

…**beast** that **ascends** from bottomless pit

FALSE PROPHET =
Counterfeit religions who are "daughters" of the "harlot."

Revelation 19:20

…**beast** was captured, and with it the **false prophet…** thrown alive into the lake of fire.

Revelation 20:10

…lake of fire… where the beast and the **false prophet** were.

Matthew 7:15,16

"Beware of **false prophets,** who come to you in sheep's clothing but inwardly are ravenous wolves. You will know them by their fruits."

FROGS – The "foul spirits" are evil angels ["demonic spirits"] who speak like frogs jump; never in a straight line! They cannot be trusted to continue in the same direction. This is a good description of how the devil operates.

Rev 16:13-16 – Deciphered

Satan spoke ["out of the mouth of the dragon"], and the **first great power spoke** [Rev 13:1], and her **apostate "daughters" spoke** ["false prophet"] – controlled by **demonic influences** ["foul spirits"], saying first one thing, and then the opposite ["like frogs"]. For they are **evil angels** ["demonic spirits"] performing convincing **miracles** and signs, who go to the **leaders** ["kings"] of the many nations of the whole world, to **organize** ["assemble"] them to fight against God and His true followers… Satan and his angels will assemble all the world leaders and armies together at the place they call **"Armageddon" = the government of God** ["mountain of God"]

Revelation 16:17-21

The 7th angel poured his bowl into the **AIR,** and a great voice out of the **TEMPLE,** from the **throne,** saying, **"It is done!"** [18] And there were flashes of **lightning,** loud noises, peals of **thunder,** and an **EARTHQUAKE** such as had never been since men were on earth, so great was that **EARTHQUAKE.** [19] The great **CITY** was **split into THREE PARTS,** and the cities of the nations fell, and God remembered great **BABYLON,** to make her drain the cup of the fury of his **WRATH.** [20] And every **ISLAND** fled away, and no **MOUNTAINS** were to be found; [21] and great **HAILSTONES,** heavy as a hundredweight, dropped on men **from heaven,** till men cursed God for the plague of the hail, so fearful was that plague.

AIR = All people of the world:

Ephesians 2:2

Satan is **"the prince of the power of the air,** the spirit that is now at work in the sons of disobedience."

Revelation 9:2

The **air** was darkened with smoke from the bottomless pit.

TEMPLE = Jesus/God:

Revelation 21:22

I saw no **temple** in the city, for its **temple** is the Lord **God** Almighty and the **Lamb.**

John 2:19,21

Jesus: "Destroy this **temple,** and in three days I will raise it up. But he spoke of the **temple of his body."**

CITY -- BABYLON =
Counterfeit church

Two symbolic "cities"
in the book of Revelation:

Jerusalem = **God's true Church**
= All Christians

Babylon = Satan's counterfeit
organizations
= Counterfeit Christians

<u>EARTHQUAKE</u> – Because this "earthquake" divided a **symbolic** city, **"Babylon,"** into **"three parts,"** it could **not** be a literal earthquake!

<u>MOUNTAINS</u> – <u>CITY</u> = **Governments.** It is not literally possible for every island and every <u>literal</u> mountain in the whole world to disappear.

<u>HAILSTONES</u> = **lies.** See <u>Dictionary</u> of <u>Symbols</u> in <u>Revelation Deciphered</u>.

<u>WRATH</u> – **See Outline No. 3**

Rev 16:17-21 – Deciphered

When the **seventh** and **final phase** of the **withdrawal** of holy angels took place – which affected **everyone everywhere** ["air"], the great voice of **God** ["temple"], the **source of all authority** ["throne"], said, "It is done." And there was increased **understanding** ["lightning"], great **commotion** ["loud noises"], **warning messages** ["thunder"], and a great **upheaval in society** – ["a great earthquake"] greater than any upheaval in society that any people had ever experienced. Satan's **counterfeit religious system** ["city" or "Babylon"] was **divided** into three parts. Whole **denominations** ceased to exist, and God allowed the **counterfeit system ["Babylon"]** to experience the **wrath of evil men** and the **wrath of evil angels.** And every **refuge – every place of safety** ["island"] **disappeared** ["fled away"], and **no nations or governments** ["mountains"] were able to rule themselves or others. And so many obvious **lies** ["hailstones"] were told in the **religious world** ["heaven"] that people cursed God because of the **lies** ["hail"].

Revelation 17:5

"Babylon the great, **mother of harlots** and of earth's abominations."

Revelation 18:2-5

"Fallen, fallen is **Babylon** the great! It has become the **dwelling place of demons**... for **all nations** have drunk the wine of her impure passion, and the **kings** of the earth have committed fornication with her... Then I heard another voice from heaven saying, **"Come out of her, my people,** lest you take part in her sins, lest you share in her plagues; for her sins are heaped high as heaven, and God has remembered her iniquities."

The word **"Armageddon"** [Greek = "Harmageddon"] is a transliteration from the Hebrew. As far as we know, no geographical location ever bore that name. As you have already learned, **"mountain"** is symbolic for government.

No <u>mountain</u> of Megiddo existed in Palestine during Bible times; however, there was the **valley of Megiddo** that is surrounded by mountains. These mountains encircled a great battlefield during Old Testament times. We can understand how people, years ago, thought that Armageddon would be a <u>literal</u> military battle between nations of the world. <u>Now</u>, with nuclear war, the idea that a military battle could be fought in such a small area is not logical nor Scriptural.

Armageddon is a spiritual battle between the <u>total</u> forces of good and the <u>total</u> forces of evil. It will include spiritual conflicts, military wars, religious persecution, miracles, suicides, mass murders, and the destructive forces of nature out of control.

According to the book of Revelation, Armageddon will begin during the 6th plague and end during the 7th plague – or, at the 2nd coming of Jesus. **God does not <u>cause</u> Armageddon, but He will <u>allow</u> evil people and evil angels to have their own way. Think what will happen just before Jesus returns when every unsaved** person will think of at least 1,000 people who, they believe, <u>deserve</u> to die – including many religious leaders! What a blood bath that will be!

When the restraints upon the wicked are removed – when holy angels cease to protect anyone but the saved -- **the <u>unsaved</u> will turn upon each other and kill each other as they have done in the past:**

Ezekiel 38:21

I will summon every kind of terror against Gog, says the Lord God; every man's **<u>sword</u>** will be against his brother.

Isaiah 9:18-20

For wickedness **<u>burns</u>** like a **fire**... Through the <u>wrath of the Lord</u> the land is <u>burned</u>, and the **people are like fuel** for the fire; **<u>no man</u> <u>spared</u> <u>his</u> <u>brother</u>...** each devours his neighbor's flesh.

Zechariah 14:12-14

This shall be the **pl<u>ague</u>** with which the <u>Lord</u> will smite all the peoples that war against Jerusalem... A great panic from the Lord shall fall upon them, so that **each will lay hold on the hand of his fellow,** and the hand of the one will be raised against the hand of the other.

Is God Really Like That?
Outline No. 29

How Will It All End for Me?

Success in this life is the finding of **happiness of the heart.** In order to be genuinely happy, each individual will:

[1] Know for sure that he or she will receive eternal life with a God of love.

[2] Enjoy his relationship with his family.

[3] Be able to provide adequately for himself and/or his family.

[4] Enjoy spending time with children.

The real reason why most people believe that a **"God of love"** would torment **"for ever"** people who have not accepted His ways of thinking, is that they have the idea that they **deserve** eternal life **because** they:

[1] Have accepted Jesus as their Savior.

[2] Have been relatively "good."

[3] Go to church every week.

[4] Pay money to the church.

FACT: No one deserves eternal life more than anyone else.

Ephesians 2:8,9

For by **grace** you have been **saved** through **faith,** and this is not of your own doing; it is the **gift** of God – **not the result of works,** so that no one may boast.

Romans 6:23

For the wages of sin is death, but the **free gift** of God is eternal life in Christ Jesus our Lord.

It is by grace that we receive from Jesus what we do not deserve!

Everyone sins! Saints are sinners who keep on surrendering. Before a person becomes a Christian he is a sinner running after sin. After a person becomes a Christian he or she is still a sinner, but running away from sin.

1 John 1:8

If we say we have no sin, we deceive ourselves.

Romans 3:10

None is righteous, no, not one.

When we, by faith, believe that Jesus will do as He has promised, He begins to create in us a new heart. The complete change takes place at His second coming when we will receive new, glorious, immortal bodies to go along with a new mind free of all negative thoughts and emotions. **Our present computer type mind will be reprogrammed by our Creator:**

Hebrews 8:10,11

This is the covenant that I will make with the house of Israel **after those days,** says the Lord. **I will put my laws in their minds,** and write them **on their hearts,** and I will be their God, and they shall be my people. And **they shall not teach one another** or say to each other, "Know the Lord," for **they shall know me,** from the least of them to the greatest.

"SAVED"

When a person talks about being "saved," he could be speaking about either of **three** different events:

[1] Justification

"I was saved" in the past when I accepted Jesus as my personal Savior. Justification is a **legal act** of heaven at which moment the **"ungodly"** are declared **"perfect"** when, in reality, we are not perfect.

Romans 4:5

And to one who does not work but trusts him who **justifies the ungodly,** his faith is reckoned as righteousness.

Romans 8:1

There is therefore now **no condemnation for those who are in Christ Jesus.**

Ephesians 2:8-10

For by **grace** you have been **saved** through **faith...** For we are His workmanship, created in Christ Jesus for **good works,** which God prepared beforehand, that we should walk in them.

"Good works" and doing right are merely the **results** of a right relationship with Jesus.

[2] Glorification

"I will be saved" in the **future** when I will receive a glorious body, and immortality, at Jesus' second coming. [See Philippians 3:21; 1 Cor. 15:51-54; 1 Thess. 4:16,17]

[3] Sanctification

"I am being saved" in the **present.**

This takes place when a Christian, setting himself apart as a disciple of Jesus, allows the Spirit of Jesus into his life so that he begins to "grow up" spiritually and emotionally into a mature adult Christian. [See John 3:5; 15:16-20; 2 Cor 4:16; Gal 2:20; Romans 15:16; 1 Corinthians 1:2]

A Christian is covered by the **symbolic robe** of Jesus' righteousness = a "robe" made to fit the Christian.

Christians are not altered to fit the robe. This **"altering"** is called **"sanctification."**

Spiritual growth during **"sanctification"** takes place **gradually** as long as a person lives. We cannot change our own hearts [Jeremiah 13:23]. The apostle **Paul** breaks down this supernatural process:

2 Corinthians 3:18

And we **all**,
[Includes everyone.]
with **unveiled face**,
[No one needs to hide in shame.]
beholding the glory of the Lord,
are **being changed**
[A gradual change]
into **his** likeness;
[To think and act as He does]
for this **comes from the Lord**,
who is the **Spirit**
[We cannot change ourselves; however, we must be willing to be changed.]

Anyone can easily become a Christian.

Jesus does not even require a sinner to repent first! A person's only requirement is to surrender and accept His promises. A change in attitude toward God and His laws comes only through the power of Jesus as He works to make changes in our innermost thinking – our hearts. God hates sin, but He loves the sinner. No one is so sinful that he or she cannot take the necessary step to receive eternal life:

Isaiah 1:18

Come now, **let us reason together,** says the Lord: though your sins are like **scarlet,** they shall be as **white as snow…**

The surrender to Jesus does not take severe mental effort and agony. Merely say to Him, **"Jesus, I accept You as my personal Savior. I am Yours. I claim Your promise that You will come into my heart and change it."** However, what you say must be from your **heart** – not merely words like a parrot!

Jesus is the One who can and does read our deepest, innermost hearts [subconscious and supra-conscious] therefore, **only He can know** whether or not we are disobeying because of human weakness, or because we have deliberately rebelled against Him and His laws. **We are always free to choose.**

After a person yields himself or herself to the Spirit of Jesus, changes for good begin to take place. Even though changes of the heart take place gradually [2 Cor. 3:18; 28-2a.9], **definite changes do take place, and are noticed by people around you** – such as family members, neighbors, and fellow workers.

In other words, regardless of what a person claims, how he or she talks and acts shows whether or not a person is a genuine Christian:

Galatians 5:22-25

The fruit of the Spirit is love, joy, peace, patience, kindness, goodness, faithfulness, gentleness, self-control... If we live by the Spirit, let us also walk by the Spirit.

How About Non-Christians?

"God is love." "God is fair."

You probably have heard preachers say that unless one accepts Jesus as his or her personal Savior, the end result will be "eternal torment" in "hell."

Who would want anything to do with a God like that?!

You have learned by studying the Bible texts in Outlines 12, 13, 14, 15, 16, & 17 that God is **NOT** like that!

It is true that the only way anyone can receive eternal life is through the merits of our Creator and Savior, Jesus; however, some will receive the free gift of eternal life who never even heard the name of Jesus!

Jews, **Moslems,** **Hindus**, and "**heathen**" who have not had the privilege of knowing who Jesus is and what He stands for, will be **judged by the law that is written on their hearts** [See Romans 2:12-16].

Every person has an inner sense of right and wrong. **For example, I** object to others stealing from me; therefore, I **know** that it is wrong to steal! **On the other hand, no one can receive eternal life who continues to knowingly and willfully reject Jesus**.

FACT: Some people will receive eternal life who never even heard of Jesus; however, no one can be saved who has knowingly rejected Jesus.

What world events will happen before Jesus returns?

No, Paul G. Sweitzer does **NOT** claim to be a psychic or modern day prophet. The following predictions are a composite of ideas gleaned from years of scientific, historical, and theological research, that includes the prophetic book of Revelation.

[1] Prediction

Natural disasters will continue to increase in number and severity. **Earthquakes** on both U.S. coasts will be far greater than we have already experienced. **Tidal waves, floods, hurricanes,** and **tornadoes** will multiply as a natural result of the imbalance of nature. The closer we get to Jesus' second coming, the greater will be the destruction of nature out of control. **What will happen to the U.S. will amaze you and frighten you!**

[2] <u>Prediction</u>

Crime will greatly increase: alcoholism, drug use, murder, rape, abnormal sexual behavior, armed robbery, and **divorce. Most of the increase in crime will be the <u>natural result</u> of the breakdown of the home.**

[3] <u>Prediction</u>

Worldwide terrorism will destroy millions. **Nuclear war** will possibly include China.

[4] <u>Prediction</u>

UFO occupants will make personal contacts with various classes of people of all religions in all parts of the world, and contacts with world political leaders, performing miracles of healing, revealing secrets of the universe [some of which will be proven true], and revealing the so-called **"facts" about God. These UFO occupants are and will be nothing more or less than <u>evil angels</u>** in a variety of human-like forms, deceiving everyone who is not firmly grounded in Bible Truth.

Fearful sights of a supernatural nature will soon be revealed in the heavens, in token of the power of miracle-working demons. The spirits of devils will go forth to the kings of the earth and to the whole world. Rulers and subjects will be deceived. They will profess to have revelations from heaven which contradict the Bible.

Satan himself will claim to be Jesus. The glory that surrounds Satan will be greater than anyone has ever seen. The shout of triumph rings out, **"Jesus has come! Jesus has come!"** But genuine Christians will not be fooled. Furthermore, Satan will not be permitted to counterfeit the exact manner of Jesus' exit from heaven.

Possibly Satan will descend in a ten mile long UFO lit up like no one has ever seen before. But no one who has studied the Bible with an open mind will be deceived! Two angels told Jesus' disciples that Jesus would return in the same way He went to heaven – which was **not** in a UFO! [See Acts 1:9-11]

Satan will then set himself up as **ruler of the world.** This will fulfill the much prophesied rule of **"antichrist."** Because most Christians believe their preachers who teach that Jesus will set up His earthly kingdom at the **<u>beginning</u>** of the Millennium, **most people will be deceived** and fall into Satan's trap. They will end up worshipping Satan, thinking they are worshipping Jesus!

2 Thessalonians 2:3,4

Let no one deceive you in any way; for that day will not come unless the rebellion comes first and the **lawless one** is revealed, the one destined for destruction. He opposes and exalts himself above every so-called god or object of worship, so that **he takes his seat in the temple of God, declaring himself to be God.**

[5] Prediction

One currency for the whole world. Also a **debit card system** [cashless society] as a method to help stop the drug traffic and tax evasion. Just before Jesus returns it will be used to try to force people to conform to the laws of the land that are contrary to the laws of God in the Bible [Rev 13:16,17].

[6] Prediction

The **United States**, the **leading power until Jesus returns** [Rev 13], will change its **constitution** in order to legally pass religious laws in an attempt to force people to conform to the teachings of certain religious leaders. These **religious leaders** will stir up the population to put pressure on the politicians to enact laws contrary to the laws of God as written in the Bible. The purpose of the religious leaders and the voters will be a misguided attempt to **appease** "God's wrath." They will fall for the **devilish propaganda that God Himself is sending trouble on this earth because He is angry with the way people are acting.**

As people in O. T. times believed they were pleasing God by sacrificing animals and infants, so people in modern times will believe they are pleasing God by trying to force people to act contrary to conscience:

John 16:2,3

Indeed, an hour is coming when **those who kill you will think that by doing so they are offering worship to God.** And they will do this **because they have not known the Father or me.**

[7] Prediction

For the sake of unity, **churches will compromise their orthodox beliefs** so as to prepare the way for **one world religion.** It's leader will be a counterfeit "antichrist." Nevertheless, this religious leader will think, act, and dictate in the same way as the real "antichrist" who will rule later on.

[8] Prediction

The following **predictions of Jesus will come true during the "last generation"** before Jesus returns:

Matthew 24:29,30

Immediately after the suffering of those days the **sun** will be darkened, and the **moon** will not give its light; the **stars** will fall from heaven, and the **powers of heaven will be shaken.** Then the sign of the Son of Man will appear in heaven, and then all the tribes of the earth will mourn, and they will see the Son of Man coming on the clouds of heaven with power and great glory.

Mark 13:24-26

But in those days, after that suffering, the **sun** will be darkened, and the **moon** will not give its light, and the **stars** will be falling from heaven, and the **powers in the heavens will be shaken.** Then they will see the Son of Man coming in clouds with great power and glory.

To fulfill Jesus' predictions, **possibly a comet** will zoom in from outer space, coming close enough to the earth to cause much destruction and loss of life. The result could be similar to the time when **Mars** came close to the earth before 701 BCE. During this time **people will be told by their religious leaders that God Himself caused the destruction** because of the corruption and wickedness on the earth. True, destruction will be **allowed** because the majority of inhabitants will have chosen lawlessness, even though there will be a **"form of godliness"** [2 Timothy 3:1-5; Matthew 7:21-23]. But the destruction will **not** be a **direct** act of God.

[9] Prediction

Before Jesus returns the world in general will have had opportunity to learn of His true character of love; that no devilish traits apply to Him. **God is not two-faced! God is love, and He always acts that way. Always!**

[10] Prediction

The second **coming of Jesus** will be **literal,** so that **everyone** will **see** Him and **hear** Him come.

Is God Really Like That?
Outline No. 30

Book Review

From your study of the first 29 outlines you have been introduced to several new ideas of God; how He thinks and acts. Even though these new ideas about God have been backed up with Holy Scripture, **it is difficult to look at God in a different way than we have been taught by preachers and relatives.** At stake is our own **personal peace of mind,** and the **peace of mind of our children.**

REMEMBER that everyone – yes, every one of us – has preconceived ideas because of what we have been taught since we were three years old.

The fact is that most people remain in the same denomination in which they were raised, with each church claiming that their doctrine is based upon what "the Bible teaches." It is extremely difficult to accept the idea that our own preacher, or parents, do not know **everything!**

Every honest Bible student, preacher or church member, changes his or her mind from time to time after prayerful study. This is why everyone, including Christians who want to know what

God is really like, will **study** the Bible evidence **for themselves.**

The revelation of Truth is progressive.

Jesus told His disciples:

John 16:12,13

"I have many things to say to you, but you cannot bear them now. When the Spirit of truth comes, he will guide you into all the truth."

The words of Jesus tell us that more information about God can be expected in our time.

Certain basics are necessary to properly evaluate the overall picture of God:

No. 1 = Personal Bible study.
No. 2 = Common sense.
No 3 = Accept the fact that God really is "love"and that he always acts like it!

Always remember: God is not two-faced. He never acts like the devil.

Our God of love places restrictions upon Himself. He does not have a split personality. He does not act like a loving God half the time, and like a devil the other half.

We know that Satan operates as a counterfeit at the present time = **"an angel of light"** [2 Cor 11:13,14]. **Satan** did the same thing during Old Testament times. **Satan** was in the **Garden of Eden** [Ezekiel 28:13]. He was a murderer and a **liar** "**from the beginning,**" according to Jesus [John 8:44]. Trouble began in Eden when Adam believed the lies of Satan in Genesis 2, rather than the truth of the true Lord God in chapter one.

Bible proof of the **counterfeit lord Satan** operating in the **Old Testament** is given in **Outlines No. 19, 20, 21, 22, 23, 24, and 30.**

The words and actions of **"God"** have been greatly misunderstood in the writings of the Old Testament. **A description of the counterfeit lord Satan operating in Genesis chapter 2 and 3, shows us how the put down of women as second class citizens began.** It was not until **Jesus** came to earth in the form of a man that the equality of women was made plain.

To get an accurate picture of how God really thinks and acts, study the life of Jesus:

John 14:7-9

"If you had known me, you would have known my Father also; henceforth you know him and have seen him... He who has seen me has seen the Father..."

> **FACT:** Everything written in the Old Testament must be compared with what Jesus did and said in the New Testament.

We have learned, from Bible texts, that the **God of the O.T.** who **gave the ten commandments,** and the God who **led Israel from the cloud** in the wilderness, was **none other than Jesus Himself** [John 8:57-59; 1 Cor 10:1-4]. **Our Creator Himself came** to earth, in the form of a man, **to redeem us** [Rev 12:16; John 1:1-5,10].

God never changes. He is the same "yesterday, today, and forever" [Hebrews 13:8; Malachi 3:6; James 1:17]. **How He was in New Testament times is how the true Lord was in Old Testament times.**

Bible writers wrote as if God actually **did** things which He merely allowed.

The people of **Israel** believed in just **one God.** They believed everything that happened, good or bad, was the result of a direct action of God

Himself. This is why Bible writers wrote as if God actually did things that He merely allowed.

Outlines 26 and 27 show that our Bible was written a little differently than we had once believed. Moses wrote much of the first four books, but they were **rewritten** because of the division of the nation of ancient Israel, and because of competition within the priesthood.

When the kingdom of ancient Israel was divided, because of the unwise actions of King Solomon, **it divided the priesthood,** which, in turn, caused the Bible stories, laws, and doctrines to be, <u>at</u> <u>times</u>, rewritten. Nevertheless, **we are able to get a clear picture of what God expects from us by comparing Holy Scripture.** God has promised that His Spirit would guide our minds as we study with a teachable attitude.

God will not <u>force</u> anyone to believe anything. Freedom of choice is something that God <u>insists</u> upon for His created beings. God lets us know His **perfect will,** but He does not <u>insist</u> that we <u>do</u> His perfect will. <u>However,</u> it should be crystal clear in our minds that God's **permissive will is something that He only <u>allows,</u> but certainly does <u>not</u> sanction.** God desires each one of us to do His **perfect will. All of God's rules are for our benefit.** The closer we follow His council the healthier and happier we will be. **In other words, God allows us to learn the hard way, by trial and error.** Sooner or later we learn that His ways are always the best ways.

God will not <u>force</u> us to follow His perfect will, even though He knows that **His perfect will is what we need, as individuals, in order to find genuine peace, success, and happiness.**

If **force** had been the method God used to overcome evil, it would have been accomplished long ago. **God always gives us liberty to do what we <u>insist</u> upon doing.**

<u>Examples</u> of people substituting God's <u>permissive</u> <u>will</u> for His **perfect will** during OT times: **Slavery, Bigamy, Divorce, Flesh eating, "Eye for an eye" philosophy, Circumcision, Animal sacrifices.** The blood of animals never took away **<u>ANY</u>** sin [Hebrews 10:4-6]. **The blood of Jesus covers <u>all</u> sins of those who will be saved.**

The more we follow God's <u>perfect</u> plan, the happier and healthier we will be.

The **"wrath of God"** is merely **God leaving people alone** who insist on doing things their way in willful opposition to His way [Romans 1:18-32].

"God's punishment" is merely God allowing enemies to do what comes naturally. **God does not make anyone sick.** He does not zap people with lung cancer because He catches them smoking! **Sickness comes as a result of** wrong eating and drinking, negative thinking, not being willing to forgive self, not being willing to forgive others, and living in an imperfect world.

Because **Jesus experienced the "wrath of God"** [Isaiah 53:4-10] does not mean that God killed Jesus! It merely means that God veiled His presence so that Jesus was not aware of His presence. **Jesus prayed, "Why have You forsaken Me," not "Why are You killing Me."**

Jesus, while in the Garden of Gethsemane and, at times, on the cross, believed, in His conscious thinking, that He was doomed to die for eternity. This will be the experience of all the unsaved when they finally realize that they have lost out on eternal life – that they have thrown away so much for so little.

Most of the fire spoken of in the Bible is NOT literal fire. There will be literal fire as a result of nature out of control around the time Jesus returns the second and third times. **18 different types of fire** are listed, along with Bible proof texts, in Outlines 6, 7, 8.

If your parents had told you that you had the **choice** of obeying their rules or not obeying their rules; then told you that **if you did not** obey their rules, they would **torment** you and **kill** you for not doing so, **would you then consider them fair and loving parents?** If not, then why would you consider God a fair and loving heavenly parent if He said and did the same thing? The fact is that **God never really said that!!** Only **tradition** has passed such blasphemy down to us.

Anyone who studies the Bible for himself or herself, with an open mind, determined to accept as fact anything the Bible teaches, regardless of what he or she has been taught earlier in life, will know for sure that God really is love, as the apostle John wrote **[1 John 4:8, 16].**

Outlines 12, 13, 14, 15, 16, & 17 cover the subjects of what happens to a person when he dies, hell, soul, spirit, the occult, the Rich Man and Lazarus, and the final end of sin and sinners. Adequate **Bible proof** is supplied.

Armageddon is a **spiritual battle** between the forces of good and the forces of evil. Some military combat will occur; however, the fight over the minds of men and women will decide who wins this spiritual battle [See Outline No. 27].

Those who believe that Jesus sets up His earthly kingdom at the **beginning** of the **Millennium,** will be deceived by Satan**,** the **antichrist.** People will fall down and worship **Satan,** thinking that they are worshiping **Jesus.**

Those who predict that **Zechariah 14** will be fulfilled [which teaches that animal sacrifices will still be made as atonement for sins] will be deceived. **Zechariah 14** will not be fulfilled because the prophecy was **given on the condition that Israel would accept Jesus** when He came as the Messiah. This Old Testament prophecy has been replaced by **Revelation 20.** It is impossible to believe and accept them both. [See Outline No. 18].

During the past few years we have been reading in the news about **water** once flowing on the planet **Mars.** By knowing that the planet **Mars** came in close proximity to our earth every 54 years until **701 BC,** and realizing that something powerful had to have happened to our earth to push its orbit out an additional 67,000 miles, **we do not find it surprising** when evidence shows that much water flowed on the planet **Mars** in the not too distant past.

The people of ancient **Israel** frequently fell back into worshiping **Mars [Baal],** even offering their infants as pagan sacrifices**! Mars was the "god of war"** to various nations around the world. **Mars came the closest to the earth at the time of Noah's flood.** God allowed it to do so because of the wickedness of man on the earth. **Because most of the earth's inhabitants rebelled against God and His laws, God did not interfere with the natural destructive forces of nature. Likewise, God will not interfere with nature out of control in the days just before His second and third comings, for the same reason.**

One lifetime here on earth is nothing compared to eternity. **No one needs to miss out on everlasting life.** God is ready and willing to give eternal life to all who ask for it, and believe, by faith, that He will fulfill all of His promises, and prepare us to live in a place where there is no sin, rebellion, discord, sickness, pain, or heartache.

No individual is so sinful that Jesus will not now accept his or her surrender. It is easy to be saved! Just ask, from your heart, for Jesus to take control of your life. Surrender your life to Him each and every day of your life – which, compared to eternity, will not be long. God is love. God is fair. God is forgiving. No one has a past so sinful that God will not forgive when asked to do so. [By the way, if you have any desire at all for Jesus to come into your life, **you can know for sure that you have not committed the "unpardonable sin."**]

Consider the following facts:

[1] God is love, and He always acts that way. Always

[2] Those who understand how God thinks and acts do not fear Him.

[3] God demands freedom of choice. He will not <u>force</u> anyone to believe anything.

[4] Jesus came to show us what the God of the Old Testament is really like, in contrast to the counterfeit lord. God is loving, kind, merciful, and forgiving.

[5] The apostle Paul wrote that Jesus was the God of the Old Testament who led Israel.

[6] God does not <u>force</u> us to do His perfect will. He allows us to learn, by trial and error, that His <u>perfect</u> ways are the only ways to receive <u>real</u> success, health, and happiness.

[7] God only uses force to prevent evil men, evil angels, and nature out of control from hurting His true followers; however this does not mean that bad things never happen to good people. God, who has His reasons for everything He allows, makes no mistakes.

[8] When Jesus, speaking to the Pharisees about their "eye for an eye" law, said, "But <u>I</u> say unto you to do the opposite, by returning good for evil," He was declaring Himself to be of greater authority than the one who gave that Old Testament law in the first place.

[9] Not <u>all</u> of the Old Testament laws were written or dictated by the <u>true</u> Lord God.

[10] God does <u>not</u> have a split personality. He is <u>not</u> loving <u>half</u> of the time, and like a devil the other half.

[11] God does not break His own laws -- the ones He has commanded us to keep.

[12] God hates sin, but loves every sinner.

[13] God is <u>always</u> willing to forgive whenever <u>anyone</u> repents and asks Him for forgiveness.

[14] The more we follow God's <u>perfect</u> will, the happier and healthier we will be.

[15] Satan will deceive most people with miracles, UFO occupants, and other evil angels in the form of men.

[16] God has promised to lead you [not drag you] into all Truth.

[17] God speaks when someone is listening with an open mind.

[18] Allah is the counterfeit lord. How do we know? Allah dictated the Koran to Mohammed. It teaches that their followers are to kill all those who do not accept their teachings. The true Lord does not kill.

[19] The "destroying angels" are the evil angels who followed Lucifer out of heaven.

[20] Being ready for Jesus to return means having a daily relationship with Him. The more we surrender our will to Jesus, the more He helps us to grow spiritually.

INDEX

Example of Page Code:
"3-2" =
3 = Outline No. 3
2 = Page 2
xxxxxxxxxxxxxxxxxxxxxxxxx

G

H

T

U

V

W

Y

Z

About the Author

An Andrews University graduate, the author, Paul G. Sweitzer, is an orthodox, born-again scholar whose research gives logical and Scriptural answers to difficult questions to which our youth expect answers.

Printed in the United States
26419LVS00001B/79-80

9 781418 421526